CHINA'S REALITY
AND
GLOBAL VISION
Management Research and
Development in China

CHINA'S REALITY
AND
GLOBAL VISION
Management Research and
Development in China

Editors

Siwei Cheng
Chinese Society for Management Modernization, China

Cunjun Zhao
Chinese Society for Management Modernization, China

Xiaohong Chen
Central South University, China

Yong Shi
Chinese Society for Management Modernization, China

 **World Scientific**

NEW JERSEY · LONDON · SINGAPORE · BEIJING · SHANGHAI · HONG KONG · TAIPEI · CHENNAI

Published by

World Scientific Publishing Co. Pte. Ltd.

5 Toh Tuck Link, Singapore 596224

USA office: 27 Warren Street, Suite 401-402, Hackensack, NJ 07601

UK office: 57 Shelton Street, Covent Garden, London WC2H 9HE

British Library Cataloguing-in-Publication Data
A catalogue record for this book is available from the British Library.

CHINA'S REALITY AND GLOBAL VISION
Management Research and Development in China

Copyright © 2012 by World Scientific Publishing Co. Pte. Ltd.

All rights reserved. This book, or parts thereof, may not be reproduced in any form or by any means, electronic or mechanical, including photocopying, recording or any information storage and retrieval system now known or to be invented, without written permission from the Publisher.

For photocopying of material in this volume, please pay a copying fee through the Copyright Clearance Center, Inc., 222 Rosewood Drive, Danvers, MA 01923, USA. In this case permission to photocopy is not required from the publisher.

ISBN-13 978-981-4287-90-6
ISBN-10 981-4287-90-3

Printed in Singapore.

Preface

The Chinese Society for Management Modernization (CSM), established in 1978, is the official body of China's National Management Association which contains all schools or colleges of management at universities around China as its associate members. The mission of CSM is to exchange and disseminate the academic findings and/or practical experiments in all aspects of management for promoting and developing China's management research and skills. CSM is also a platform for management researchers, practitioners, business leaders as well as governmental officers to communicate and share their common interests of management. In December 2006, CSM has held its first national annual conference at Beijing with Guanghua School of Management, Beijing University as the local host where over 1,000 scholars, CEOs and entrepreneurs attended. In November 2007, the second national annual conference was held in Nanjing by the School of Management, Nanjing University. There were over 600 attendees.

During November 1–2, 2008, the third CSM national annual conference was held at the School of Business, Central South University, Changsha, Hunan, China. The total number of attendees for this conference was more than 700. A number of well-known international scholars in management and CEOs of multi-national and national corporations have been invited and they delivered keynote or plenary speeches. There were more than 11 parallel sessions covering strategic management, organizational behaviors, accounting, finance, operations, marketing, management science, information management, public affairs, innovations, and technology management at the conference. The aim of the conference is to seek the solutions to deal with management challenges from both China's reality and global concerns. This book presents the highlight of the third CSM national annual conference. The papers were either based on keynote speeches or selected from the submissions that have been peer reviewed. The purpose of the book is to disseminate the cutting-edge findings of management research in China, through this conference, to the rest of the world given the fact that the Chinese economy is one of the fastest growing in the world.

Siwei Cheng, Cunjun Zhao, Xiaohong Chen, and Yong Shi
March 2010
Zhongguanchun, Beijing

Contents

Part 5: Management Challenges from Chinese Society

Part 1

Current Issues in China's Economic Development

Fundamental Theory and Research Methodologies for Fictitious Economy

Siwei Cheng

CAS Research Center on Fictitious Economy and Data Science,
School of Management, Graduate University of
Chinese Academy of Sciences, Beijing 100080, China
chengsw@gucas.ac.cn

In this paper, the author describes the fundamental theory and research methodologies in the field of fictitious economy. Fictitious economy refers to all activities of fictitious capital mainly based on financial platform. Compared with real economy, fictitious economy is another economic pattern, including its structure and evolution, existing at economic system, which can be viewed as "software" of economy. Although the concept of fictitious capital was initiated by Karl Marx, it has been expanded to include credit capital, knowledge capital, and social capital. According to this, the development of fictitious economy has five stages: (i) capitalization of spare money, (ii) socialization of profitable capital, (iii) marketization of priced security, (iv) internationalization of financial market, and (v) integration of global finance. The exchange and re-exchange are a major movement of fictitious capital. While the uncertain price of fictitious capital creates the possibility of profitable investment, its expansion produces risk and its movement could not directly increase social wealth. The system of fictitious economy has five characteristics such as complexity, stability, high-risk, parasitism, and periodicity. This paper outlines the challenging research problems, including relationships between fictitious economy and real economy, regulatory factors, risk analysis and prevention, and evaluation system in fictitious economy. In addition, it elaborates on six research methods, known as complexity science, decision making under uncertainty, group decision making, complex data analysis for decision support, mathematical finance, and computer simulation to deal with fictitious economy problems.

Keywords: Fictitious capital; Fictitious economy; Complexity; Financial markets.

1. Introduction

Study on fictitious economy has being gradually recognized by international community. There are three kinds of categories that belong to the term equal to "fictitious economy" in Chinese translation (Cheng, 1999). The first one is fictitious economy, which refers to all activities of fictitious capital that is mainly based on financial platform. The second one is virtual economy, which refers to the economic activities performed on the basis of information technology, including the well-known e-commerce. It should be translated as "reality-simulating economy" in Chinese. The third one is visual economy, which refers to the visualized economic activities that are simulated with computer. It means a model of a kind of economic activity will be established before using the model for computer simulation. For example, some economic policies may be simulated on the computer before the implementation is carried out. It can also be considered as visualized economy. There are some internal relations between the three categories. The fictitious economy discussed in this paper mainly refers to the first category (fictitious economy).

According to the author's preliminary investigation on this subject, the most common concept is the virtual economy. But, there are so many different descriptions on the notations and extensions of this concept. It not only includes the above categories, but also the economic activities, such as the online games. In recent years, the international community tends to define it as the creation and transfer of the virtual wealth in the online games. For example, Wikipedia explains the virtual economy as "A virtual economy (or sometimes synthetic economy) is an emergent economy existing in a virtual persistent world, usually exchanging virtual goods in the context of an Internet game. People enter these virtual economies for recreation and entertainment rather than necessity, which means that virtual economies lack the aspects of a real economy that are not considered to be 'fun' (for instance, players in a virtual economy do not need to buy food in order to survive, and usually do not have any biological needs at all). However, some people do interact with virtual economies for 'real' economic benefit (Wikipedia)". On the homepage of Virtual Economy Research Network, it explicitly says: "Some online resources, such as domain name, virtual items in community address, powerful characters in online game, etc. are similar to the real goods that may only be under the control of a single person during a period. Nowadays, this virtual assets are brought and sold by thousands of people in many markets around the world (Virtual-Economy)". This kind of virtual economy is also developed rapidly in China (Xu, 2008). Although some domestic scholars suggest use virtual economy as the equivalent English terms for Chinese words "Xuni Jingji", the author insists to use "fictitious economy". In this way, it not only shows a preciseness in the field of science study, but also inherits the concept of fictitious capital that was initiated by Karl Marx.

The domestic study on fictitious economy began from 1997. At that time, the author took the official position as Director of Management Science Department, National Natural Science Foundation of China. Our department and the Mathematics and Physics Department jointly started a major subject — Finance Mathematics, Finance Engineering, and Finance Management — at the beginning of 1997. After the breaking out of the East-Asian financial crisis in July 1997, some scholars tried to analyze the crisis with the theory of fictitious economy (Liu, 1998; Cheng et al., 1999). Especially, after the principle of "properly dealing with the relationship between fictitious economy and real economy" (Jiang, 2002) was proposed at the Sixteenth National Congress of CPC, the study on the fictitious economy has been developed vigorously. Up to now, five nationwide fictitious economy forums had been held. There are thousands of papers on fictitious economy published in domestic newspapers and periodicals.

The domestic study on fictitious economy can be roughly divided into three academic schools, or three kinds of academic viewpoints.

First, fictitious economy is considered as a fictitious value system. This kind of viewpoint is mainly held by traditional economists. It is due to the traditional economics which considered economy as a value system.

In this way, the fictitious economy should be a fictitious economy value system.

Second, fictitious economy is considered as finance itself. This viewpoint mainly comes from the scholars of finance community. From their viewpoint, they are actually talking about finance when talking about fictitious economy. Some of them even think that it is unnecessary to use the term "fictitious economy".

Third, fictitious economy is considered as an economic activity pattern, which includes structure and its evolution, existing in the economic system as opposed to real economy. The fictitious economy is the "software" in the economy. This viewpoint is proposed by the author in this article and is agreed by a number of scholars in the field of system engineering and natural science and technology.

In my opinion, the domestic research on fictitious economy is now at the beginning stage. There is no fixed paradigm. It is better to freely discuss it from different viewpoints of the scholars and put their opinions under a comprehensive consideration to obtain a consistent view on it. But, the three categories have different thinks and methods. Some of these thinks and methods can be mutually complementary. Some of them may only reach a comparative knowledge after putting them into practice.

Author has been made some studies on the fictitious economy. These studies mainly try to discuss the chaos and self-organization issues in security market, currency market, foreign currency market, future and option market, equity transaction market, financial crisis, inflation and deflation, commercial bank transform, countryside financing, real-estate financing, etc. They also involve the theory and method for fictitious economy (Cheng, 2003, 2007). It is hoped that these studies will help drive the economic and financial reforms. This article tries to present author's study results and understandings on the fundamental theory and research methods of fictitious economy.

2. Initiation and Development of Fictitious Capital

2.1. *Karl Marx's fictitious capital theory*

Karl Marx initiated the fictitious capital theory in volume III of his great works *Das Capital* (Marx, 1957). Volume III was published after his death by his friend Friedrich Engels based on the collection of his scripts. There is also some of Friedrich Engels' contribution to this theory.

According to Karl Marx's quotation, the term fictitious capital was used by Wee Liseem (a banker of Yorkshire) in 1840 in his *Letter About Currency Issues* (2nd enlarged edition in London, 1840). It mainly referred to accommodation bill (bill). In Part 5 of Volume III in his *Das Capital*, especially after Chapter 25, Karl Marx made a thorough study on fictitious capital. His theory on fictitious capital can be briefly concluded into two main viewpoints.

First, he thought that fictitious capital is generated on the basis of loan capital (i.e., interest-bearing capital) and bank credit system (Samezo, 1989). On the basis of the capitalist production, money can be transformed into capital. By the transform, money changes from a fixed value to a self-increasing value. At this time, the use value of money is that it can be transformed into capital to generate profit. Under this meaning, money can be considered as a special commodity. The owner of it can loan it to person who needs capital with some legal forms and conditions. It will be returned to the owner with interests after a period according to the arrangement. Money has become a capital that can bring the interest. Credit is the foundation of loaning.

However, when money is loaned as interest-bearing capitals, the owner cannot get any equivalent as payment as for any normal commodity exchange. They only get a guarantee in some forms that the capital and interest will be paid back in the future. This guarantee (normally in writing) is fictitious capital. After the emerging of bank, it collected a large part of the idle money in society to transform the money into interest-bearing capital. As the enlargement of the credit system, banks began to distribute credits in addition to cash currency, which enable the increasing of the types of fictitious capital. At his time, Karl Marx thought that fictitious capital included the loaning credit of banks (such as bank bills, etc.), capitalized value (such as valuable securities, etc.), and real-estate mortgage bill, etc.

Second, Karl Marx thought the fictitious capital has no value for itself. But, it can bring profit through circular movement, that is, produce some kinds of surplus value.

According to Karl Marx's labor value theory, it is stipulated that the value quantity in use value is the social necessary labor time used for the production of the use value. Because there is no labor quantity in the fictitious capital itself, there is no value in fictitious capital.

In *Das Capital*, Karl Marx viewed that surplus value can only be generated through activities of real economy. It means that the capitalist will use currency as capital. They will turn the capital into production elements through exchange, including hiring of workers, purchase of raw materials, erection of plants, purchase of machines, etc. Then, they will produce products though production process; the product will be changed into commodity through circulation process; the commodity will get currency back through exchange. In this circulation of real economy, profits are produced due to the surplus value. This is a very important fundamental viewpoint in *Das Capital*.

In Volume III of *Das Capital*, Karl Marx pointed out that fictitious capital can produce surplus value in some forms through circular movement. But in strictly means, this surplus value is not produced by the fictitious capital itself. They are paid to the owner of fictitious capital by the functional capitalist (industry capitalist or commercial capitalist) from their profits (surplus value) according to the arrangement in the form of interest. So, Karl Marx used "some form" to describe this concept.

Karl Marx described that capital must have two characteristics. First, it must have value. Second, it must be able to produce surplus value. Because the fictitious capital has the second character, it can be considered as capital. But it does not have the first character; that is, it cannot be used to purchase production elements by direct exchange, so it can only be fictitious capital.

We should admit that Karl Marx had strong predictability. It is very uneasy for him to initial the fictitious capital theory in 19th century (he was born on 5 May 1818 and died on 14 March 1883). Of course, after more than 100 years later, we have broader and deeper knowledge on fictitious capital.

2.2. *The definition of fictitious capital*

The author thinks that fictitious capital is a resource established on the basis of trust relationship that does not have a material form or currency form with uncertain value but can produce profits. They can be used to obtain the usage rights of real capital. But, it has to promise to give a return to the owner of real capital, or share risks, and profits with the owner of real capital. For example, security promises to pay a return to the owner of real capital. Stock shares risks and profits with the owner of real capital. Most importantly, the emerging of the certificate of title shows the double properties of the capital rights belongings, realizes the separation of the ownership and uses rights, and finally causes the generation of fictitious capital.

As we all know, in real economy, the ownership and the use rights of money are both exchanged with the commodity it purchased during the exchange process. The ownership and the use rights of money are not separated. When somebody uses some money to purchase a kind of commodity, he will lose the ownership and use rights both at the same time. But capital has two characteristics that can be divided into ownership and use rights that can be separated from each other. For example, if somebody uses money to purchase a bond issued by an enterprise, he transfers the use rights of the money to the enterprise. The enterprise gives him a certificate of title, i.e., bond, to certify that the ownership of the money belongs to him. So, he has rights to ask the enterprise to pay back the principal and interest. But stock certifies that the owner of the stock has the rights of a shareholder and bears the liability of shareholder. The mortgage bill of real estate certifies that the ownership of the real estate is transferred to the financial institution or private person and the mortgager who gets the loan only holds the use rights of the real estate. If the mortgager cannot pay back the loan after expiration, the use rights will lose. So, we can see the separation of ownership and use right cause the generation of fictitious capital. It is a very important viewpoint. We can analyze many related issues from this viewpoint.

2.3. *Main types of fictitious capital*

Fictitious capital has two important supporting points. One of them is that the real capital is assessed and measured by generally accepted symbols of value. Another one is the capitalization of the "soft" elements that relates to technology, education, management, etc. This means we can observe and assess all kinds of "soft" elements in the way that observes and assesses capital in traditional meanings, and conclude these elements as fictitious capital. This construction mode will enable all kinds of fictitious capital and real capital that has been assessed by the symbols of value to have a match relationship on the economic meanings. We can observe the operational mechanism and efficiency of fictitious capital system through this relationship. So, the relationship becomes the core relationship among the many relationships of fictitious economy.

From the viewpoint of "soft" elements, there are three major types of fictitious capital.

First one is credit capital. The kind of fictitious capital already existed at the age of Karl Marx. Nowadays, it has been developed into the foundation of financial industry. For example, bank absorbs deposits by its credit. Enterprises issue bonds and stocks by their credit. The borrower obtains loan from the bank by his credit. A lot of domestic banks ask the borrower to provide guarantee or mortgage. These banks almost become financial house or hock shop. The bank should give loan according to the credit of the borrower. So, credit capital refers to the use right of real capital that is obtained by the credit of fund raiser.

The second is intellectual capital. Intellectual capital refers to the use right of the capital is obtained by the fund raiser on the basis of his knowledge, technology, trademark, or even consolidated knowledge as standards. The most obvious example is venture capital. The venture capital is the creator uses his creative results to obtain capital from the venture investor. If it failed after investment of the capital, both parties will share the risks. If success, both parties will enjoy the benefits. Venture capital itself embodies the combination of real capital and fictitious capital. The social wealth can only be produced through the combination of these two kinds of capital (Cheng, 2008).

The third one is social capital. The concept of social capital is at first initiated by sociologists. It comes from the theory developed in 1970s on the basis of social network studies. It mainly refers to the relationships in the same social network and among different networks (Portes, 1998). In recent 30 years, the theory and practice of social capital have obtained many developments and renewed of their scopes. The sociology community still has arguments on the definition and effect of social capital. Although some economists pay attention on the effect of social capital on the economy. It is still not popular in economics community. The author transplants the concept of social capital into the fictitious capital to define it as social capital refers to corporation relationship and institutions formed by the interaction of members of society. In simple words, social capital is the "relationship". In China, relationship becomes a negative word due to the serious corruption in our society. But whether in China or not, relationship is also a rather important elements in economical life. The member of society will improve the mutual understanding and friendship, strengthen mutual trust and establish corporation relationship during their contacts and social intercourses. It is also possible to institutionalize this relationship and forms the social capital. Social capital had positive effect on the development of economy. For example, someone points out that the northern part of Italy is better developed than southern part due to the original system of the north is republic system and the south is monarchy. As for the private equity fund developed rapidly in recent years, the capital is raised privately by the general partner of the fund from the limited partner. The investor will only give capital to the general partner for him to earning profit for them on the basis of trusts on his ability and moral character.

In summary, the owner of credit capital, intellectual capital, and social capital has no real capital himself. But, he can obtain the use right of real capital. But, he has to give certificate of title to the owner of real capital to admit his ownership and promise some return or sharing of risk and profits with him. The value of these fictitious capitals is uncertain and can only be determined after combined with real capital and liquidated.

In the course of the combination of these three fictitious capitals with the real capital, the title of them will be solidified into the certificate of title. For example, it should stipulate the share percentage of the fund raiser or admit that the profits beside the interest will belong to the fund raiser. Because the certificate of title has no value for itself and only the carrier of fictitious capital, so it can be called as secondary fictitious capital. The credit capital, intellectual capital, and social capital can be called as original fictitious capital. The fictitious capital referred thereafter in the paper mainly referred to the secondary fictitious capital represented by the certificate of title.

3. Definition and Features of Fictitious Economy

Fictitious economy is a mode of economic activities that are compared with real economy. It refers to economic activities that are performed by the fictitious capital, which uses the financial platform as a main support and the synthesis of all relationship existing in it. In the activities of real economy, capital can only produce profits through a circulation from exchange to production, to circulation, and finally to exchange. But in the process of the activities in fictitious economy, the capital can produce profits without through this circulation.

3.1. *Development process of fictitious economy*

The development process of fictitious economy can mainly be divided into the following five stages.

The first stage is the capitalization of idle money. This means the people's idle money becomes capital that can produce interest. The earliest origin of fictitious economy can be traced back to the commercial loan behavior among the individuals. For example, Mr. A is urged to purchase some kind of goods but has not enough capital. Mr. B has some amount of idle money. So Mr. A borrows some amount of money from Mr. B. Mr. A promises to pay back the principal and interest in a fixed period. Through this activity, Mr. A gets the use right of this amount of money and can use the property of medium of payment of the money to get profit through actual operating activities. Mr. B remains the title of the money with the promissory note as a certificate and obtained the right to ask for the principal and interest from Mr. A at expiry. The promissory note is an embryonic form of the fictitious capital. This fictitious capital can get increment from the circulation of the lending and repaying. During this process, Mr. B does not do actual economic activities but earns his profits through a kind of fictitious economic activities.

The second stage is the socialization of the interest-bearing capital. That is, the bank acts as an intermediary institution to borrow idle money from people and loan it out to get interest. Besides, enterprises can raise fund by issuing of bond and stock and promise to pay back the principle and interest after a fixed period or share the risks and profits with investors. People can use their own idle money to buy some kinds of valuable securities such as stock and bonds to get interest. According to this, the socialization of interest-bearing capital brings out the banks and fictitious capital in the different forms such as bonds and stocks. The socialization of the interest-bearing capital can lead the social capital from the people who do not perform real economic activities such as production, circulation, and exchange to the people who perform real economic activities. The capital distributed in individuals can be collected together to perform economic activities of larger scale and high profits. It optimizes the investment direction and improves the usage efficiency of the capital.

The third stage is the marketization of valuable security. The biggest problem of fictitious capital in its early stage is the lack of liquidity. It is hard to be changed into cash when the owner needs the money urgently. This problem becomes the handicap in the process of transforming the idle money to interest-bearing capital. After the marketization of valuable security, they can be bought and sold freely according to its expected gains. Therefore, the financial markets, such as stock market, bond market, and currency market, used for the transaction of fictitious capital, are generated. The marketization not only can enable the valuable security held by people to be transformed into cash at any time which dramatically improves the liquidity of fictitious capital, but also can lead the capital to flow into the industries and enterprises with better expected profit, which further improves the usage efficiency of the capital. But it also creates possibilities for the speculation with the price fluctuation in security market. In 1898, future exchange of agricultural products was introduced. The future exchange progressively spread to industrial raw materials such as nonferrous metal, crude oil, etc. They became new forms of fictitious capital.

The fourth stage is the internationalization of financial market. It means that fictitious capital can be exchanged across the country boundary. This process can be traced back the fixed rate bond issued by debtor counties and railway companies on the financial market of Britain, France, and German in the middle of the 19th century. But large-scale multinational investment began in 1920s. It stagnated due to the economic recession in the United States in 1930s and the World War II. After 1944, the international financial market with huge scale has been progressively built up with the drive of Bretton Woods Agreements and GATT. The internationalization of financial market can lead the international capital to flow into the industry with better profits and dramatically improve the capital utilization efficiency. At the same time, a new financial market — foreign currency market — was also established. The future exchange becomes more and more virtualized, i.e., purchasing of future becomes a method for speculation. After 1960s, the exchange of stock, future, and foreign currency all has prompt and future exchange methods. Option exchange appeared in 1973.

The fifth stage is the integration of international finance. It refers to the increasingly closer relationship between the domestic financial markets of countries to the international financial market with increasingly influence on each other. Since 1980s, the flow rate of fictitious capital in financial market kept on increasing because: (1) the dependency among the economy of various countries has been greatly increased with the development of economic globalization; (2) the scale of fictitious economy has been enlarged with the enhancements on financial innovations and the forming of floating exchange rate system after US dollar's separation with Gold Standards; (3) the flow rate and flow speed of the fictitious capital in financial market has been kept on growing faster with the development of information technology (IT). The three factors accelerated the progressive integration of financial markets of various countries. It makes the relationship between domestic financial market of various countries with the international market become closer with more interaction. Even we can say, one tiny part of its change will bring changes on the whole of it. As we observed from the East Asia Financial Crisis began in 1997, a liquidity crisis in Tailand brings significant influences on the whole East Asia, Asian, and even to the World.

3.2. Movement principle of fictitious capital

3.2.1. Exchange–re-exchange is the main movement process of fictitious capital

The purchasing of bonds or stock is to transfer the use right of real capital for exchange of a certificate of title. After a fixed period, this certificate of title will be exchanged again to get back the use right of the real capital with possible profits. This kind of fictitious capital can enable the capital to bring money from money without the circulation in real economy.

The movement process of fictitious capital includes two parts: exchange and re-exchange. The Exchange not only includes the exchange between the real capital and the certificate of title (virtualization of real capital), but also the exchange between original fictitious capital and the certificate of title (secondarilization of original fictitious capital). The re-exchange process is the liquidation process of the fictitious capital, and includes the selling it in public market or between individuals.

3.2.2. Uncertainty of the price of fictitious capital makes the speculation possible

The theory of neo-classical economics considers the person who performs economic activities as "economic person". They pursue the maximization of their own benefits. Their behavior is completely rational. According to this theory, the price of stock is the rational expectation on the future value of the real economic variants that influence the stock price. That is, the rational price of a stock should equal to the present value of its future gains. However, Nobel Laureate in Economic Sciences Herbert Simon pointed out that the person who performs the economic activities is only partially rational. It is difficult for people to know and predict all kind of results with the limitation on the information and knowledge. They usually make decisions on their own subjective judgment. It is also difficult for them to take consideration on all possible solutions during the decision-making process (Simon, 1976). Besides, people's sense on value and words and behaviors of other people may also affect his correctness on decision making.

The exchange of stock happened in the stock market is due to the differences on the rational prices of same stock by different investors. Some investors think the price of a stock is higher than its' rational price and decide to sell it. Other investors think its' price is lower than its' rational price and decide to buy it. If all investors are rational, then there will be no transaction.

Any stock market is a place for investment and at the same time a place for speculation. Generally, "investment" refers to a long-term investment behavior that plans to enjoy higher dividends and increase on the enterprise's value after buying of the stock. "speculation" refers to a short-term investment behavior that expects to sell it under favorable conditions after buying it.

Normally, right-sized speculation will not damage the security market but benefit the operation of it. First, it helps increase the transaction of stock to improve the liquidity of market and speed up the turnover of capital. Second, the issue of new stock will be put forward due to the speculators who are more easily taking the risk for issue of new stock. Third, the speculation that selling at higher price and buying at lower price can regulate the supply and demand relationship in the market and help stabilize the price. The author thinks, that a mature stock market is a market with right scale of speculation. The dynamic balance will be maintained between investment and speculation. Although the market may fluctuate due to the influence from external environment. Normally, the market can maintain a relatively stable operation. It will bring more satisfied return for a large part of investors while promoting the economic development.

In fact, many investors in the stock market have motivation for both investment and speculation. The ratio between them is depended on specific conditions of the individuals and stock markets. If most investor has a significant more speculator behavior, the market will become a market with excessive speculation. As this time, the investor will not care about the operation results of enterprises. The blue chips are ignored. The stocks with larger possibility for speculation will attract investors. Excessive speculation will also boost the short-term behavior in the market and provide conditions for the manipulation of the market. The huge risk with the excessive speculation will become the potential problem that may cause serious fluctuations and further damage to the economy and society.

3.2.3. *The expansion of fictitious capital brings related risks*

The production base of the fictitious capital is the trust of investing party given to the fund-raising party and the profit-earning perspective invested project. The certificate of title given by the fund-raising party to the investing party has no relationship with the own value and currency assets of the fund-raising party. If expectation of the investing party (or fund-raising party) on the profit-earning perspective of the invested project is too optimistic, it will usually bring excessive investment or fund-raising that causes the expansion of the fictitious capital. When the optimistic estimation fails due to subjective or objective reasons, related risks will be generated.

As the development of the science and technology and financial innovation, there are too many kinds of financial derivative products for people to understand and utilize. The original purpose of the financial derivatives is (1) to meet the different preference on safety, profitability, and liquidity of various investors; (2) to reduce the risks through hedging. But they will provide the market with all kinds of speculation tools that bring a rapid expansion of fictitious capital.

The expansion of fictitious capital can be divided mainly into the following types:

(a) Over-valuation: if investors over-value the value of a certificate of title, the fictitious capital will be expanded. For example, in stock market, if the investors have excessive optimistic evaluation on the profit expectation of a public-listed company, they will purchase its' stock with higher price. Especially in bull market, many investors will purchase this stock based on ideas of "follow the trend" or "bigger fool theory" (believes some will buy it at higher price) and cause bubble on it. These investors will definitely lose money when the bubble breaks.

(b) Over-debt: the fund-raising party will normally borrow a lot if he thinks his return on asset is higher than the borrowing rate to make more profits. This may result the ratio of his debt to the asset up to several tens or hundreds. When the investor asks for the return of loan due to the bad expectation or refuse to give new loan, the fund-raising party will often be faced with the risk of bankruptcy.

(c) High guarantee ratio: the transaction with larger amount can be performed with lower guarantee. For example, only 5% guarantee is paid for one future contract in the future market of commodities.

(d) Multiplier effect: as we all know, the original currency money supply can be multiplied several times to finally form social currency supply due to the currency multiplier effect. Similar to this, the fictitious capital can also be kept on enlarge through multiplier effect. For example, the holder of a kind of bonds can get cash from a bank after pledging these bonds to the bank. Then, he can use this cash to purchase futures and financial derivatives. So the capital used to buy the bonds can be calculated with the unpaid bonds, unclosed future contract (the amount of it may be higher than up to 20 times of the guarantee), and unclosed financial derivatives. It can be enlarged to several tens times on the book value. But the low risks of holding bonds is also becoming the high risks for the futures and financial derivatives. He may get higher payment or lose it all.

3.2.4. *The movement of fictitious capital cannot produce social wealth*

Because the movement of fictitious capital (fictitious economy activities) is not included in the material production activities, so it cannot produce social wealth. The effect of the fictitious economy is to redistribute of the wealth produced by the real economy. For example, the stock market can only redistribute the wealth that exists in it. The real wealth comes from the listed companies. The speculation on stock may bring someone more wealth. But the winners earn this part of wealth from the losers (after deducting the stamp duty, commission fee of security agency, and the administration fee of stock exchange). So, it is just a redistribution of wealth. When stock market is in a fast bull market, the rapid increase of the stock price brings more capital into the market. It seems that there are only winners, no losers. But when the stock market falls suddenly, the last one enters the market may become the losers. The dividends of the stock comes from a part of the profit distributed to the shareholders after the production of wealth by the listed companies as the repayment for the utilization of the capital. But the fictitious economy can indirectly produce wealth by its optimization on the real economy. For example, the stock market should help the company with good profits and get off the company with bad profits. It should utilize its function on optimization on resources configuration. It should make the enterprises with good performance which needs capital to raise fund at a lower cost than from the bank. It should also make the enterprises with bad profits to be marginalized before they are eliminated from the market.

3.3. *Features of fictitious economy system*

The fictitious economy system has five features: complexity, metastability, high-risks, parasitism, and periodicity.

3.3.1. *Complexity*

The normal features of a complex system include huge scale, high degree of coupling, low transparency, dynamics, and openness. But the most essential feature is that its components have some kinds of intelligence. That is the ability to understand its environment, predict the changes of the environment, and take actions on the predefined targets. This is the internal reason for the organic evolution, technological innovation, economic development, and social progress.

Stock market is a kind of complex system. The main components are natural person and legal person (buyer, seller, and agency). They perform stock transaction in the stock market according to a set of rules. Although everyone of them has the freedom to make decision independently according to their own understanding of the environment and development perspective and their predetermined targets, their decision cannot avoid the influence from the decisions of others and external environment. Although there is easily to have chaos in the system due to the nonlinear interactions among the components, the self-organization effect of the system will make the system show a degree of order and stability in a macro and long-term scope.

In the stock transaction, investors only have a far less than enough understating on the conditions and price changes of the present market and future market. Their investment capability and risk-bearing ability are not the same. There are many differences on their understanding and evaluation on the investment value. The targets and expectations on the investment are also different in many ways. There are many investors who do not know analysis methods on the technical trends of the market. They even do not have basis knowledge of the investment in stock market. They are lack of the ability to recognize and judge the huge market information. So they will follow the trends in blindness and believe all rumors or even make decision on their own instincts and impulses. Therefore, there must be a large amount of chaos in the stock market. But the mutual influences on each other and the leading effect of external environment on peoples' behavior make the stock market show a certain kind of big trends from the aspect of macro and long term. Thus, these trends will be maintained relatively stable in a period, that is, bull market and bear market.

3.3.2. Metastability

Meta-stable system refers to a kind of system that stays in a status far from balance, but can maintain relative stability through exchange of material and energy with external environment. It is called system with dissipative structure in system science. Although this system can reach a stability though self-organization effect, but the stability is very easy to be destroyed by minor disturbances from outside. After destroy of the stability, the system may walk in a certain scope and enters into status of stability or walking in an alternative ways. From a macro-viewpoint, it can be considered as being stabilized in certain scope, i.e., regional stability. But the system may change dramatically or even corrupt after losing of stability. After the corruption, the system may restore its meta-stable with deep structural adjustment. It is also possible for the system to die away. Normally, the system has smaller possibility to corrupt when it has larger inertia.

The stock market is a meta-stable system that has to maintain its relative stability by exchanging the capital with external environment. There are many causes that may be the market meta-stable. But the most essential cause is the instability of the fictitious capital.

The internal instability of the fictitious capital comes from the fictitious nature itself. For example, the stock itself does not have any real value but represent a right to obtain incomes and a certificate of title. It makes the holder of it have the right to claim the part of the surplus value corresponding to his capital paid when he purchases the valuable security. After the stock is traded in the stock market, the prices of the stock will be determined by the subjective prediction of people on its future price. It is because the stock does not have any value itself. Its price cannot be determined by the objective value principle. It is also affected by the conditions of supply and demand. These all make the stock price go far away from the performance of actual economic activities. When the stock price is much higher than its rational expectation, the bubble is formed. The bubble can only be maintained stable by the inflow of capital from outside. But, it is only a kind of false stability that is very easy to be broken. When the inflow of the capital is not sufficient, its price will fall down.

The instability of the fictitious economy system also comes from the virtualization of the currency. It means that currency itself did not really have value. After the separation of the currency from the Gold Standard and Gold Exchange Standard, although the currency still has its value in use as an instrument of payment, it has no value that can be really measured with any kind of commodity. At this condition, the value of currency can only be measured by its purchasing power. The purchasing power is affected by various factors, such as amount of money issued, interest rate, exchange rate, people's consuming behavior, etc. Therefore, the virtualization of currency will enhance the instability of the fictitious economy. The positive-feedback existing in the fictitious economy system will also enhance the instability of this system. For example, a stock will be bought by more people if it had been bought by a lot of people. This kind of interaction is a positive-feedback effect. This effect will cause enlarging effects that make the price of the stock go down and up in large extent.

3.3.3. High-risk

The risks in economic activities refer to the difference between the expected profits from the actual profits. These risks come from the uncertainty of objective world and people's limitation on their cognitive ability for the objective world. It also comes from the subjective evaluation error of people on the expected earnings. The stock market has high risks but also has the possibility to get high earnings.

The high risks of fictitious economy system come from its complexity and metastability. First, the internal instability results in the unpredictable changes on its price. The enlarging of the transaction scale in financial market and the increasing types of the transaction also make the system more complex. Second, people's predictability is insufficient for the market and environment changes. So far, we still cannot find a better prediction method for expected earnings. Therefore, people are easily to make wrong decisions. Third, many people have limited capability to bear the risks and have no idea when faced with big risks. They may even enlarge the risk through positive feedback effect. At last, many people are willing to take more risks for higher earning. It makes the unstopped innovation with high risks and high return, including various futures, options, forward options, swap options, etc.

Besides, some illegal behaviors also cause the high risks in the financial market. First, untrue disclosure of information that misleads the investors; Second, the insider trading will always make the benefits of medium and small investors to be damaged; Third, the vicious market manipulation will make the banker earn huge profits. According to some studies, people tend to over-estimate their risk-bearing ability and make themselves bankrupted due to the over-venture. For example, if there are several projects that have the same investment amount of 1,000,000 yuan, with the risk ratio of 80% and 5,000,000 earnings for each project. Because the risks are matched with returns, people always think if they put 5,000,000 yuan in these five projects, the success of one project of them is enough to bearing all the risks. But when it is calculated with "venture bankruptcy rule", there is only 67% opportunity for one of them to be succeeded with 5,000,000 yuan investment. If you want to get the 95% opportunity for at least one of these kind projects to be succeeded, you need to put 14,000,000 yuan to 14 projects. As we can see, only 5,000,000 yuan is far from enough to bear the risks in them.

3.3.4. *Parasitism*

There are close relationships between the fictitious economy system and real economy system. The fictitious economy system is generated on the basis of real economy system and is attached to it.

There are close associations between the fictitious economy and real economy. The risks in the real economy system, such as products overstock, bankruptcy of enterprise, will all be transferred into the fictitious economy and make it lose its stability. The risks in the fictitious economy system, such as large falling down of stock index, rapid fall down of real estate price, great increase of bad debt in banks, serious depreciation of currency, will also cause serious influence on the real economy. These are the action and reaction between the real economy and fictitious economy. Nowadays, the finance becomes the core of the economy. The real economy cannot be operated by itself without the fictitious economy. Therefore, if we consider the real economy as the hardware of the economy system, then the fictitious economy can be considered as the software of the economy system. Any one of them will not operate well without the other. The software can only be operated when attached to the hardware.

The stock is the stock certificate issued by the limited liability company to the investor. It represents the ownership of their holder (shareholder) to the limited liability company. Because the stock is a kind of valuable security without repayment terms, it can only be sold to other investors in the secondary market without the rights to ask for withdrawal after purchasing them in the primary market. Theoretically speaking, the value of stock is mainly determined by the future performance of the listed company whether in primary market or secondary market. In other words, it should be the present value of future earnings. In spite of the irregular fluctuations of the price on stock market, the stock is essentially parasitic to the listed company. The stock market is parasitic to the real economy. Therefore, the listed companies are the foundation of the stock market.

Because the investor's judgment on the prices of any stock is based on the predication on its future performance, the parasitism of the stock is mainly showed when the market price of the stock usually is affected by the information on the limited liability company that issues this stock. The information includes the information disclosed by the company itself, information on the changes of external environment and the information go around in the society, etc.

On the other hand, stock market has a significant reaction on real economy. The raising of the stock market will strengthen peoples' confidence on economy perspective. People will increase their consumption under the influence of "wealth effect". The consumption will drive the economy up. On the contrary, when the bubbles in stock market breaks, people will not only reduce consumption but also undersell the financial assets. These behavior will cause economic recession or even economic crisis.

3.3.5. *Periodicity*

The evolution of fictitious economy system generally shows some features of periodicity. These features normally include stages such as the accelerated growth of real economy, beginning of the forming of economic bubbles, progressive expansion of currency and credit, general raising of all kinds of financial assets, the optimistic mood spread all over, the price of stock and real estate keep on raising, the economic bubble breaks under the external disturbs, all kind of financial index drops rapidly, people all sell real assets and financial assets, deceleration of real economy or negative growth, etc. But this periodicity is not a simply circulation and reciprocation. It is a wavy, spiral up periodicity.

The operation of the stock market also has periodicity. The bull market and bear market will appear alternatively. The stock market is mainly built upon investor's optimistic expectation on the future earnings (after all the optimistic expectation on the economic development). From the macroview, there is definitely some bubble in the stock market. The expansion and break of the bubble cause the fluctuation of the market. But this fluctuation is a wavy and spiral-up trends. For example, when the US stock market falls dramatically on 19 October 1987 (Black Monday), the Dow Jones Index was under 3,000 points. But 13 years later, the Dow Jones Index reaches over 12,000 points.

4. Research Fields of Fictitious Economy

The research fields of fictitious economy generally include four aspects.

4.1. The relationship between fictitious economy and real economy

First of all, the relationship between fictitious economy price and the corresponding entity price is considered. Fictitious capital in itself has no value, and the intrinsic value of an ownership certificate is only that of a piece of paper. However, the price bases on people's confidence with the entity which attaches to. For example, generally speaking, the PE ratio of one stock should not exceed the inverse of Bank Interest Rate. If the stock return is only equal to interest income on bank deposits, there was no need for people to buy stocks. Even though many listed companies in our country have the PE ratio higher than the inverse of Bank Interest Rate, some people who buy stock are not optimistic about its current value, but the value in the future. In other words, they estimate that the future value of the fictitious capital would be higher than today's price of the entity. Another example is in the future market, where the difference between commodity future price and spot price also exists.

Second is the relationship in the operation cycle between fictitious and real economy. As it is well known, real economy appears periodic, and there are cycle theories in short, medium, and long term. The author considers that the fictitious economy also has periodicity, but the cycle is not entirely consistent with real economy, as it is affected by many factors.

The analysis of the cycles of fictitious and real economy in our country presents that sometimes the two cycles were consistent, but sometimes not. Usually, the stock market is regarded as the economic climate. There is some truth in this, but not absolute. In some cases, the cyclical behavior in stock market is depended on that in real economy. For example, as the stock market is based on the listed company and real economy, the situation of the stock market should approximately reflect the real economy from the point of macro and long term. The real economy can be indicated by the GDP, while the stock market is normally represented by the stock index (e.g., Dow Jones Index). Although the cycle of the stock market may lead over or lag behind the economic cycle, the deviation in long term is abnormal. It should also be noted that the stock index is only compiled by several weighted stocks with statistical methods, as there are so many stocks in the market, it cannot comprehensively reflect the whole.

In recent years, some people challenged the statement that the stock market was economic climate. They considered that the stock market situation had no necessary connection with the economy, as the deviation had actually happened that the stock market raised its price while the economy was slowdown. From the point of view of complex science, the stock market and real economy is not a simple linear relation, but intricate nonlinear relation with multifactor. First, the GDP and stock index cannot adequately represent the status of real economy and stock market; secondly, both of them are affected by many factors, e.g., economic environment, social institution, government's policy, public confidence, and so on, which do asymmetrical and asynchronous influence on GDP and stock index; thirdly, status in stock market often deviates from real economy in short or long term, and their developments are not synchronous as a result of many factors; finally, the reaction that stock market appears to economy makes the relationship and interaction much more uncertain and obscure. It is emphasized that, when the excessive speculation, black manipulation, and oversize policy implication, do present in the stock market, the deviation from real economy will appear.

In addition, the impact of the stock market on real economy is also up to its scale. The total market value is around 93% of its GDP in the stock market all over the world, this figure is 130% in developed countries. The scale of circulating share is less than 50% of GDP in our country as the majority of shares are not yet in circulation. As a result, the stock market cannot be the economic climate. For example, during the rapid growth in our economy from 2001 to 2005, the stock market was in a bear market.

However, while the slight increase in 2006–2007, the stock market boomed. Then, the Shanghai Composite Index is a poor representation. On one hand, stocks in Shenzhen Stock Exchange are not included in this index that can only represent about 70% of the stock market. On the other hand, it is made up of the weighted total market value of all the listed companies in Shanghai Stock Exchange, so the grail stock has a very large weight, which brings out virtual rising and falling.

The risk in real economy may transmit to the fictitious economy, and vice versa. So some topics, e.g., the procedure, mechanism, influence factors, etc. should be investigated in the risk transference.

Fictitious economy is a double-edged sword, which has not only promoting effect, but also has untoward effect to real economy. In this respect, how to go after profits and avoid disadvantages should be discussed.

4.2. Institutional factors in fictitious economy activity

Even though the word "institution" was in common use for the past few years, the understanding of the essence varied with each individual. Generally, institution is considered as the norms for all the people to observe. In academic circles, it is often regarded as the system of politics, economy, culture, etc. forming in a specific historical condition. At the beginning of the 20th century, institutionalism rising in America focused on institution research, and analyzed the important role of institutional factors in economic and social development. They thought organization and regulation of economy were much more important than resource allocation, income distribution, and the level of income, product, commodity price, etc. They stressed the great role of factors relating to society, history, politics, psychology, culture, etc. to the social and economic life. They also advocated institutionalism and structured analytical method. The inspiration of institutional economics is that the fictitious economy research must pay special attention to the role of institutional elements.

The author ever uses the complex science to analyze the institutional problem, and considers that institution should include both aspects of the regime and mechanism. Regime is the status and structure of the system at a certain time point and mechanism refers to the process and dynamics of the system evolution. The regime and mechanism are interdependent that the regime is the starting point and the result of the system evolution, while the mechanism is the evolution path. Owing to the interaction between the system and external conditions as well as between different agents within the system, self-organization should emerge, leading to the formation of the hierarchical structure and function structure, and promote the system evolution in a certain direction.

In the eyes of fictitious economy development, the institution in fictitious economy is the result of evolution; meanwhile, the proposition that "transaction priors to the rules" is still true in the fictitious economy. For example, the "South Sea Bubble" had already generated in Britain before the equity financing regulation was issued. The "South Sea Bubble" was the result of failure to make timely control after the fictitious capital transaction emerged. But it proved that transaction could in advance exist without institution. After the "Mississippi Bubble", although politicians in France extremely objected to the stock market and equity financing, the Credit Mobilier founded by Peter Laird Brothers also involved in investment banking steering clear of the financial control. Consequently, it is difficult to find fictitious institution at least for the formal rules unless the transaction involved.

On the other hand, we must also focus on the reaction of institution to the transaction behavior. After the interaction between institution and transaction can be available, institution often becomes a crucial factor in further development of the fictitious economy, even in the change of the development path. Examples of macrocontrol were too numerous to mention individually after the popularity of Keynesian, while monetarism, financial, and monetary policy managed by supply-side economist had greatly changed the internal operational locus of financial system as well as the impact of financial system on real economy in the United States and Europe. After the middle of the 20th century, the supervision models and the corresponding supervision rules had an increasingly effect on the activities of agents in the fictitious economy system.

The author believes the institution in fictitious economy could be divided into three levels. The first level is formal legal system rooted in different cultures to regulate the behavior of the market players, the basic relationship in the market and the competitive order, which plays a fundamental role in fictitious economy transaction. The second level is related supervision including various regulation, direction, suggestion, and recommendation that we sketched by the executive supervision authority considering the legal principles and administrative discretional power. The third level is the so-called "hidden rules" developing on the basis of day-to-day trading habits in fictitious economy. There is a certain and complementary relationship in these three levels so that they can arise from compulsive institutional change (external-organization), as well as evolving from the induced institutional change (self-organization).

In accordance with the complex science point of view, a certain institution for fictitious economy can stabilize the expectation of the main market players. Under the given institutional framework, the market players know others' rule of action as all of them are rational. If so, the institution should be appropriate and stable. Otherwise, if the market players are difficult to play their roles, while the business opportunities are hard to achieve under such framework, the institution must be changed. It is through the interaction between the institutional environment and the market players that the integration of self-organization and external-organization promotes the development and evolution of fictitious economy.

The study of financial institution should integrate normative approach and empirical approach, and widely absorb the theories and research methods in psychology, sociology, management, mathematical finance, behavioral finance, decision-making technique of uncertainty, computer simulation, etc. Both microfoundation and macroeffect should be investigated. The policy research should object the trend of simple explanation, mechanical copy and vulgarization, attach particular importance to the validity of research results, enhance its persuasiveness and make contributions to improve the institutional environment of fictitious economy.

4.3. *Generation and precaution of risk in fictitious economy*

Risk is defined as difference between expected return and actual return. There are some debates today about this definition. Some people consider only negative difference as risk not the positive one. In other words, lower-than-expected earnings is risk, the contrary is not. This in fact is to consider unilaterally or bilaterally to evaluate the risk. At present, although the unilateral method is the mainstream, the author does not agree. An actual return over the expected one means an excessive amount of input, as the expected return can be achieved using less input, so that the risk of wasting resource also exists. Considering the risk unilaterally may encourage people to waste resource to chase "safety". However, the bilateral consideration could encourage people to try to make the expected return correspond closely to the actual one and get a reasonable balance in safety and profitability.

The risk originates from the uncertainty of the objective world and the limitation of people's cognitive ability, as well as the subjective estimate error of the expected return. The author divides the risk into two types: one is called objective risk and the other one is subjective risk. The objective risk derives from the uncertainty of the objective world and the limitation of people's cognitive ability as the objective world moves and changes so continuously that people cannot fully understand it. As Lenin said, "To really understand things needs to master and study clearly all aspects, relationships and 'mediators' of it. We could never achieve this completely" (Lenin, 1986). While the surrounding environment and the objects themselves are changing all the time, we cannot get an absolute "real-time" result, as well as "reconstructing" the status of that moment because we do study in a certain point of time. In addition, as indicated in the chaos theory, the deterministic system still has uncertainty. For example, the butterfly effect is superposition of a series of small probability events, but may bring about the result that "the flap of a butterfly's wing may cause a big storm". Consequently, the uncertainty of the objective world cannot be grasped completely by people.

For example, the rational price of stock should be the present value of the future earnings of the listed company. The price depends on the future earnings and discount rate related to the economic fundamentals, so that it must be predicted using past and current data. In fact, the future earnings depend on business performance of the listed company, which is indeterminate. The discount rate is based on interest rate, which is also affected by the market fluctuations. As a result, the future earnings and the discount rate are both uncertain since the rational price cannot be figured out. Both of the uncertainty will cause the risk, which is objective and independent of people's will, as we cannot fully understand the changes in fundamentals of real and fictitious economy. In recent years, the forecasting techniques have made significant progress, such as technologies in data mining, knowledge discovery in database, symbolic data analysis, group decision making, etc. There have been considerable improvements in forecasting using the historical data and the experience of experts. However, the future cannot be predicted with total accuracy as the objective risk always exists.

The subjective risk derives from the subjective estimate error of the expected return. Because the development of the stock market relies on the positive psychological expectancy, it could not be without speculation, bubble, and risk. If all the investors are rational and predict the future accurately, the share price would be fixed so that the trading volume would be zero. The speculators focus on the bid-offer spread, not the future discounted earnings. The existence of the spread is based on the estimation for the future price of some people, who may buy the stock over its rational price while they are over-optimistic. Therefore, coming with speculation, there is bubble, consequently, the risk, which dubbed the subjective risk. This kind of risk is easy to be magnified as the result of its positive feedback. As a general rule, people often tend to overestimate their risk tolerance that means ability to protect the security under a certain degree of probability and normal luck which is often overlooked. Taking the classical coin case for instance, getting the head and win one dollar, vice versa. How much should one prepare to prevent from losing all at the 90% probability when the Jesus stands just in the center of two guys? It is said that because the probability of head and tail sides are both 50%, people dare to gamble while they have two dollars. But the fact is that the probability of no less than once head in twice throws is only 75%, so one should prepare four dollars to get the 90% probability in normal luck according to the binomial theorem. As throwing coins for 1000 times, the opportunity of head is generally equal to the tail following the law of large numbers. But it is not true while throwing only twice. It is very likely to gamble away while throwing for fourth tail side. Therefore, people often over-estimate their risk tolerance. For example, it is precarious to speculate in stocks with mortgage loan, while people only have a thought of making money and do not fully considerate their risk tolerance.

Based on the principles of complex science, the subjective estimates of future are various in a complex system including people. A kind of self-organization which allows the system to continuously move in one direction could emerge as a result of the interaction between different people and the direction of the external environment. The subjective risk will accumulate gradually in the presence of self-organization, as well as constantly enlarge due to the role of positive feedback. Consequently, the stock price is much higher than its rational price.

4.4. Evaluation system of fictitious economy

The establishment of one evaluation system follows five steps in accordance with the principle of system engineering. First, the index system including many indicators should be established; the second is the determination of the measurement method for each indicator; the third is expressions of the measurement results that some could be expressed in a quantitative way and others in a qualitative way; the fourth is a judging method of the quality for each measurement result; finally, the integrated judging method for the measurement results should be determined to get the quality evaluation of the entire system. The weighted aggregate method is generally used which gets the summation of each indicator multiplied by the corresponding weight. Actually, this method has some limitations as ignoring the interaction between each indicator, so that the further research and improvement should be proposed.

5. Research Methodology of Fictitious Economy

There are six kinds of methods to research fictitious economy.

5.1. Complexity science methodology

Complexity science aims to study complexity and complex systems, which is the advanced stage of system science. Because of the interaction among elements of the system, as well as between systems and the external environment, the system will produce a self-organizing effect. It will form hierarchy and functional structure of the system and promote the system evolution in some direction. At present, there are five genres in complexity science in general. Among them the prevailing theory is self-organizing, self-learning, and adaptive theory, advocated by the Santa Fe Institute, the United States. For example, in the market economy, each enterprise is autonomous decision making, managing its own business. However, in fact, the decision making in each business is inevitably influenced by other company's decisions and also by the external environment. To some enterprise the system, when the emergence of new competitors, the company can change the behavior, that may need to improve quality, reduce production, or develop new products. From the external environment, when the banks tighten or easing money supply and cause changes in loan costs, the company's decision making usually will be changed accordingly. Because of blind expansion, some enterprises in our country are plunged into liquidity crisis at the circumstances of tightening the money supply, resulting in a loss or even bankruptcy. From a macroview, the self-organization effect should have a certain direction in a long time, which forms the ascending or decline phase of business cycle. It is the same in the stock market. For each person, making the decisions of what stocks to buy, when to buy, when to sell is his personal behavior. But he could have been influenced by the surrounding people — if most people buy, he may not sell. Consensus is also a kind of important influencing factor. For example, if public opinion is advocating "the expected ten thousand points" or "ten years of gold bull market", the investor may feel that we should buy. Affected by self-organization, the stock market will form bull or bear market.

Firstly, we have to study how the self-organization effect forms structure (Ilya and Nicolis, 1977). There are two types of structure, which are hierarchical structure and functional structure. For example, the organizational structure of an enterprise is probably such a hierarchy that includes the team, workshop, factory, the division, and the headquarters. Besides, there will form a kind of cross-hierarchical functional structure in the enterprise, such as financial subsystem, personnel subsystem, production subsystem, logistics subsystem, and so on.

Secondly, we need to study how the self-organization effect promotes the system evolution, which is self-organizing, self-learning, and adaptive. That means the system is not only able to self-organize, but also to obtain experience and lessons through self-learning and adapt to environmental changes, since the components in the system are intelligent. Any effective policy must be able to influence the behavior of members within the system. If the policy cannot change the behavior of members, the effect of this policy is small. Some government departments in our country always regard the policy as panacea and think policy can change the behavior of market players. But in fact it is not necessary. As pointed out by Mao Zedong: "external factors are conditions causing changes; internal changes are basis of changes; external factors work via internal factors" (Mao, 1991). If policy is exogenous, it has to work via changing behavior of the members in the system. For example, when the stock market soared during the first half of 2007, the government has taken some actions, including raising interest rates several times, raising the stamp duty, issuing special treasury bonds and so on. These actions in fact aims to prevent the stock market overheating. Chinese people are generally agreed that the market will not fall before 17th CPC National Congress or the Olympic Games. Based on this consideration, the policy cannot change people's expectations, and they will continue to buy at the high point till the bubble crash at 6,100 point, which caused the stock market slump and investors suffer enormous losses.

We will not only study the behavior of individuals, but also investigate the organizational behavior. Organizational behavior depends on the self-organization effect among the members in this organization, between individuals and groups (a group of people in organizations) as well as between organizations and external environment. Organizational behavior will react to the behavior of its members. To our opinion, we will study organizational behavior based on the characteristics of fictitious economy and the theory of Institutional Economics.

The basic methods of researching complexity science include the following four methods (Cheng, 1999).

(1) Combining qualitative determination and quantitative calculation. Some of the economists in our country decline to qualitative analysis, and some decline to quantitative analysis. One type is the researchers to study Marxist economics, including some famous economists. They usually are not good at quantitative analysis, and hardly use any mathematical tools in their published papers. They often have enough knowledge and experience of economics and can make sharp, qualitative judgments. Another type is the economic researchers who used to study engineering before. They usually

do well in quantitative tools, but are limited in knowledge of economics, which causes their calculated results often hard to be explained. Therefore, we must combine these two. We have to learn quantitative methods and cultivate common sense of economics in the meantime. We need to set up the conceptual model of the system and subsystem by qualitative judgments, then transform it into mathematical model and solve the problems by calculation or simulation. At last, we should summarize the conclusions derived from quantitative tools by qualitative analysis, to form a proposal to solve the problem.

(2) Combining microscopic and macroscopic analysis. Microanalysis aims to research the system elements and their hierarchical structure, while macroanalysis aims to understand the functional structure of the system and its formation process. For example, when we research the stock market, it is necessary to research both individual stocks and the overall stock market. The overall stock market is definitely not the sum of individual stocks. Certainly bubble of the stock market begins from some individual stock. When the evaluation of a stock is on the high side, it will produce foam, and the people holding this stock will sell it to make money. In a bull market, people earning money will not quit the stock market, but speculate those potential soaring stocks including rubbish shares, conceptual shares and so on, which cause bubble to those individual stocks. Finally we will see the bubble of overall stock market. The bubble of an individual stock is different with the whole market. Some excuse for the stock market bubble is said, "The bubble of China's stock market is structural", which is nonsense indeed. In any stock market, it is impossible that all of the listed companies have bubble. There is always part of them are good. Even in the stock market crash of "Black Monday", in 1987, in the United States, there were still 16 shares gained.

(3) Combining reductionism and Holism. Reductionism gives emphasis to microstructure and seeks explanation of the macrosituation based on it, such as explaining the biological phenomenon through physical–chemical laws. Holism thinks that the relationship and interaction among the members in the system determine the macronature of the system. However, it is difficult to grasp the overall system if there is no deep understanding of the system's microstructure. Complexity science is to discover the overall

property and behavior of the system by deeply studying individuals. It can be said that Reductionism is the prevailing methodology since Newton's times. From the view of Reductionism, divide a system into several subsystems, and then research every subsystem respectively. In this way, the issue has been thoroughly studied. But, in fact Reductionism cannot really solve the problem. It is necessary to combine it with Holism, which is one of the backgrounds of complexity science establishment. Holism is not only to look at each part, but also to study the interaction and influence between each part, which is the principle that the whole is larger than the total of the parts. Researching fictitious economy, we should not only study stock market, exchange rate market, and currency market respectively, but also explore their mutual contact and influence. For example, the changes of money market, foreign exchange market, and real estate market will affect the stock market, and they also affect each other.

(4) Combining scientific reasoning with philosophical speculation. Scientific theory is a conceptual system with some logical structure and tested by experiment. Scientists are always striving to explain some scientific theory with symbolic expression to make it an Axiomatic system. However, the development of science has proved that any theory is often not seamless and there exist some "anomalies". At this time, we must explain them with philosophical thought, such as the laws of individual and general, inevitability and contingency, as well as opposite, unity, and negation of negation.

5.2. Decision making method under uncertainty

Fictitious economy is high risk, and it faces the subjective and objective risk, that is, it faces the problem of uncertain decision making. There are following four methods of uncertain decision making.

(1) Quantify qualitative variables. Variables can be divided into quantitative, semiquantitative, and qualitative variables. Qualitative variables have two types — order variable and nominal variable. The so-called order variables are not numerical, but have differences with each other, and can be sorted according to some index, such as high, medium, and low. The order variables can be treated by a certain method, such

as multidimensional scaling or generalized quantization techniques. The variable of a nominal variable does not have any meaning itself, for example, the 5th basketball player does not mean he is better than the 1st. Illustrated in traffic study, it is necessary to assign a value to every transport mode, such as 1 for road transportation, 2 for railway, 3 for water, 4 for airlines, 5 for pipeline, and so on. It facilitates modeling and operation in computer.

(2) Determining the experience probability. This includes data mining, knowledge discovery in databases, intelligent mining, and so on. That is to infer the future based on the historical and existed data. It is usually the longer time span to infer, the greater its margin of error. Hence this method is suitable for short term prediction, not for the medium, or long-term prediction.

(3) Improvement of subjective probability. Subjective probability is given by experts based on their determination and analysis. Improvement of subjective probability means to improve the subjective probability by group decision making.

(4) Case study and integration of priori information. Case study is very important. Research work requires the researchers to master statistical data, has the ability to forecast, and is to be able to study the case. Though case study is individual, a "drop of water" can often reflect "the whole world". The individual case can discover a lot of specific problems, even some special cases not in conformity with common sense. Of course, we should not regard the results of case study as a universal law, because after all it is the individual event. Now some researchers abuse induction and treat illustration as a proof. That is wrong. If illustration equal proof, we can prove Sichuanese does not eat chili, for example. It is not difficult to find out several persons eating no chili from tens of millions Sichuaneses. Mr. Chang is Sichuanese and he does not eat chili; Mr. Wang is Sichuanese and he does not eat chili too; Mr. Li is Sichuanese and he does not eat chili either, which comes to the conclusion: Sichuaneses do not eat chili. Obviously this is wrong. Therefore, example cannot be taken as proof. In addition to case study, priori information is also very important. In the above case, Sichuaneses like chili is a priori information. Thus, we will doubt the conclusions that Sichuaneses do not eat chili. With priori information, case study cannot be puzzled by some superficies.

5.3. *Group decision making method*

In the decision-making process, the judgment of experts is very important. Group decision making is an effective means of improving expert judgments. The author sorts group decision making into two types, collaborative, and coordinative decision making.

Collaborative decision making is to study how to centralize the scattered views to form the optimal collective decision while the decision makers have the consistent goal, when the effect of group decision making will be better than any individual personal decision making. Delphi method is a practice of collaborative decision making in the early time. The process is to ask experts make their own judgments, then integrate their views and back to the experts. Each expert can revise his judgments according to the feedback. Slowly the dispersive views concentrate and finally a conclusion with majority agreement can be obtained. Now the decision makers have access to adequate information in advance by various means such as computers, and can gradually arrive at optimal decisions via integration of computer.

Coordinative decision making is to study how the participants with conflict of interest make a satisfactory decision making. That requires find a compromise point using cooperative game theory, such as the Shapley value solution and Nash agreement. For example, budget assignment is a typical case of coordinative decision making. When several departments discuss budget assignment, each department expects more. In the meantime, each department hopes to arrive at a result; otherwise they all cannot get money. Therefore, interest conflict and appropriate compromise both exist in coordinative decision making. There are many problems worthy of study.

In group decision making, we should consider the difference of knowledge and experience of all participants, the influence of information asymmetry between each other, and their behavior in the decision-making groups, to prevent the drift of the optimal decision point because of authority or herd effect. Probably, there are authoritative decision makers in the group, and others do not dare to oppose their points. That is so-called authority effect. In this circumstance, group decision making does not work. The so-called herd effect refers everybody go with the stream, which also cannot take the role of group decision making. In addition, we should develop and improve democratic centralism relying on modern decision-making science, to make it the decision-making system with Chinese characteristics.

5.4. Complex data analysis for decision support

Decision-making needs two types of knowledge for evaluation and prediction, knowledge about system quality and evolution. These two types of knowledge are both extracted from the data, for which the complex data analysis methods are necessary for research. There are now commonly used principal component analysis, factor analysis, cluster analysis, correlation analysis, regression analysis, regression tree, the logic of data analysis. There is a relatively new method of partial least squares, symbols, data analysis, data analysis functions, and so on.

5.5. Mathematical finance methods

Mathematical finance is to apply mathematical tools and models to study the financial problems. The following four methods research should be mastered in fictitious economy research.

(1) According to the principle of fictitious economy, the pricing of financial assets has relationship with the adhered real economy. For example, pricing of a company's stock has relationship with the enterprise's assets and performance. In fact, there are three types of enterprise assets pricing. The first is pricing of tangible assets, which has mature theories and methods in Accounting and Finance, including depreciation, tangible and intangible loss, and so on. The second is the pricing of intangible assets. Now, there are many state-owned enterprises in China, whose tangible assets almost have been depleted after the decades' depreciation. Their values lie in the intangible assets, such as its trademark, customers, technology, skilled workers, and so on. At present, people are still willing to merger and acquisition to those state-owned enterprises with very few tangible assets, because of achieving their intangible assets. However, the pricing of intangible assets has always been a problem. For lower price may cause loss of state-owned assets and higher price will stop people to buy. The third is dynamic pricing, which is to expect the future value. Many equity investments, especially private fund investment, depend on

the future value of investing object. The major roles of private fund are mergers and acquisitions. After M&A business, private fund will enhance the value through improving management and related systems, and then sell it again. Therefore, private fund has no interest in enterprise operation and development. Similar with venture capital funds, private fund aims to find the future value of the object. There is no good solution for how to find the future value of enterprises, which is exactly what we should study deeply. It is meaningless to discuss whether suffering disadvantage in M&A, when there is no proper evaluation methods, because we do not know the exact value of companies. If the future value of enterprise will have significant growth after M&A, it will be worthy. Both two sides have received corresponding return. However, if the future value of enterprise after M&A has no or little growth, it is not a successful M&A.

(2) Fractal market analyses (Peters, 2002; Yang *et al.*, 2008) are a branch of nonlinear science to describe complex system with irregular structure. Fractal refers to the frame that has some similarity (usually from the view of statistics) between some parts and the overall of the system. Fractal dimension, which is noninteger dimension, is quantitative characterization and basic parameter of fractal. Fractal market hypothesis is proposed since the traditional efficient market hypothesis is difficult to explain the trend of price behavior in capital market. Fractal market analysis tries to analyze the generalized capital markets on holism theory, which can better explain the diversity of investors. Fractal market analysis has overcome the limitations of efficient market theory, and taken into account nonrational expectations of investors and the nonlinear relationship of market reacting to information. The most important finding of fractal market analysis is that the stability of market is based on the diversity of investors. When there are many investors with different investment periods to participate, it can ensure the market stable.

(3) Autoregressive Conditional Heteroscedasticity Analysis (ARCH) (Mills, 2002) was introduced in 1982. It has been considered by many researchers as a better nonlinear financial time series model. To obtain more flexibility, some researchers extended ARCH further to GARCH (General Autoregressive Conditional Heteroscedasticity). Many empirical studies have shown that the volatility of stock returns is time-varying (conditional heteroskedasticity) and nonlinear characters. Single variable

model of GARCH has captured this dynamic behavior of volatility to a certain extent by the means of describing volatility as a linear equation of past forecasting mean square error. But, the parameters of GARCH are not stable in the time dimension. Some research has also pointed out that sometimes the predicted results based on simple GARCH model are poor. Therefore, all sorts of improvements have been performed to ARCH, including nonlinear ARCH (NARCH), threshold ARCH (TARCH), asymmetric ARCH (AARCH), quadratic ARCH (QARCH), noninteger integral ARCH (FIGARCH), ARMA-ARCH, and so on. ARCH is an important method of mathematical finance, which has been widely used in financial analysis such as futures analysis, stock market analysis. But we also realize its limitation as a black-box method. We must explore the methods combining ARCH analysis and mechanism analysis, and do not rely too much on the conclusions of ARCH analysis.

(4) Financial risk theory covers definition, measurement, processing, control, and management of risk. With accumulation of the financial data and development of statistical methods, the traditional financial risks theory, such as option pricing and hedging theory, is facing challenge (Phillipe and Marc, 2002).

5.6. *Computer simulation methods*

The final method of complexity sciences is computer simulation. Computer simulation methods generally have two types. One is the so-called discrete event simulation, which is traditional methods of computer simulation, such as GPSS, symscript, and so on. The other is agent-based simulation, which has been widely used in complex sciences research. There are two tools in agent-based simulation. One is Swarm Simulation Toolkit, developed by Santa Fe Institute, the United States. The other is NetLogo, developed by Northwestern University. Other well-known relative simulation tools include Artificial Life, Cellular Automata, Co-opetition, and so on.

References

Cheng, S., 1999. Fictitious economy and financial crisis. *Journal of Management Sciences in China*, 2(1), 1–6.

Cheng, S., 1999. *Complex Science and Management, Included in Exploring Complexity Science*. Beijing: Democracy and Construction Press, pp. 1–15.

Cheng, S., 2003. *On Fictitious Economy*. Beijing: Democracy and Construction Press.

Cheng, S., 2007. *On Financial Reforms*. Beijing: China People's University Press.

Cheng, S., 2008. *On Venture Capital Investment*. Beijing: China People's University Press.

Cheng, S. *et al.*, 1999. *Analysis and Implications of the Financial Crisis in East Asia*. Beijing: Democracy and Construction Press.

Ilya, P. and Nicolis, G., 1977. *Self-Organization in Non-Equilibrium Systems*. Wiley.

Jiang, Z., 2002. Build a well-off society in an all-round way, and create a new situation in building socialism with chinese characteristics — delivered at the opening of the 16th CPC Party Congress (November 8, 2002).

Lenin, Vl., 1986. More on Union, Current Situation and the Mistakes Taken by Comrade Trotsky and Bukharinite, in *The Collected Works of Lenin* (Vol X). Beijing: People Press, 291.

Liu, J.M., 1998. *From Fictitious Capital to Fictitious Economy*. Jinan: Shandong People's Publishing House.

Marx, K., 1957. *Das Kapital*, 1st edn., Vol. III. Translated by the Compilation and Translation Bureau of the CPC Central Committee. Beijing: People Press, 525–670.

Mills, T.C., 2002. *The Econometric Modeling of Financial Time Series*, 1999, 2nd edn. Translated by Yu Zhuojing. Beijing: Economic Science Press.

Peters, E.E., 2002. *Fractal Market Analysis*. Translated by Chu Hailin, Yin Qin. Beijing: Economic Science Press.

Phillipe, B.J. and Marc, P., 2002. *Theory of Financial Risks*. Translated by Zhou Weiqun. Beijing: Economic Science Press.

Portes, A., 1998. Social capital: Its origins and applications in modern sociology. *Annual Review of Sociology*, 24, 1–24.

Samezo, K., 1989. *Dictionary of Das Kapital*. Translated by Xue Jingxiao *et al.*, Nankai University Press.

Simon, H., 1976. *Administrative Behavior*, 3rd edn. New York: The Free Press.

Mao, T., 1991. *On Contradiction, Selected Works of Mao Tsetung*, 2nd edn., Vol. I. Beijing: People Press, p. 302.

Virtual-Economy. http://virtual-economy.org/.

Wikipedia. http://en.wikipedia.org/wiki/Virtual_economy.

Xu, J., 2008. *Virtual Monetary and Virtual Bank*. Shanghai: Shanghai Jiao Tong University Press.

Yang, X., Qian, L., and Lijun, W., 2008. Theoretic discussion on fractal market analysis in capital market. *Finance and Economy*, 16, 85–86.

Mutual Funds Performance Evaluation Based on Endogenous Benchmarks[*]

Xiujuan Zhao[†], Shouyang Wang[‡], Wuyi Yue[§], and Hong Yan[¶]

[†] *School of Economics and Management,*
Beijing University of Posts and Telecommunication,
Beijing 100876, China

[‡] *Academy of Mathematics and Systems Science,*
Chinese Academy of Sciences, Beijing 100080, China

[§] *Department of Intelligence and Informatics,*
Konan University, Kobe 658–8501, Japan

[¶] *Faculty of Business, The Hong Kong Polytechnic University,*
Hung Hom, Kowloon, Hong Kong

This article proposes two quadratic-constrained Data Envelopment Analysis (DEA) models for the evaluation of mutual funds, from a perspective of evaluation based on endogenous benchmarks. In comparison to the previous studies, this article decomposes the two vital factors for mutual funds performance, i.e., risk and return, in these quadratic-constrained DEA models, one of which is a partly controllable quadratic-constrained programming, in order to construct mutual funds' endogenous benchmarks and give insight management suggestions. The approach is illustrated using a sample of 25 actual mutual funds in the China market. It identifies the root reasons for inefficiency and the ways for improving the performance. The result shows that although the market environment in year 2006 is much better than that in 2005, the average efficiency score declines in year 2006 due to the relaxing of system risk control. The majority of mutual funds do not show persistence in efficiency ranking.

*This research is in part supported by Grant-in-Aid for Science Research (No. 19500070) and MEXT.ORC (2004–2008) of Japan, the Hong Kong UGC CERG Fund PolyU5457/06H and the National Natural Science Foundation of China (No. 70801006).

The most important conclusion is that the ranking of mutual funds in China depends mostly on the system risk control.

Keywords: Mutual funds; Data envelopment analysis (DEA); Performance evaluation; Efficiency; Persistence.

1. Introduction

Mutual funds have become one of the most important investment tools for most people as these enable them to take part in diversified investment. Assets managed by mutual funds are increasing and their types and demands are getting diversified; therefore, how to evaluate funds' performance has become a question of consequence. Since the important work of Markowitz (1952), Sharp (1964, 1966), Treyner (1965), and Jensen (1968, 1969), numerous studies have been concerned with measuring performance in two aspects, risk and return, mainly based on the mean-variance (MV) framework. The evaluation results of these studies appear to depend, to a large extent, on the exterior benchmark used (1978).

In the most recent decade, there have emerged some studies based on data envelopment analysis (DEA) methodologies to evaluate mutual funds' performance. Introduced by Charnes and colleagues (CCR) (1978), DEA is a mathematical programming method for measuring the relative efficiency of decision-making units (DMUs). Since it is a nonparameter method capable of comparative evaluation, it is able to give assessments based on multi-inputs and multi-outputs and enables managements to benchmark the best-practices of mutual funds by calculating scores denoting their efficiencies.

In order to assess 11 funds engaging in finance and metal industries in International Bargainers Research Database, Wilkens and Zhu (2001) chose the standard deviation of returns and the proportion of negative monthly return in the year as inputs, monthly return, skewness of return distribution and the minimum return in the year as outputs. Murthi and colleagues (1997) put forwarded a portfolio performance measurement based on DEA in 1997, called DEA portfolio efficiency index (DPEI), with the standard deviation and transaction loads as inputs, excess return as outputs to investigate 2,083 mutual funds in the third quarter of year 1993.

Choi and Murthi (2001) used the same inputs and outputs but with a different DEA formulation. McMullen and Strong (1998) analyzed and compared the comparative effectiveness of 135 American stock funds with the data of the past one year, the past three years, and the past five years based on DPEI index. Sedzro and Sardano (1999), on the other hand, analyzed 58 US equity funds that exist in Canada using DEA with annual return, expense ratio, minimum initial investment, and a proxy for risk as factors associated with fund performance. Galagedera and Silvapulle (2002) analyzed and measured comparative effectiveness of 257 Australian mutual funds during years 1995–1999 in different combinations of inputs and outputs. Basso and Funari (2001) used several risk measures (standard deviation, standard semi-deviation, and beta) and subscription and redemption costs as inputs and the mean return and the fraction of periods in which the mutual fund was nondominated as outputs. Basso and Funari (2003), for assessing ethical funds, substituted the fraction of nondominated periods for an ethical score of the mutual fund. Luo and colleagues (2003) used the integrated DEA index to evaluate the comparative performance of 33 closed-end funds, which come into the Chinese market before 2001. They found that the ranking differs much from that of Jessen index, which indicates that index selecting is very important in funds' performance evaluation. Chang (2004) used a nonstandard DEA formulation (based on minimum convex input requirement set) with mean return as output and standard deviation, beta, total assets, and load as inputs. Zhao and colleagues (2007) evaluated Chinese mutual funds in DEA model with value-at-risk (VaR) under asymmetry Laplace distribution, cost and total return, and also investigated their scale efficiencies. Furthermore, Luo *et al.* (2003), Han and Liu (2003), Ma and colleagues (2003) also studied the performance of closed-end funds in the Chinese market with improved DEA model. Chen (2003) summed up DEA models applied in mutual funds performance evaluation.

Most of these researches were based on conventional linear envelopment model, and the major differences between them are the consideration of variables and data samples. As is known to all, that DEA approaches provide each inefficient DMU's endogenous benchmark and estimates of the potential improvement that can be made. In mutual funds' evaluation in DEA models, the endogenous benchmarks are portfolios of funds. It is one of the advantages of DEA approaches. However, conventional DEA approaches do not compute correctly the risk of the target portfolios, as in the above references. These approaches compute the risk measure of the benchmark against which the mutual fund is compared as a linear combination of the risk measures of the intervening mutual funds. This does not take into account the diversification effects and the resulting overestimation of the risk measure usually leads to underestimate the efficiency scores. To make up for this consideration, Morey and Morey (1999) and Briec *et al.* (2004) proposed quadratic-constrained DEA models that use an MV approach with variance as input and mean return as output. But there is still space to improve. Their input is total risk and output is total return. This makes sense, but still is not explicit enough in management. A good evaluation should be able to tell the root reason for different performances.

This article is going to dig the problem deeper and gives two quadratic-constrained envelopment models with information of system risk, nonsystem risk, excess return from timing and excess return from selecting. Our purpose is to investigate the root reason of each mutual fund's relative efficiency, present its endogenous benchmark, and further to give performance improvement suggestions. Considering that the two kinds of risk are a little different from each other, system risk cannot be lessened with diversification while nonsystem risk can, we give a quadratic constrain for nonsystem risk in the envelopment evaluation model. While constrains of system risk, of excess returns should be handled as linear. In addition, since the system risk is an uncontrollable factor, we take uncontrollable factor technology in our quadratic-constrained DEA models. The two models proposed in this article are from the perspective of input orientation and the perspective of output orientation respectively. With this approach, investors will be more capable to assess mutual funds or make funds portfolios to the best with their endogenous benchmarks.

The rest of this article is organized as follows. Section 2 describes measures of risk and excess return. Section 3 presents the two quadratic-constrained envelopment evaluation models for mutual funds' endogenous benchmarks. Section 4 makes an empirical study of mutual funds in China and Sec. 5 draws some insightful conclusions.

2. Measures for Risk and Excess Return

2.1. *Excess return*

Different mutual funds differ in investment proportions due to different assets collocation. Most existing quantitative researches of asset collocation are based on the frame of Brinson *et al.* (1986). Actual collocation is a course of timing and equity selection, which defines extended and steady strategic structure originally, and then adjusts each kind of asset's proportion including stock, bond, and money dynamically. Asset collocating is the principle step of investment decision. Decomposing and measuring the excess return from asset collocation can help managers find out the reasons for performance differences and movement as time changing, and identify its performance improvement in the future.

According to Brinson and colleagues, suppose that there is a market benchmark M with g kinds of assets and a mutual fund P with the same g kinds of assets. g is a positive integrity. These g kinds may be stock, bond, or money etc. The return of the ith asset in P is denoted as R_{pi} and that in M is denoted as R_{mi} ($i = 1, 2, \ldots, g$). The ith asset proportion in P is denoted as W_{pi} and in M is denoted as W_{mi}, respectively. Then mutual fund P's excess return from timing R_{PT} can be represented as follows:

$$R_{PT} = \sum_{i=1}^{g} R_{mi} \times (W_{Pi} - W_{mi}), \tag{1}$$

Mutual fund P's excess return from selecting R_{PS} can be represented as follows:

$$R_{PS} = \sum_{i=1}^{g} (R_{pi} - R_{mi}) \times W_{pi}. \tag{2}$$

For practical conveniences, the original proportion allocation of the mutual funds P at the beginning of some given time horizon is regarded as benchmark M's collation proportion. And we suppose the benchmark will not change its asset allocation during this horizon. Therefore, we can investigate mutual fund P's excess return from asset collation adjustment, or we can say, timing during the given period via formula (1). However, since it is very hard for us to get the actual return R_{pi}, excess return from selecting cannot be computed directly. Here, we get a substitute in an indirect way for selecting by excluding timing as follows:

$$R_{PQ} = R_P - R_M - R_{PT}, \qquad (3)$$

where R_P is mutual fund P's actual total return, and R_M is the benchmark's total return. R_{PQ} can be regarded approximately as the excess return from selecting during the given period.

2.2. Risks

Risk is a vital factor affecting the return. As a professional financing instrument, one of mutual funds' basic functions is to manage portfolio's risk. According to Capital Asset Pricing Model (CAPM), investment risk can be decomposed into system risk and nonsystem risk. System risk is from market's integral changing, impossible to be diversified by the portfolio. Nonsystem risk is the risk that only affects some industry or some company, able to be counteracted by diversified investment. System risk can be computed as follows according to CAPM:

$$R_P = \alpha_P + \beta_P R_M + \varepsilon_P, \qquad (4)$$

where R_P denotes the mutual fund's total return and R_M denotes the benchmark's total return. β_P is a measure of system risk. The bigger β_P value is, the higher system risk this mutual fund takes. Equation (4) can be solved by Least-Squares Method. The standard deviation $\sigma(\varepsilon_P)$ of stochastic error series ε_P is regarded as nonsystem risk.

Though the transaction loads is also what investors concern about and it is a necessary payout in mutual fund operation, high initial commission and redemption commission are a severe intimidation and erosion to investment return. It needs not to be considered solely, because mutual funds' returns have already subtracted it.

In summary, in our programming evaluation model for mutual funds, we will consider system risk indicator β_P, nonsystem risk indicator $\sigma(\varepsilon_P)$, excess return from timing and excess return from selecting.

3. Modeling

3.1. *Related models*

The conventional DEA model that was employed in previous related studies is the CCR model (1978) or BCC model (1984), which are both linear DEA models and going to be illustrated as follows: Suppose that there are n mutual funds. Each one has m inputs and s outputs. $\mathbf{x}_j$ is the input vector and $\mathbf{y}_j$ is the output vector of the jth mutual fund, $\mathbf{x}_j = (x_{1j}, x_{2j}, \ldots, x_{mj})$, $\mathbf{y}_j = (y_{1j}, y_{2j}, \ldots, y_{sj})$. The state possibility set made of inputs and outputs is $T = \{(\mathbf{x}, \mathbf{y}) | \mathbf{x} \geq \sum_{j=1}^{n} \lambda_j \mathbf{x}_j, \mathbf{y} \leq \sum_{j=1}^{n} \lambda_j \mathbf{y}_j, j = 1, 2, \ldots, n\}$. Then, the comparative efficiency of mutual fund $j_0 (1 \leq j_0 \leq n)$ can be defined as

$$\theta^* = \min \theta$$

subject to

$$\sum_{j=1}^{n} \lambda_j x_{ij} \leq \theta x_{ij_0}, \quad i = 1, 2, \ldots, m,$$

$$\sum_{j=1}^{n} \lambda_j y_{rj} \geq y_{rj_0}, \quad r = 1, 2, \ldots, s, \tag{5}$$

$$\sum_{j=1}^{n} \lambda_j = 1,$$

$$\lambda_j \geq 0.$$

It is easily seen that linear model provides a subsection production surface, which denotes a production frontier in economics: the most outputs on given inputs or the least inputs on given outputs. Projection of inefficient units (funds) actually provides a feasible scenario to improve performance, since it points out the reason and extent of inefficiency, as is also one of DEA model's advantages. Here, the projection of an inefficient point $(\mathbf{x}_{j_0}, \mathbf{y}_{j_0})$ is

$$\begin{cases} \hat{\mathbf{x}}_{j_0} = \theta^* \mathbf{x}_{j_0} - \mathbf{s}^{*+} = \sum_{j=1}^{n} \lambda_j^* \mathbf{x}_j \\ \hat{\mathbf{y}}_{j_0} = \mathbf{y}_{j_0} + \mathbf{s}^{*-} = \sum_{j=1}^{n} \lambda_j^* \mathbf{y}_j, \end{cases} \tag{6}$$

where s^{*+}, s^{*-} are the corresponding optimal relax and optimal surplus for constraints of model (5). $(\hat{x}_{j_0}, \hat{y}_{j_0})$ denotes a new comparatively DEA efficient fund against the original n funds.

Apparently, DEA models provide endogenous benchmarks for each inefficient mutual fund and estimates of the potential improvement that can be made. The endogenous benchmarks are portfolios of mutual funds in the evaluation. The inputs of the benchmark against which the mutual fund is compared are a linear combination of the inputs of the intervening mutual funds, so are the outputs. However, when risk measure is as one of inputs, linear DEA model cannot compute correctly the risk of the target portfolios, as in the related references. It does not take into account the diversification effects and the resulting overestimation of the risk measure usually leads to underestimate the efficiency scores. To make up for this consideration, Morey and Morey (1999) and Briec and colleagues (2004) proposed quadratic-constrained DEA models that use an MV approach with variance as input and mean return as output. Suppose there is only risk as an input and total return as an output, determine $\omega_j \geq 0$ ($j = 1, 2, \ldots, j_0, \ldots, n$) and $\theta \geq 1$, so that

$$\theta^* = \max \theta$$
subject to
$$\sum_{j=1}^{n} \omega_j^2 \sigma_j^2 + \sum_{\substack{k=1 \\ k \neq j}}^{n} \sum_{j=1}^{n} \omega_k \omega_j \text{Cov}(R_k, R_j) \leq \sigma_{j_0}^2,$$
$$\sum_{j=1}^{n} \omega_j E(R_j) \geq \theta E(R_{j_0}), \tag{7}$$
$$\sum_{j=1}^{n} \omega_j = 1,$$
$$\omega_j \geq 0,$$

where σ_j^2 is the jth mutual fund's return deviation variance to measure the total risk, $\sigma_{j_0}^2$ is fund j_0's return deviation variance, $\text{Cov}(R_k, R_j)$ is the covariance between the ith mutual fund and the jth mutual fund, $E(R_j)$

and $E(R_{j_0})$ are the expectations of the ith and the jth mutual fund's return respectively.

3.2. Proposed model

Model (7) is more scientific and accords with reality, concerning about funds' risk and return. It takes the diversification effect for risk into consideration. On the other hand, since there is only total risk and total return measure concerned, even though the model can provide much insightful information to improve performance, it is still not clear enough and practical enough. For example, a relative inefficient fund has a target portfolio of mutual funds as an endogenous benchmark. If the model tells that it needs to lower its total risk at some extent to be relatively efficient, say 10% compared to its original level, then how should we realize it? Both the fund's risk measure and the target portfolio's risk measure are total risk, wherein actually, nonsystem risk is avoidable or diversified and system risk is unavoidable.

The similar situation happens to return the measure. Investors care about the excess return of mutual funds more than total return, as a matter of fact. The excess return is the substantial reason that they invest on mutual funds. Even we take excess return as an output in model (7) and model (7) gives us suggestions on how much to improve on excess return to get better performance, it does not provide ultimate help in mutual fund's management. Because it can only tell the extent of improvement needed, but not the specific way to improve. That is why we are going to describe our quadratic-constrained envelopment models as follows.

It is also based on model (7).

$$\theta^* = \max(\theta_1 + \theta_2)/2$$

subject to

$$\sum_{j=1}^{n} \omega_j^2 \sigma^2(\varepsilon_j) + \sum_{\substack{k=1 \\ k \neq j}}^{n} \sum_{j=1}^{n} \omega_k \omega_j \mathrm{Cov}(\varepsilon_k, \varepsilon_j) \leq \sigma^2(\varepsilon_{j_0}),$$

$$\sum_{j=1}^{n} \omega_j \beta_j \leq \beta_{j_0},$$

$$\sum_{j=1}^{n} \omega_j R_{jT} \geq \theta_1 R_{j_0 T},$$

$$\sum_{j=1}^{n} \omega_j R_{jQ} \geq \theta_2 R_{j_0 Q},$$

$$\sum_{j=1}^{n} \omega_j = 1,$$

$$\omega_j \geq 1, \tag{8}$$

where $\sigma^2(\varepsilon_j)$ $(j = 1, 2, \ldots, j_0, \ldots, n)$ is the variance of ε_j and β_j $(j = 1, 2, \ldots, j_0, \ldots, n)$ denotes the jth mutual fund's system risk level. Both ε_j and β_j come from the following Eq. (9). $\text{Cov}(\varepsilon_k, \varepsilon_j)$ is the covariance between ε_k and ε_j.

$$R_j = \alpha_j + \beta_j R_M + \varepsilon_j, \quad j = 1, 2, \ldots, j_0, \ldots, n. \tag{9}$$

And R_{jT} $(j = 1, 2, \ldots, j_0, \ldots, n)$ in Eq. (8) comes from the following Eq. (10) and $R_{jQ}(j = 1, 2, \ldots, j_0, \ldots, n)$ in Eq. (8) comes from the following Eq. (11).

$$R_{jT} = \sum_{i=1}^{g} R_{mi} \times (W_{ji} - W_{mi}), \quad j = 1, 2, \ldots, j_0, \ldots, n, \tag{10}$$

$$R_{jQ} = R_j - R_M - R_{jT}, \quad j = 1, 2, \ldots, j_0, \ldots, n. \tag{11}$$

R_j is the jth mutual fund's return and R_M is the return of the market benchmark.

Model (8) considers the problem from an output perspective. It tries to keep the fund's risk level and increases its excess returns as much as possible. θ^* represents the relative performance. According to classical data envelopment analysis methodology, θ^* in output forms will be larger than or equal to 1, which means that the larger θ^* is, the poorer performance the fund has.

On the contrary, when it comes to input perspective, we could constitute another quadratic-constrained envelopment model as follows to settle the same problem.

$$\varphi^* = \min \varphi$$

subject to

$$\sum_{j=1}^{n} \omega_j^2 \sigma^2(\varepsilon_j) + \sum_{\substack{k=1 \\ k \neq j}}^{n} \sum_{j=1}^{n} \omega_k \omega_j \text{Cov}(\varepsilon_k, \varepsilon_j) \leq \varphi \sigma^2(\varepsilon_{j_0}),$$

$$\sum_{j=1}^{n} \omega_j \beta_j \leq \beta_{j_0},$$

$$\sum_{j=1}^{n} \omega_j R_{jT} \geq R_{j_0 T}, \tag{12}$$

$$\sum_{j=1}^{n} \omega_j R_{jQ} \geq R_{j_0 Q},$$

$$\sum_{j=1}^{n} \omega_j = 1,$$

$$\omega_j \geq 1.$$

Considering that one of inputs, system risk cannot be diversified by portfolio, we are not able to change the system risk level unless changing volumes, which means system risk is uncontrollable. Therefore, improvement indicator φ is not multiplied to the right side of the system risk constraint. There is only nonsystem risk is controllable in model (12). Model (12) actually describes a scene that decreases nonsystem risk as much as possible without lessening any of excess return by constituting a new portfolio of mutual funds. Apparently, φ^* is less than 1 and the less φ^* value is, the poorer performance is.

Models (8) and (12) can be converted into their equivalents as models (13) and (14) respectively.

$$\theta^* = \max(\theta_1 + \theta_2)/2$$

subject to

$$\sum_{j=1}^{n} \omega_j^2 \sigma^2(\varepsilon_j) + \sum_{\substack{k=1 \\ k \neq j}}^{n} \sum_{j=1}^{n} \omega_k \omega_j \text{Cov}(\varepsilon_k, \varepsilon_j) + s_1^+ = \sigma^2(\varepsilon_{j_0}),$$

$$\sum_{j=1}^{n} \omega_j \beta_j + s_2^+ = \beta_{j_0},$$

$$\sum_{j=1}^{n} \omega_j R_{jT} - s_1^- = \theta_1 R_{j_0T},$$

$$\sum_{j=1}^{n} \omega_j R_{jQ} - s_2^- = \theta_2 R_{j_0Q}, \tag{13}$$

$$\sum_{j=1}^{n} \omega_j = 1,$$

$$\omega_j \geq 1$$

$$\varphi^* = \min \varphi$$

subject to

$$\sum_{j=1}^{n} \omega_j^2 \sigma^2(\varepsilon_j) + \sum_{\substack{k=1 \\ k \neq j}}^{n} \sum_{j=1}^{n} \omega_k \omega_j \mathrm{Cov}(\varepsilon_k, \varepsilon_j) + s_1^+ = \varphi \sigma^2(\varepsilon_{j_0}),$$

$$\sum_{j=1}^{n} \omega_j \beta_j + s_2^+ = \beta_{j_0},$$

$$\sum_{j=1}^{n} \omega_j R_{jT} - s_1^- = R_{j_0T}, \tag{14}$$

$$\sum_{j=1}^{n} \omega_j R_{jQ} - s_2^- = R_{j_0Q},$$

$$\sum_{j=1}^{n} \omega_j = 1,$$

$$\omega_j \geq 1,$$

where s_1^+, s_2^+, s_1^-, and s_2^- are the corresponding relax and optimal surplus for the constraints.

The projection of an inefficient mutual fund can be attained by the following equations:

$$
\begin{cases}
\hat{\sigma}^2(\varepsilon_{j_0}) = \varphi\sigma^2(\varepsilon_{j_0}) - s_1^{*+} = \sum_{j=1}^{n}(\omega_j^*)^2\sigma^2(\varepsilon_j) \\
\qquad + \sum_{\substack{k=1 \\ k \neq j}}^{n}\sum_{j=1}^{n}\omega_k^*\omega_j^*\mathrm{Cov}(\varepsilon_k, \varepsilon_j) \\
\hat{\beta}_{j_0} = \beta_{j_0} - s_2^{*+} = \sum_{j=1}^{n}\omega_j^*\beta_j \\
\hat{R}_{j_0 T} = R_{j_0 T} + s_1^{*-} = \sum_{j=1}^{n}\omega_j^* R_{j T} \\
\hat{R}_{j_0 Q} = R_{j_0 Q} + s_2^{*-} = \sum_{j=1}^{n}\omega_j^* R_{j Q},
\end{cases}
\tag{15}
$$

where $s_1^{*+}, s_2^{*+}, s_1^{*-}$, and s_2^{*-} are the corresponding optimal relax and optimal surplus for the constraints. ω_j^* $(j = 1, 2, \ldots, n)$ are the optimal weights for each unit. $\hat{\sigma}^2(\varepsilon_{j_0})$, $\hat{\beta}_{j_0}$, $\hat{R}_{j_0 T}$, and $\hat{R}_{j_0 Q}$ actually constitute a new target portfolio for mutual fund j_0. With these parameters, mutual fund j_0 is able to identify the essential reason for poor performance and later to improve it.

$$
\begin{cases}
\Delta\sigma^2(\varepsilon_{j_0}) = \sigma^2(\varepsilon_{j_0}) - \hat{\sigma}^2(\varepsilon_{j_0}) = (1 - \varphi)\sigma^2(\varepsilon_{j_0}) + s_1^{*+} \\
\Delta\beta_{j_0} = \beta_{j_0} - \hat{\beta}_{j_0} = s_2^{*+} \\
\Delta R_{j_0 T} = \hat{R}_{j_0 T} - R_{j_0 T} = s_1^{*-} \\
\Delta R_{j_0 Q} = R_{j_0 Q} - \hat{R}_{j_0 Q} = s_2^{*-}.
\end{cases}
\tag{16}
$$

4. Empirical Study

4.1. *Data*

With the financial market liberalization and globalization, foreign investors' interest in the Chinese financial market is growing considerably. Therefore, ranking in mutual fund industry would be of international interest.

Since open-ended mutual funds in China are required to publish their asset collocation data from year 2004, only asset data from year 2005 to year 2007 is available when this paper is done. To insure all evaluated funds are in the same market environment and policy circumstance, 25 open-end mutual funds of stock type which have the required data in years 2005 and 2006 are selected to do empirical study here, all of which were issued before year 2004.

According to the prescription of stock-typed mutual funds by CERC[1], we construct the virtual exterior benchmark, i.e., market benchmark as 80% × contemporary stock market return + 15% × contemporary bond market return + 5% × money return, among which contemporary stock market return refers to 50% of ISA[2] return and 50% ISIA[3] return, contemporary bond market return refers to CBI[4] return. The virtual benchmark is designed to reflect the Chinese security market comprehensively and accurately. All data come from Tianxiang Investment Analysis System.

Disposed data are shown as Table 1.

The stock market in year 2005 was still in vale, when most funds were cautious to control their risk and restricted β_j ($1 \leq j \leq 25$) less than 1 to avoid more loss in course of market falling down. That is why Chinese mutual funds' system risks were lower than the benchmark. While in year 2006 when bull market came, the funds' risk control slacked off to share benefits of grail rising, therefore β_js were exalted.

4.2. Ranking

Evaluating 25 mutual funds' performance both in years 2005 and 2006 in model (14), the outcome is shown as Table 2.

The evaluation of each fund's comparative performance reveals the ones settled on the production frontier, and points out each fund's performance changing and their comparative rankings movement in the given set.

---

[1] Asset on stock not less than 60% and not more than 95%, regulated in Management Methods of Equity Investment Funds Operation, 29th June, 2004.
[2] Index of Shanghai A-shares that is the signal index of Shanghai Stock Exchange.
[3] Index of Shenzhen Ingredients A-shares that is the signal index of Shenzhen Stock Exchange.
[4] The Chinese Bond Index that is the signal index of Chinese bond market.

Table 1. Inputs and outputs of 25 mutual funds.

Fund Name	β_P 2005	β_P 2006	$\sigma^2(\varepsilon_P)$ 2005	$\sigma^2(\varepsilon_P)$ 2006	R_{PT} 2005	R_{PT} 2006	R_{PQ} 2005	R_{PQ} 2006
Huaanchuangxin	0.6098	0.7208	0.006	0.0074	0.500877	-8.84208	-0.4173	8.888619
Huaxiachengzhang	0.5932	0.7634	0.0048	0.0071	0.727706	0.796419	-0.58849	-0.76601
Guotaijinying	0.5571	0.797	0.0056	0.0072	-2.55794	19.83804	2.682034	-19.6411
Xinlanchou	0.6132	0.7853	0.0056	0.0067	0.852928	-2.82101	-0.76504	2.805617
Changshengchengzhang	0.5789	0.6946	0.0047	0.0052	0.544688	-6.6933	-0.44124	6.477621
Baoyinghongli	0.5982	0.7694	0.0048	0.0089	0.025801	-18.3518	0.025952	18.68587
Dachengjiazhi	0.5653	0.7673	0.0044	0.0068	-0.53951	-7.68092	0.654394	7.711403
Jiashichengzhang	0.5665	0.7071	0.0058	0.0083	0.37455	-17.5095	-0.25179	17.63945
Huaan MSCI	0.7537	0.8949	0.0029	0.0047	-3.93021	-1.60627	3.949763	1.749488
Wanjia 180	0.7144	0.9021	0.0019	0.0046	-3.40292	3.961437	3.41861	-3.80676
Zhaoshanggupiao	0.5836	0.7154	0.0047	0.0062	0.018714	-0.72987	0.109939	0.727443
Hefengchengzhang	0.6113	0.7316	0.0049	0.008	0.573651	18.12505	-0.30043	-18.3777
Hefengzhouqi	0.6625	0.7284	0.0056	0.0084	-0.86473	11.03235	1.004541	-10.7496
Hefengwending	0.5919	0.6844	0.0053	0.0075	1.15508	15.99596	-1.03283	-15.7377
Jinyingyouxuan	0.6714	0.7143	0.0043	0.0087	0.502953	-5.32444	-0.44693	5.018644
Penghuashouyi	0.5818	0.6203	0.0049	0.0095	-1.02203	-20.0305	1.132801	20.08416
Jiashiwenjian	0.5241	0.6881	0.005	0.0058	-1.05893	-2.01028	1.185118	1.794744
Jiashizengzhang	0.5458	0.6695	0.0056	0.0073	-1.37267	-14.4914	1.627866	14.53621
Baokangxiaofeipin	0.5492	0.6205	0.004	0.0054	-1.01097	5.69089	1.19733	-5.715
Yinhewenjian	0.6817	0.7278	0.0048	0.008	1.651603	-4.5717	-1.63975	4.812023
Haifutongjingxuan	0.6136	0.7083	0.0043	0.0054	-1.0157	-8.32626	1.162452	8.350115
Rongtongshen 100	0.8154	0.9586	0.0032	0.0073	-3.31979	-1.38137	3.3554	1.386394
Rongtongchengzhang	0.6862	0.5429	0.0048	0.0066	1.374613	24.78204	-1.26444	-25.0454
Jingshenyouxuan	0.5579	0.6873	0.0053	0.0074	-0.26128	5.480109	0.441939	-5.24595
Guotaijingxuan	0.5507	0.6253	0.0053	0.0053	-0.2968	-7.49238	0.396312	7.508311

Table 2. Outcome of stock-typed funds evaluation in 2005–2006.

	Efficiency in 2005	Ranking in 2005	Efficiency in 2006	Ranking in 2006
Huaanchuangxin	0.810648	29	0.823323	24
Huaxiachengzhang	1.000000	1	0.777108	33
Guotaijinying	0.925428	10	0.772355	34
Xinlanchou	0.806414	30	0.678474	45
Changshengchengzhang	0.853918	18	0.894465	14
Baoyinghongli	0.82955	21	0.989521	7
Dachengjiazhi	0.905965	12	0.791685	31
Jiashichengzhang	0.87261	17	1.000000	1
Huaan MSCI	0.905724	13	0.664417	46
Wanjia 180	1.000000	1	0.688776	43
Zhaoshanggupiao	0.851633	19	0.699035	42
Hefengchengzhang	0.812159	28	0.702294	41
Hefengzhouqi	0.760803	35	0.687915	44
Hefengwending	0.835763	20	0.736832	38
Jinyingyouxuan	0.814566	27	0.747648	37
Penghuashouyi	0.815283	26	1.000000	1
Jiashiwenjian	0.961097	8	0.752677	36
Jiashizengzhang	0.929304	9	0.995191	6
Baokangxiaofeipin	0.783887	32	0.66361	47
Yinhewenjian	0.52611	49	0.5055	50
Haifutongjingxuan	0.877733	16	0.918385	11
Rongtongshen 100	0.818806	25	0.55146	48
Rongtongchengzhang	0.826961	22	1.000000	1
Jingshenyouxuan	0.892329	15	0.723826	39
Guotaijingxuan	0.723811	40	0.825624	23

In Table 2, among 25 mutual funds, there were two comparatively efficient in year 2005, namely, Huaxiachengzhang and Wanjia 180, and three efficient in year 2006, namely, Jiashichengzhang, Penghuashouyi, and Rongtongchengzhang. Sixteen funds' investment efficiency scores were lower in year 2006 than in 2005, nine funds' efficiency scores are higher in year 2006 than in 2005. Obviously, the average efficiency of the 25 open-end funds descended in 2006. Among them, Yinhewenjian was the most persistent one, whose efficiency scores of the two years were almost the same.

4.3. *Management information*

Each fund's information of projections on DEA comparative effective frontier provides further useful information to improve their management. Generally, the more times to stand on the efficient frontier, the more predominant and more competitive the target fund is. Therefore, funds constructing efficient frontier are ideal to the evaluated one. That is to say, they are the powerful competitors on the relationship of inputs and outputs this paper suggests. Take Huanchuangxin as example, Huaxiachengzhang was its powerful competitor in year 2005, while Xinlanchou, Dachengjiazhi, and Yinhewenjian were its competitors in year 2006. Huaxiachengzhang constituted other funds' frontier 44 times as a most competitive one; however, its efficiency score dropped to 78% in year 2006. Similarly, Wanjia 180 performed well to constitute other funds' frontier 29 times in year 2005, while its efficiency score in year 2006 was only 69%. On the contrary, Fund Penghuashouyi's efficiency score in year 2005 was 81%, but it constituted other funds' frontier 28 times in year 2006 with the efficiency score 100%. So was Rongtongchengzhan, 83% in year 2005 and 100% in year 2006, constituting other funds' frontiers many times.

By calculating difference between inefficient funds and their projections on the efficient frontier via formula (16), we can get the improvement distance for the inefficient funds and find out the reason of inefficiency, exaltation, or descendant.

Table 3 lists each fund's inadequacy or excess in inputs and outputs according to formula (16). It shows that system risk all needs to be depressed. At the same time, depression of system risk will bring large increasing for excess returns, so that some fund's excess return would even goes to 10 times higher. Seen from Table 3, the nonsystem risk is far from the same important with system risk. Therefore, it is concluded that differences of comparative efficiency mainly result from system risk controlling.

Table 3 also indicates that many funds' efficiency changing in year 2006 result from risk control. For example, Jiashiwenjian ranked the 8th among 25 funds in year 2005, it needed to cut down 3.89% of its system risk to attain the comparative effectiveness; while its rank dropped to 36 in year 2006, it needed to cut down 24.73% to be efficient. Huaxiachengzhang,

Table 3. Changes needed for inputs and outputs.

	2005				2006			
	$\Delta\beta_{j0}$ (%)	$\Delta\sigma^2(\varepsilon_{j0})$ (%)	$\Delta R_{j0}T$ (%)	$\Delta R_{j0}Q$ (%)	$\Delta\beta_{j0}$ (%)	$\Delta\sigma^2(\varepsilon_{j0})$ (%)	$\Delta R_{j0}T$ (%)	$\Delta R_{j0}Q$ (%)
Huaanchuangxin	−18.94	0.00	21.07	0.00	−17.67	0.00	999.90	0.00
Huaxiachengzhang	0.00	0.00	0.00	0.00	−22.29	0.00	0.00	0.00
Guotaijinying	−7.46	0.00	999.90	0.00	−32.37	0.00	0.00	999.90
Xinlanchou	−19.36	0.00	0.00	0.00	−32.15	0.00	999.90	0.00
Changshengchengzhang	−14.61	0.00	11.33	0.00	−10.55	0.00	999.90	0.00
Baoyinghongli	−17.05	0.00	999.90	0.00	−9.59	0.00	0.00	0.00
Dachengjiazhi	−9.40	0.00	999.90	0.00	−20.83	0.00	999.90	0.00
Jiashichengzhang	−12.74	0.00	61.91	0.00	0.00	0.00	0.00	0.00
Huaan MSCI	−9.43	0.00	999.90	0.00	−33.56	0.00	0.00	0.00
Wanjia 180	0.00	0.00	0.00	0.00	−31.12	0.00	0.00	999.90
Zhaoshanggupiao	−14.84	0.00	999.90	0.00	−30.10	0.00	999.90	0.00
Hefengchengzhang	−18.78	0.00	4.68	999.90	−29.77	0.00	0.00	999.90
Hefengzhouqi	−23.92	0.00	999.90	0.00	−31.21	0.00	0.00	0.00
Hefengwending	−16.42	0.00	0.00	0.00	−26.32	0.00	0.00	0.00
Jinyingyouxuan	−18.54	0.00	0.00	999.90	−25.24	0.00	999.90	0.00
Penghuashouyi	−18.47	0.00	999.90	0.00	0.00	0.00	0.00	0.00
Jiashiwenjian	−3.89	0.00	999.90	0.00	−24.73	0.00	999.90	0.00
Jiashizengzhang	−7.07	0.00	999.90	0.00	0.00	0.00	999.90	0.00
Baokangxiaofeipin	−21.61	0.00	999.90	0.00	−33.64	0.00	0.00	999.90
Yinhewenjian	−47.39	0.00	0.00	999.90	−49.45	0.00	999.90	0.00
Haifutongjingxuan	−12.23	0.00	999.90	0.00	−8.16	0.00	999.90	0.00
Rongtongshen 100	−18.12	0.00	999.90	0.00	−44.85	0.00	999.90	0.00
Rongtongchengzhang	−17.30	0.00	0.00	999.90	0.00	0.00	0.00	0.00
Jingshenyouxuan	−10.77	0.00	999.90	0.00	−27.62	0.00	0.00	0.00
Guotaijingxuan	−27.62	0.00	999.90	0.00	−17.44	0.00	999.90	0.00

Table 4. Correlation test of different indexes rankings.

	Treynor ratio	Sharpe ratio	Jensen Alpha	IR	M-2	RAC
Comparative efficiency	−0.153595	−0.208934	0.203713	0.178612	0.230667	0.254441
Treynor ratio	1.000000	0.986394	0.444335	−0.569889	−0.339328	−0.576269
Sharpe ratio	0.986394	1.000000	0.379945	−0.593425	−0.341626	−0.558684
Jensen alpha	0.444335	0.379945	1.000000	0.388877	0.612123	0.155704
IR	−0.569889	−0.593425	0.388877	1.000000	0.821699	0.615461
M-2	−0.339328	−0.341626	0.612123	0.821699	1.000000	0.729650
RAC	−0.576269	−0.558684	0.155704	0.615461	0.729650	1.000000

Wanjia 180, Penghuashouyi, Rongtongchengzhang, etc. were all similar to the fund Jiashiwenjian, changing much in their comparative efficiency scores in the two years, resulting from the controlling of system risk not persistent.

4.4. *Comparison with other methods*

We then compare efficiency ranking of these 25 open-ended funds in years 2005 and 2006 with rankings of their Sharp ratios, Treynor ratios, Jensen Alphas, information ratios (IR), M-2s and risk adjustment capacity (RAC), which are classical mutual funds evaluation methods in correlation test. The results are listed as follows:

By regressing comparative efficiency ranking on the other six series, the coefficients are not significant. Therefore, it is concluded that the comparative efficiency scores do not necessarily have the relationship with the traditional fund performance index. The traditional indexes only consider the difference between the average market return and the fund portfolio's return adjusted by risk, without weighing the other factors such as load that also affects performance in course of investment; while DEA approach pays attention to these two or more things. DEA based on multiple inputs and multiple outputs is much different in computing the principle from the single factor ratio index under the hypothesis of CAPM. There is no surprise to see their outcomes' deviation. Besides, Sharp ratio, Treynor ratio, Jensen Alpha, IC, M-2,[5] RAC do not always have significant positive or negative relations among themselves.

5. Conclusions

Data envelopment analysis is a systematic analysis method and usually applied to comparative performance evaluation. This article proposes two quadratic-constrained DEA models for the evaluation of mutual funds, from a perspective of evaluation based on endogenous benchmarks. In comparison to the previous studies, this article decomposes the two vital factors for mutual funds performance, i.e., risk and return, in these quadratic-constrained DEA models, one of which is a partly controllable quadratic-constrained programming, to construct mutual funds' endogenous benchmarks and give insight management suggestions. These two models with inputs of system risk and nonsystem risk, outputs of timing excess returns and selecting excess return, among which system risk is an uncontrollable variable, are applied to evaluate 25 open-end mutual funds' performance during years 2005, 2006, all of which were issued before year 2004. With weights and slack variables, we track down the reason of bad performance and the improvement orientation. Compared with traditional methods, data envelopment analysis in mutual fund performance evaluation can obtain more management information for regulators and fund management companies to take measures to boost funds' operation efficiency.

The empirical results show that, although the Chinese financial market in year 2006 is much better than that in year 2005 for mutual funds, the average efficiency scores in year 2006 were lower than in 2005, which results from poor system risk control. Most mutual funds relaxed their control on system risk in year 2006 and the comparative efficiency changed a lot with not any persistence. System risk control affects comparative effectiveness greatly. The difference of evaluation principles leads to no correlations between DEA rankings and traditional rankings, though it is logistical.

---

[5]M-2 is a common index in fund evaluation, which is based on CAPM and APT theory, with risk-free equities' joining, adjusting portfolio's risk equal to benchmark, then comparing their returns on the same risk level.

References

Banker, R., Charnes, A., and Cooper, W.W., 1984. Some models for estimating technical and scale inefficiencies in data envelopment analysis. *Management Science*, 30, 1078–1092.

Basso, A. and Funari, S., 2001. A data envelopment analysis approach to measure the mutual fund performance. *European Journal of Operational Research*, 135, 477–492.

Basso, A. and Funari, S., 2003. Measuring the performance of ethical mutual funds: A DEA approach. *Journal of the Operational Research Society*, 54, 521–531.

Briec, W., Kerstens, K., and Lesourd, J.B., 2004. Single-period markowitz portfolio selection, performance gauging, and duality: A variation on the luenberger shortage function. *Journal of Optimization Theory and Applications*, 120, 1–27.

Brinson, G.P., Hood, L.R., and Beebower, G.L., 1986. Determinants of portfolio performance. *Financial Analysts Journal*, 42, 39–44.

Chang, K.P., 2004. Evaluating mutual fund performance: An application of minimum convex input requirement set approach. *Computers and Operations Research*, 31, 929–940.

Charnes, A., Cooper, W.W. and Rhodes, E., 1978. Measuring the efficiency of decision making units. *European Journal of Operational Research*, 2, 429–444.

Chen, G., 2003. Non-parameter method for equity investment fund appraisal. *Forum of Statistics and Information*, 18, 64–68.

Choi, Y. and Murthi, B., 2001. Relative performance evaluation of mutual funds: A nonparametric approach. *Journal of Business Finance and Accounting*, 28, 853–876.

Galagedera, D. and Silvapulle, P., 2002. Australian mutual fund performance appraisal using data envelopment analysis. *Managerial Finance*, 28, 60–73.

Han, Z.X. and Liu, B., 2003. Comparative performance appraisal for closed-end funds based on data envelopment analysis. *Management Review*, 15, 17–21.

Jensen, M., 1968. The performance of mutual funds in the period 1945–1964. *Journal of Finance*, 23, 389–416.

Jensen, M., 1969. Risk, the pricing of capital assets, and the evaluation of investment portfolios. *Journal of Finance*, April, 167–247.

Lin, Z.P. and Lin, R.Y., 2005. Main approaches for fund performance appraisal based on DEA models. *Journal of Systems Engineering*, 20, 73–74.

Luo, H.L., Wang, H.C., and Tian, Z.J., 2003. Data envelopment analysis for closed-end funds performance with double risk measurements. *Systems Engineering* (in Chinese), 21, 94–100.

Ma, L.J., Wu, J., and Cheng, X.J., 2003. Investment funds performance assessment approach based on DEA. *Value Engineering*, 4, 63–65.

Markowitz, H., 1952. Portfolio selection. *Journal of Finance*, 7, 77–91.

McMullen, P. and Strong, R., 1998. Selection of mutual fund using data envelopment analysis. *Journal of Business and Economic Studies*, 4, 1–12.

Morey, M. and Morey, R., 1999. Mutual fund performance appraisals: A multihorizon perspective with endogenous benchmarking. *International Journal of Management Science*, 27, 241–258.

Murthi, B., Choi, Y., and Desai, P., 1997. Efficiency of mutual funds and portfolio performance measurement: A non-parametric approach. *European Journal of Operational Research*, 98, 408–418.

Roll, R., 1978. Ambiguity when performance is measured by the security market line. *Journal of Finance*, 33, 1051–1069.

Sedzro, K. and Sardano, D., 1999. Mutual fund performance evaluation using data envelopment analysis. Working Paper, School of Business, University of Quebec at Montreal, Canada.

Sharpe, W., 1964. Capital asset prices: A theory of market equilibrium under condition of risk. *Journal of Finance*, 19, 425–442.

Sharp, W., 1966. Mutual fund performance. *Journal of Business*, 39, 119–138.

Treynor, J., 1965. How to rate management investment funds. *Harvard Business Review*, January/February, 63–75.

Wilkens, K., and Zhu, J., 2001. Portfolio evaluation and benchmark selection: A mathematical programming approach. *Journal of Alternative Investments*, 4, 9–20.

Zhao, X.J., Zhang, H.S., Lai, K.K., and Wang, S.Y., 2007. A method for evaluating mutual funds' performance based on asymmetric laplace distribution and DEA approach. *Systems Engineering: Theory and Practice*, 27, 1–10.

Structural Breaks, Adaptive Expectations, and Risk Premium: The Information Content in the Mispricing of the USD/RMB Forward Rates

Rong Chen* and Zhenlong Zheng[†]

Department of Finance, Xiamen University,
Xiamen, Fujian, 361005, China
*aronge@xmu.edu.cn
[†]zlzheng@xmu.edu.cn

This paper explores the information content in the mispricing of the USD/RMB forward rates with different maturities in the deliverable forward (DF) and non-deliverable forward (NDF) markets. First, we find that the USD/RMB forward basis series are all non-stationary ones with structural breaks in both markets. This indicates the CIP does not hold in USD/RMB forward markets, either onshore or offshore. In essence, the USD/RMB forward basis is the difference of the expectation of the depreciation of the US dollar against the RMB controlled by China's Central Bank and the expected return of the US dollar as an investment asset. Second, main factors influencing the behavior of the USD/RMB forward basis are the expectation of the appreciation of the RMB controlled by China's Central Bank and the risk premium. Third, adaptive expectations play an important role in the change of the USD/RMB forward basis, particularly in NDF markets. Also the information of the NDF basis could be used to predict the spot rates in a short future. Finally, our study reveals that the risk premium of the RMB is positive for global investors in the USD/RMB NDF markets.

Keywords: Forward basis; Structural breaks; Adaptive expectations; Predictability; Risk premium.

1. Introduction

Financial markets are the center of information exchange and trading is the reflection of information. No matter whether it is recognized, what most financial studies attempt to do is to explore and interpret useful information from market variables, such as prices and trading volume. For example, much effort has been devoted to obtaining the information of systemic risk and risk aversion from stock prices. Nowadays using advanced techniques, we could get more complicated information such as price volatility and tail risk, etc.

This paper is an attempt to explore the information content in the deviations from no-arbitrage prices, which is usually called the forward/cash basis or the futures/cash basis (henceforth, termed "the basis"), in USD/RMB forward markets. This is not a neglected area in financial researches. To the best of our knowledge, previous studies usually attribute the existence of such deviations to transaction frictions, for example, trading costs, delayed arbitrage, short-sale constraints, and liquidity. This is because the markets they examine are all developed forward or futures markets where arbitrage trading is effective. The basis behavior in USD/RMB forward markets is different due to arbitrage constraints. The USD/RMB forward basis is persistently large and does not follow a mean-reverting process as the basis in developed forward markets does. This makes it a new interesting issue: we find that we could obtain information, such as expectations, risk premiums, and prediction, from the USD/RMB forward basis.

Another motivation for our study derives from the simultaneous existence of USD/RMB deliverable forward (DF) and non-deliverable forward (NDF) markets. The former is the onshore interbank FX forward market in China. DF contracts are FX forwards traded in the onshore interbank market in which physical delivery is allowed. NDFs are quite similar to DFs except that at maturity they are settled in a freely convertible currency, typically the US dollar. The difference is due to the fact that NDFs are traded offshore and the RMB is subject to capital controls. Is the basis behavior in USD/RMB DF and NDF markets different or not? It is also an interesting issue.

Our analysis proceeds in two stages. In the first stage, we analyze the possible information contained in the USD/RMB forward basis in theory given the existence of arbitrage constraints and market interventions by the central bank. We propose that we might obtain the information of rational expectations, adaptive expectations, risk premiums, and the prediction of spot FX rates from the USD/RMB forward basis. In the second stage, the practical USD/RMB forward basis behavior in our sample periods is examined and the theoretical views proposed in the first stage are testified.

The conclusion of our study can be summarized as: First, the existence of mispricing in USD/RMB forward markets is inevitable due to the official daily foreign exchange market intervention operations in China. In essence, the USD/RMB forward basis is the difference of the expectation of the depreciation of the US dollar against the RMB controlled by China's Central Bank and the expected return of the US dollar as an investment asset. The wider the difference, the farther the basis will be away from zero.

Second, main factors influencing the behavior of the USD/RMB forward basis are the expectation of the appreciation of the RMB controlled by China's Central Bank and the risk premium.

Third, adaptive expectations play an important role in the change of the USD/RMB forward basis, particular in NDF markets. This suggests that investors adjust their expectations dynamically using the latest information. However, rational expectations are hard to be testified.

Fourth, the change of the USD/RMB NDF basis could be used to predict the spot rates in next few days. In our samples, the one-month USD/RMB NDF rate is a good but not perfect unbiased estimator of the future spot rate at maturity.

Last, we get some information of the risk premium of the RMB. Our results show that for global investors in the one-month USD/RMB NDF market, the systemic risk and the risk premium of the RMB are positive.

The rest of the paper is organized as follows. Section 2 reviews related literature. Section 3 defines the USD/RMB forward basis and describes the data. Section 4 is the theoretical analysis of the USD/RMB forward basis. Sections 5, 6, and 7 present the empirical results in different ways. Section 8 concludes.

2. Literature Review

There have been some insightful studies about the futures/cash basis. Cornell and French (1983), Modest and Sundaresan (1983), and Figlewski

(1984) are among the first ones who report deviations from no-arbitrage prices appear frequently in futures markets. However, MacKinlay and Ramaswamy (1988), Brennan and Schwartz (1990), Yadav and Pope (1990), and Sofianos (1993) find such deviations do not persist too long before they disappear and mispricing is just a temporary phenomenon. Furthermore, MacKinlay and Ramaswamy (1988), Brennan and Schwartz (1990), Yadav and Pope (1990, 1994), Sofianos (1993), Lim (1992), and Strickland and Xu (1990) illustrate that the futures basis in most developed futures markets follows a mean reverting process with the mean quite close to zero. This suggests that, on average, in these markets, arbitrage activities are quite effective and there is no persistent mispricing. Accordingly, most arguments about the basis relate the futures basis with transaction frictions, such as trading costs, delayed arbitrage, and short-sale constraints, etc. The research of Roll and colleagues (2007) represents the latest development in this area, which explores the relations between the basis and market liquidity.

Obviously, the focus of these studies is different from ours. Due to the effective arbitrage activities in developed markets, what these researches examine are factors leading to temporary deviations which could be used to explain the persistent large gap between the practical USD/RMB forward rates and their "fair values". That is why new factors such as expectations and risk premium have to be introduced to explore the information contained in the USD/RMB forward basis.

3. Definition and Data

3.1. *The definition of the USD/RMB forward basis*

According to the covered interest rate parity (CIP), the forward rate should satisfy

$$F_t = S_t e^{(r_d - r_f)(T-t)}, \tag{1}$$

where S_t and F_t are the USD/RMB spot rate and forward rate at time t, respectively. The forward contract matures at time T. r_d and r_f represent the continuously compounded risk-free rates per annum of the RMB and the US dollar, respectively, over the period of $T - t$. Thus, the USD/RMB forward basis is defined as

$$B_t = \ln(F_t) - \ln(S_t) - (r_d - r_f)(T - t). \tag{2}$$

Obviously, if the CIP holds, the basis should be zero.

3.2. Data

To conduct empirical tests, the data of USD/RMB spot rates, the Dollar Index, USD/RMB DF and NDF rates, the US risk-free interest rates, and the China risk-free interest rates are collected on a daily basis. To obtain as much information as possible, we collect DF and NDF rates with different maturities, from 1, 3, 6, 9 to 12 months. For the same purpose, we employ the longest sample periods available: for the 12-month data, the sample period is from May 12, 2006 to August 8, 2008; for other data, the sample periods are all from March 1, 2006 to August 8, 2008. In our research, we use the USD Libor rates and the spot rates calculated from the prices of the Central Bank Notes traded in the Chinese interbank money market as the US and China risk-free interest rates, respectively.[1] All data about FX are obtained from the Reuters Market Data System while the data of interest rates is from the Wind Info.

4. The Theoretical Analysis

In theory, it has been recognized that the expected future spot rate $\ln(E(S_T))$ is different from the forward rate $\ln(F_t)$ as long as the risk premium of S, ρ_t is not zero

$$\ln(E(S_T)) - \ln(F_t) = \rho_t(T - t). \tag{3}$$

It is due to the fact that speculators in forward markets claim risk premium to assume systemic risk of the underlying assets.[2]

In a "free" market without interventions, we have

$$\ln(E(S_T)) = \ln(S_t) + y_t(T - t), \tag{4}$$

---

[1] In this paper, all the interest rates and yields are computed continuously compounded.
[2] See Engle (1996) and Chen and Zhenlong (2007, 2008).

where y_t, the expected return per annum of the underlying asset, is equal to $(r_t - q_t) + \rho_t$ with q_t the known yield per annum on the underlying asset over the remaining period of forwards. From (3) and (4), we get

$$\ln(F_t) = \ln(S_t) + (r_t - q_t)(T - t). \tag{5}$$

That is the no-arbitrage relation between the forward prices and the cash prices. In FX markets, it is the CIP.

However, if there are persistent market interventions, Eqs. (4) and (5) will not hold any more. That is the case of the USD/RMB spot markets. With capital control and the persistent interventions of the Central Bank in the USD/RMB spot market, the US dollar could not be regarded as a pure investment asset and the expectations of future USD/RMB spot rate will not satisfy Eq. (4) anymore. The difference between $\ln(E(S_T))$ and $\ln(S_t)$ is the expectation of China's exchange rate policy objective. However, the relations described in Eq. (3) will not be affected because the investors in the forward markets are still pursuing the risk premium. Thus, we get

$$
\begin{aligned}
B_t &= \ln(F_t) - \ln(S_t) - (r_d - r_f)(T - t) \\
&= \ln(E(S_T)) - \rho_t(T - t) - \ln(S_t) - (r_d - r_f)(T - t) \\
&= [\ln(E(S_T)) - \ln(S_t)] - [(r_d - r_f)(T - t) + \rho_t(T - t)] \\
&= [\ln(E(S_T)) - \ln(S_t)] - y_t(T - t). \tag{6}
\end{aligned}
$$

Equation (6) suggests that when the market expectation of the depreciation of the US dollar against the RMB controlled by China's Central Bank, $\ln(E(S_T)) - \ln(S_t)$, is different from the expected return of the US dollar as an investment asset, $y_t(T - t)$, the existence of mispricing is inevitable. The wider the difference, the farther the basis will be away from zero. This is the first proposition we want to testify in this paper.

Next, as $\ln(S_t)$ and $(r_d - r_f)(T - t)$ are usually known, Eqs. (3) and (6) illustrate that two factors influencing USD/RMB forward rates and the forward basis are the expectation of the appreciation of the RMB controlled by China's Central Bank, $\ln(E(S_T)) - \ln(S_t)$, and the risk premium of the US dollar, ρ_t. With one of them given, we could get the other from the forward basis. That is the second thing we want to do in this paper: with the hypothesis of rational expectation, we attempt to separate the information of the risk premium from the USD/RMB forward rates or the forward basis.

However, do there really exist rational expectations? If not, what kind of expectation is it? That is the third issue we hope to study in this paper.

In following sections, based on the above analysis, our work is to employ the data of the USD/RMB FX markets to reveal information contained in the USD/RMB forward basis as much as possible.

5. Empirical Study I: Does the CIP Hold?

In this section, our task is to testify the proposition that the USD/RMB forward basis is the difference of the expectation of the depreciation of the US dollar against the RMB controlled by China's Central Bank and the expected return of the US dollar as an investment asset. The wider the difference, the farther the basis will be away from zero. So whether the CIP holds and whether the basis is equal to zero in the USD/RMB DF and NDF markets needs to be tested.

Table 1 illustrates in our samples, the means of all the basis series in either USD/RMB DF or NDF markets are negative. However, it is impossible to test whether these means are different from zero significantly by t-statistic since all the basis series could not reject the unit root hypothesis at even the 10% level. But all the forward basis are nonstationary time series, which suggests there does not exist a long-term equilibrium relationship among $\ln F_t$, $\ln S_t$, and $(r_d - r_f)(T - t)$. This also indicates that in our samples, for all USD/RMB forward rates in both DF and NDF markets, the CIP does not hold and the basis is not zero.

However, when we observe the basis behavior more closely, we find that all the basis series remain quite close to zero at first, and then shift to negative values just as illustrated in Fig. 1. These occasional, but violent, changes seem to be more the structural breaks proposed by Perron (1989) than the accumulation of frequent random small changes of unit root process. Since classical ADF tests tend to incorrectly classify stationary time series with structural breaking trends as integrated, it is necessary to conduct more tests of stationarity to avoid incorrect inferences and inappropriate following steps such as cointegration analysis.

Table 1. Means and the ADF unit root tests of the foreign exchange rates series.

	Mean	Lag length	ADF	ΔADF
DFB_{1m}	-0.00186	1	-2.54	-21.63***
DFB_{3m}	-0.00562	1	-1.46	-30.01***
DFB_{6m}	-0.01246	1	-0.97	-30.83***
DFB_{9m}	-0.02079	1	-0.86	-30.17***
DFB_{12m}	-0.030072	1	-0.46	-27.33***
$NDFB_{1m}$	-0.00353	2	-3.04	-21.92***
$NDFB_{3m}$	-0.0101	1	-2.53	-27.40***
$NDFB_{6m}$	-0.0206	0	-2.01	-24.48***
$NDFB_{9m}$	-0.03131	0	-1.47	-24.60***
$NDFB_{12m}$	-0.045357	0	-0.80	-22.91***
$\ln(S)$	2.024348	0	-1.56	-23.83***
$\ln(S)_{12m}$	2.019481	0	-1.72	-22.80***
$\ln(DI)$	4.389992	0	-2.14	-24.70***
$\ln(DI)_{12m}$	4.381883	0	-2.69	-24.37***

1. DFB and NDFB represent the forward basis of DF and NDF rates respectively. $\ln(S)$ and $\ln(DI)$ represent the log of the USD/RMB spot rates and the log of the Dollar Index. Subscripts 1m, 3m, 6m, 9m, and 12m mean the series correspond to the samples of 1-, 3-, 6-, 9-, and 12-month forwards.

2. ADF and ΔADF are the unit root statistics for the exchange rate series and the first difference of the exchange rate series respectively. In the unit root test, we employ the ADF tests with a constant and a time trend in the regression. The null hypothesis in the ADF unit root tests is the time series data have a unit-root. Lag length is determined by the Akaike and Schwarz information criteria. ***denotes significance at 1% level. The critical value at the 10% level is -3.13.

We employ the sequential test of the unit root raised by Banerjee and colleagues (1992) to check the stationarity of the USD/RMB forward basis. A dummy variable D_t is introduced in the ADF tests with a constant and a time trend in the regression,

$$\Delta B_\tau = \psi B_{\tau-1} + \mu + \alpha \tau + \sum_{i=1}^{p} \beta_i \Delta B_{\tau-1} + \gamma_k D_\tau$$
$$+ \varepsilon_\tau \varepsilon_\tau - IID(0, \sigma^2),$$

where D_τ captures the possibility of structural breaks at time τ and the lag length of p is determined by the Akaike and Schwarz information criteria. Consider two cases:

$$\begin{cases} \text{Case A (break in mean): } D_\tau = I_{(\tau > k)} \\ \text{Case B (break in trend): } D_\tau = (\tau - k)I_{(\tau > k)}, \end{cases}$$

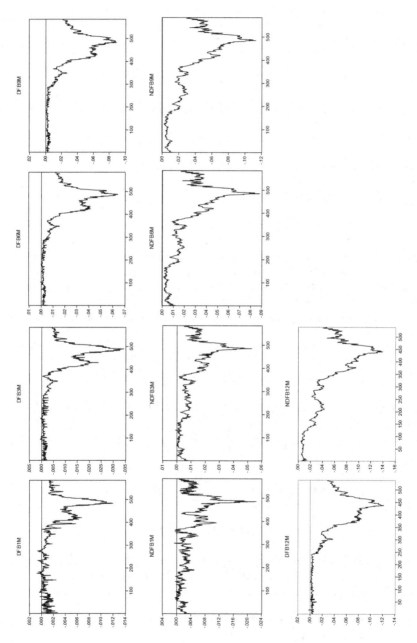

Fig. 1. The USD/RMB forward basis series.

where $I\,(\cdot)$ is the indicator function. For case A, the t-statistic testing $\gamma_k = 0$ provides information about whether there has been a break or shift in the intercept; for case B, this t-statistic provides information about whether there has been a change in the slope in the trend. Thus the t-statistic testing $\psi = 0$ provides the information about whether B_t is stationary after controlling the influence of structural breaks. The estimators and test statistics are computed using 30% of the full N observation, that is $k = k_0, k_0 + 1, \ldots, k_T$, where $k_0 = 0.15N$ and $k_t = 0.85N$. The resulting statistics are thus sequential since we conduct the test day by day from k_0 to k_t. If there are more than one structural breaks, the day when the maximum and minimum t-statistic appear will be chosen as the ultimate structural break points.

Figure 2 and Table 2 show the results of the sequential tests. For all the forward basis either in DF or NDF markets, again we fail to reject the unit root hypothesis at even the 10% level although there do exist structural breaks. These results support the conclusion that the CIP does not hold in both the USD/RMB DF and NDF markets.

Besides, the results of the sequential tests show all the forward basis series share the following two features:

Firstly, the structural break points of all the forward basis series appear almost at the same time. In the tests of case A, all the minimum t-statistic of γ_k (that is negative) appear in the period from September 6, 2007 to September 17, 2007. This significantly negative shift in mean of B_t suggests a negative structural break to the USD/RMB forward rates. This means that after the break, the USD/RMB forward rates are significantly below the fair value. And all the maximum t-statistic of γ_k (that is positive) in the test of case A also appear together, from March 10, 2008 to March 27, 2008, which indicates that the USD/RMB forward rates shift up suddenly back to the fair value. In the tests of case B, although there are only positive structural break points, they appear together again, from February 22, 2008 to March 6, 2008, which suggests during this period, the changing speed of the USD/RMB forward basis rise suddenly.

All these results highly coincide with the market reality. On September 15, 2007, China's Central Bank declared to raise interest rates by 0.27 percentage points. Only three days after that, the US Federal

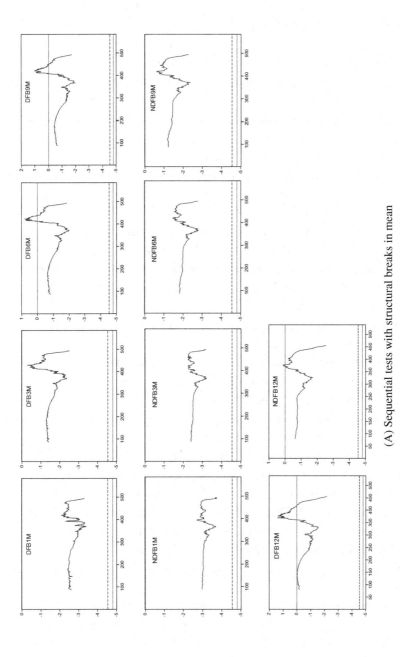

Fig. 2. The ADF statistics in sequential tests.

(A) Sequential tests with structural breaks in mean

Note: Except the line of zero, real lines, and dashed lines in the lower part of the figures are the critical values at the 5% and 10% level calculated by Banerjee *et al.* (1992). The critical values of the 10% level in figure A and B are −4.55 and −4.11 respectively.

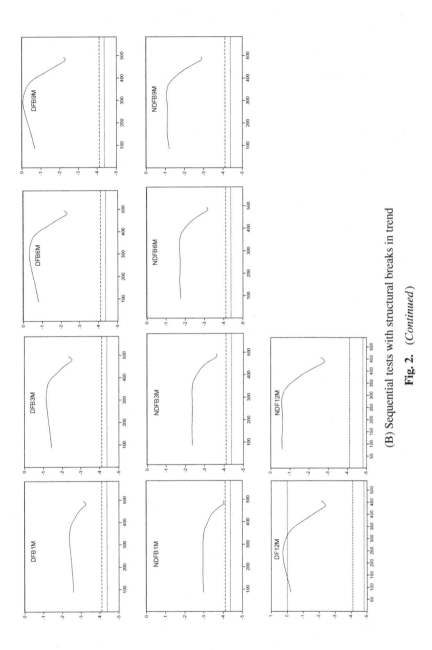

(B) Sequential tests with structural breaks in trend

Fig. 2. (*Continued*)

Table 2. Structural break points in the sequential tests.

	Case A: breaks in mean		Case B: breaks in the slope	
	Structural break points	ADF > 0	Structural break points	ADF > 0
DFB_{1m}	2007/9/13 2008/3/27	—	2008/3/3	—
$NDFB_{1m}$	2007/9/6 2008/3/13	—	2008/3/6	—
DFB_{3m}	2007/9/13 2008/3/19	—	2008/2/25	—
$NDFB_{3m}$	2007/9/6 2008/3/13	—	2008/3/6	—
DFB_{6m}	2007/9/17 2008/3/18	2007/11/20–2008/1/2	2008/2/25	—
$NDFB_{6m}$	2007/9/6 2008/3/13	—	2008/3/5	—
DFB_{9m}	2007/9/11 2008/3/19	2007/11/16–2008/1/18	2008/2/22	—
$NDFB_{9m}$	2007/9/17 2008/3/13	—	2008/3/5	—
DFB_{12m}	2007/9/19 2008/3/10	2007/11/12–2008/2/13	2008/2/22	2006/12/5–2007/8/24
$NDFB_{12m}$	2007/9/17 2008/3/13	2007/11/27–2007/12/4	2008/3/5	—

1. This table illustrate the structural break points of all the forward basis series in the sequential tests

$$\Delta B_\tau = \psi B_{\tau-1} + \mu + \alpha\tau + \sum_{i=1}^{p} \beta_i \Delta B_{\tau-1} + \gamma_k D_\tau + \varepsilon_\tau \varepsilon_\tau - IID(0, \sigma^2)$$

In case A, $D_\tau = I_{(\tau > k)}$, this test captures the structural break points in the mean of the forward basis. In case B, $D_\tau = (\tau - k)I_{(\tau > k)}$, this test captures the structural break points in the trend slope of the forward basis.

2. The periods of ADF > 0 are the periods when the ADF statistic is greater than zero in our tests.

Reserve cut interest rates by 0.5 percentage points. This led to a big rise in interest rate difference between China and the United States, which has been negative for a long time. According to the CIP, the increase of interest rate differences should lead to the appreciation of the USD forward rates.

However, that was the period people began worrying about the potential hurt of the Subprime Mortgage Crisis to the American economy, and was also the period that the market believed China's Central Bank was going to accelerate the appreciation of RMB. This is consistent with the negative shift in mean of B_t. In the period from February 2008 to March 2008, after six interest rate cuts of the US Federal Reserve, the view that the US dollar would stop depreciation temporarily was quite popular. This is again consistent with the sudden rise of the mean and the slope of B_t.

Secondly, the ADF statistics of the six-month, nine-month, and twelve-month DF basis and twelve-month NDF basis are positive from the middle of November 2007 to the middle of February 2008. Positive ADF statistics means explosive processes, that is, the influence of one shock to the series will increase explosively instead of disappear with time elapsing. This could also be explained by the market reality. This is the period that China's Central Bank accelerated the appreciation of the RMB against the US dollar. This led to temporary market panic to sell the US dollar, which is consistent with the explosive feature of the basis.

In all, we find that in our sample periods, the CIP does not hold in either USD/RMB DF or NDF markets. The empirical results in both markets support the proposition in the previous section. That is, anytime when the interest rate difference between China and the United States is different from the expected appreciation of the US dollar against the RMB controlled by China's Central Bank, the forward rates tend to follow the market expectation instead of the CIP. This leads to those structural breaks we observe in the basis series.

6. Empirical Study II: Rational Expectations and Risk Premium

As illustrated in Sec. 4, two factors influencing USD/RMB forward rates and the forward basis are the expectation of the appreciation of the RMB controlled by China's Central Bank and the risk premium of the US dollar. With one of them given, we could get the other from the forward basis. However, it is hard to implement due to the unobservabilities of the expectation and risk premium.

One possible solution is to assume rational expectation, that is,

$$\ln(S_T) = \ln(E(S_T)) + \varepsilon_T$$

in which ε_T is a Gaussian white noise process. Thus, we could replace $\ln(E(S_T)) - \ln(S_t)$ in Eq. (6) by $\ln(S_T) - \ln(S_t)$ and separate the information of risk premium from the forward basis. Equation (6) could be turned into the corresponding econometrics model

$$\ln(S_T) - \ln(S_t) = \beta_0 + \beta_1[\ln(F_t) - \ln(S_t)] + u_T, \qquad (7)$$

where β_0 reflects the constant component in $\rho_t(T - t)$, u_T is the sum of the time-varying component in risk premium and the stochastic disturbance. The t-statistic testing $\beta_1 = 0$ provides information about whether $\ln(F_t)$ is the unbiased expectation of the future spot rate at time T.

Table 3 reports the results of ADF tests and cointegration tests. Unfortunately, except for one-month NDF forward rates, all time series of $\ln(S_T) - \ln(S_t)$ and $\ln(F_t) - \ln(S_t)$ in our samples could not be used to conduct regression (7) because neither they are stationary nor we could reject the hypothesis of non-cointegration. This means that we could only separate the information of risk premium in one-month NDF market with the assumption of rational expectation. This is quite different from the empirical results of developed markets. We believe the main reason is the low efficiency of the USD/RMB FX markets.

When we run regression (7) using the data of one-month NDF forward rates, we use the Newey-West procedure to get standard errors that are robust against heteroskedasticity and autocorrelation in the error terms. The results are reported in Table 4.

The null hypothesis of $\beta_1 = 0$ and $\beta_1 = 1$ are both rejected at the 1% level, indicating that the one-month NDF rate, $\ln(F_t)$, is a rather good estimator of the future spot rate in one month, but not a perfect unbiased one. At the same time, the null hypothesis of $\beta_0 = 0$ is also rejected at the 1% level. Since β_0 reflects the constant component in $\rho_t(T - t)$, to some extent these results verify that assuming rational expectation, the expected future spot rate $\ln(E(S_T))$ is the sum of the forward rate $\ln(F_t)$ and the risk premium. At the same time, we find β_0 is less than zero, the error term

Table 3. Rational expectations and risk premium: ADF tests and Johansen cointegration tests.

	ADF tests		Hypothesis of 0 cointegration vector		Hypothesis of at most 1 cointegration vector	
	$\ln(F_t) - \ln(S_t)$	$\ln(S_T) - \ln(S_t)$	Trace statistic	Max-Eigen	Trace statistic	Max-Eigen
DFB$_{1m}$	−2.177886	−4.307339***	—	—	—	—
DFB$_{3m}$	−1.986229	−2.486799	13.08694	10.47171	2.615227	2.615227
DFB$_{6m}$	−1.446510	−1.603071	6.930845	4.895674	2.035171	2.035171
DFB$_{9m}$	−2.515198	−1.832725	9.581118	7.661866	1.919252	1.919252
DFB$_{12m}$	0.132560	−1.911447	9.939930	7.965630	1.974300	1.974300
NDFB$_{1m}$	−3.592710**	−4.307339***	—	—	—	—
NDFB$_{3m}$	−3.616845**	−2.486799	—	—	—	—
NDFB$_{6m}$	−3.117203	−1.603071	12.08312	8.905495	3.177628	3.177628
NDFB$_{9m}$	−2.271688	−1.832725	4.211797	4.176849	0.034949	0.034949
NDFB$_{12m}$	−2.339929	−1.911447	7.096333	7.018956	0.077377	0.077377

1. *** and ** denote significance at 1% and 5% levels respectively.
2. "—" suggests that cointegration tests could not be conducted because two variables are not both I(1).

Table 4. Rational expectation and risk premium: one-month NDF market.

Regression with Newey-West estimator	Mean of residuals	ADF test to residual series
$\ln(S_T) - \ln(S_t) = \begin{array}{c} -0.002710 \\ {\scriptstyle(-3.217029^{***})} \end{array}$		
$\begin{array}{c} + \quad 0.595330 \\ {\scriptstyle(3.982319^{***})} \\ {\scriptstyle(-2.70695^{***})} \end{array} [\ln(F_t) - \ln(S_t)]$	$-5.13E{-}19$	-3.697053^{***}
$\bar{R}^2 = 0.127663$	$(-2.81E{-}15)$	

1. The number in the second line below the coefficients is the t-statistic with the null hypothesis of $\beta_1 = 1$. Other numbers in parentheses represents the t-statistic with the null hypothesis of 0.
2. $***$ denotes significance at 1%.

containing the time-varying components of risk premium is stationary and the null hypothesis of the mean of the error term is equal to zero could not be rejected. All these results suggest that for global investors in the one-month NDF market, the risk premium of the RMB as an investment asset is relatively constant and the systemic risk is positive.

7. Empirical Study III: Adaptive Expectations and Predictability

In Sec. 6, we obtain some information of the risk premium with the assumption of rational expectations. However, one may ask: is the expectation really rational expectation? Or, are investors able to predict future spot rate rationally? A more reasonable assumption might be adaptive expectations rather than rational expectations. With adaptive expectations, market participants always adjust their expectations dynamically based on the latest information. There could be several ways to investigate adaptive expectations. In this paper, we explore this by examining the joint dynamic structure of the changes of the USD/RMB forward basis, the changes of the USD/RMB spot rates, and the changes of Dollar Index. The idea is that the most important part of the information set about the future USD/RMB spot rate obtained by market participants is the information of the latest changes of the USD/RMB spot rates and the Dollar Index. If there exist adaptive expectations, this information should be reflected in the changes of the USD/RMB forward basis because the expectation is one of the most important factors determining the forward basis.

Table 5. Adaptive expectations and predictability: Granger Causality Tests.

	Lag length	d(B)		d(lns)		d(lndi)	
		d(lns)	d(lndi)	d(B)	d(lndi)	d(B)	d(lns)
DFB$_{1m}$	3	0.874902	0.954789	1.631403	312.5144***	6.518235**	0.085142
DFB$_{3m}$	4	7.562009*	12.24220***	7.086853*	308.5754***	1.289178	0.519834
DFB$_{6m}$	4	14.59849***	6.958080*	8.791102**	306.7463***	2.623660	0.540139
DFB$_{9m}$	3	2.970160	2.459039	1.898264	303.9733***	2.019971	0.023202
DFB$_{12m}$	3	0.612151	1.238907	2.231819	305.8830***	6.070498**	0.132261
NDFB$_{1m}$	4	9.483556**	34.65919***	16.98054***	258.3271***	1.774110	0.877168
NDFB$_{3m}$	5	19.48180***	19.62126***	11.36582**	272.6048***	5.186750	0.207288
NDFB$_{6m}$	5	12.76552**	8.614036*	13.09048**	277.0446***	4.283696	0.363074
NDFB$_{9m}$	3	2.825244	3.283097	5.234946*	281.2512***	0.077822	0.031959
NDFB$_{12m}$	5	11.62083**	8.951395*	9.519520**	268.2179***	5.094530	1.132364

1. d(B), d(lns), and d(lndi) are one differences of the USD/RMB forward basis, the log of the USD/RMB spot rates and the log of the USD/RMB Dollar Index respectively.

2. The numbers in the table are the value of the statistic of Granger Causality Tests with the null hypothesis that the coefficients are zero. ***, **, and * denote significance at 1%, 5%, and 10% levels respectively.

Since all these three series are non-stationary, we conduct cointegration tests before Granger Causality tests are performed. If there exist cointegration relationships among these three variables, Granger Causality tests will be conducted based on VEC models. If not, Granger Causality tests will be conducted with first difference of the variables.

The results in Table 5 show there do exist adaptive expectations in the USD/RMB NDF markets widely. Except for nine-month NDF contracts, the changes of other USD/RMB NDF basis are all positively and significantly related to 3–5 lags of the changes of USD/RMB spot rates and the Dollar Index. This indicates that the more quickly the USD/RMB spot rates appreciate in the past few days, the lower the return of the Dollar Index, the less the basis will be than zero and the more the RMB will appreciate against the US dollar in NDF markets. This suggests that NDF investors do trade with adaptive expectations. However, we find evidence of adaptive expectations only in three-month and six-month DF markets.

The other result revealed in Table 5 is the two-way Granger Causality between the NDF basis and the USD/RMB spot rates. The changes of the USD/RMB spot rates are all positively and significantly related to 3–5 lags of the changes of USD/RMB NDF basis. This suggests that in the NDF markets there exist not only adaptive expectations but also predictions about the spot rates in next few days. Again in the DF markets, only three-month and six-month forward basis have this function of prediction. The NDF markets seem to be more sensitive in adaptive expectations and predictability than the DF markets.

8. Conclusion

In this paper, we explore the information content in the deviations from no-arbitrage prices in the USD/RMB DF and NDF markets and get some interesting conclusions:

First, the USD/RMB forward basis series are all non-stationary series with structural breaks in either DF or NDF market. This indicates that the CIP does not hold in both markets. The reason lies in the official daily foreign exchange market intervention operations in China.

Second, in essence, the USD/RMB forward basis is the difference of the expectation of the depreciation of the US dollar against the RMB controlled by China's Central Bank and the expected return of the US dollar as an investment asset. The wider the difference, the farther the basis will be away from zero. Sometimes the basis might be close to zero. But it is not the evidence that the CIP holds but a coincidence. Since arbitrage activities are nearly impossible in the USD/RMB FX markets, what determine the forward rate are no longer the CIP but the expectations and the risk premium.

Third, in the USD/RMB NDF markets, there exist significant adaptive expectations and predictions about the spot rates in next few days. Investors usually adjust their own expectations dynamically according to the behavior of China's Central Bank and the short-term tendency of the US dollar in the global markets. NDF investors are more sensitive than DF investors to the fluctuations in the market. In our sample, the one-month NDF rate is a good but not unbiased estimator of the future spot rates in one month.

Last, we reveal that in one-month NDF markets, the risk premium of the RMB for global investors is positive.

References

Banerjee, A., Lumsdaine, R.L., and Stock James, H., 1992. Recursive and sequential tests of the unit root and trend break hypotheses: theory and international evidence. *Journal of Business and Economic Statistics*, 10, 271–287.

Brennan, M.J. and Schwartz, E.S., 1990. Arbitrage in stock index futures. *Journal of Business*, 62, S7–S31.

Chen, R. and Zhenlong, Z., 2007. Can futures price discover the future spot price in the future? *Studies of International Finance*, 9, 70–74.

Chen, R. and Zhenlong, Z., 2008. Unbiased estimation, price discovery and market efficiency: the relationship between futures prices and spot prices. *Systems Engineering — Theory & Practice*, 8, 2–11.

Chung, Y.P., 1991. A transactions data test of stock index futures market efficiency and index arbitrage profitability. *Journal of Finance*, 46, 1791–1809.

Cornell, B. and French, K.R., 1983. The pricing of stock index futures. *The Journal of Futures Markets*, 3, 1–14.

Engel, C., 1996. The forward discount anomaly and the risk premium: a survey of recent evidence. *Journal of Empirical Finance*, 3, 123–192.

Figlewski, S., 1984. Explaining the early discounts on stock index futures: the case for disequilibrium. *Financial Analysts Journal*, 40, 43–47.

Klemkosky, R.C. and Lee, J.H., 1991. The intraday ex post and ex ante profitability of index arbitrage. *Journal of Futures Markets*, 11, 291–311.

Lim, K., 1992. Arbitrage and price behavior of the Nikkei Stock Index futures. *Journal of Futures Markets*, 12, 151–161.

MacKinlay, A.C. and Ramaswamy, K., 1988. Index-futures arbitrage and the behavior of stock index futures prices. *Review of Financial Studies*, 1, 137–158.

Modest, D.M. and Sundaresan, M., 1983. The relationship between spot and futures prices in stock index futures markets: some preliminary evidence. *Journal of Futures Markets*, 3, 15–41.

Perron, P., 1989. The great crash, the oil shock and the unit root hypothesis. *Econometrica*, 57, 1361–402.

Roll, R., Schwartz, E., and Subrahmanyam, A., 2007. Liquidity and the law of one price: the case of the futures-cash basis. *The Journal of Finance*, 62, 2201–2234.

Sofianos, G., 1993. Index arbitrage profitability. *The Journal of Derivative*, 1, 6–20.

Strickland, C. and Xu, X., 1990. Behavior of the FTSE 100 basis. Universidad de Warwick: Financial Options Research Center.

Yadav, P.K. and Pope, P.F., 1990. Stock index futures arbitrage: international evidence. *Journal of Futures Markets*, 10, 573–603.

Yadav, P.K. and Pope, P.F., 1994. Stock index futures mispricing: profit opportunities or risk premia? *Journal of Banking and Finance*, 18, 921–953.

Part 2

Management Innovations

The Chinese Management Mode in the Era of Globalization

Shaochun Xu

Chair of Board of Directors,
Kingdee International Software Group Company Limited,
Shenzhen 518057, China
ping_xu@kingdee.com

This paper divides the reform and open-door policies endorsed by China in the past 30 years into five development stages: Period of Management Enlightenment, Period of System Innovation, Period of Chinese-Western Fusion, Period of Compliance with International Practices, and Budding Period of Chinese Management Mode. This paper analyzes briefly the main characteristics of each period and lists the symbolic enterprises and events in each stage. The paper proposes three key integral elements of the Chinese Management Mode: modern Chinese ethical philosophy, modern management thinking, and successful management practice. The paper goes further ahead to analyze and describe the basic integral elements of the successful management practice. In conclusion, the paper holds that the use of the Chinese management mode can explain properly the 30-year continuous growth of China's economy and Chinese enterprises. The paper also believes that the Chinese management mode provides a theoretical reference to the fact that Chinese enterprises will become market leaders in the future global economy.

Keywords: Globalization; China; Management mode; Zheng He.

1. Major Transformation Faced by China and Chinese Enterprises

By the end of 2008, I attended the global Asian leaders' conference in New York. At this conference, some experts forecasted that China would become the world's largest economic entity in the future with its gross domestic products (GDP) to exceed America's. In the meanwhile, many people also raised some questions: how can the Chinese economy and Chinese enterprises become the market leader in the process of globalization? How can the Chinese enterprises become the equal partner in the global ecosystem? How can China achieve the sustainable economic growth and development? These have reminded me of the story of Zheng He's voyages to the Western Ocean.

In 1405, Zheng He started the initial voyage to the Western Ocean together with more than 27,000 warriors, followed by another six voyages to the Western Ocean within 28 years, which shocked the entire world. What were the reasons for Zheng He's success? I think there were three reasons: First, Zheng He conceived the grand ideal and shouldered a mission, that is, spread the cultures of the Grand Ming Dynasty. Second, he had a personal faith. Zheng He was a Hui Muslim. It was a limitless glory for a Muslim to pay a pilgrimage to Mecca. These two points became the spiritual pillars for his success. Third, Zheng He had the most solid and strongest "treasure ship" in the world. According to the historical record, Zheng He's ship, 148 meters in length and 60 meters in width, was the biggest sail vessel in the world at that time. It was strong enough to resist huge winds and waves and sail through winds and waves. It could absolutely be termed as an "aircraft carrier" at that time.

In fact, the enterprise development was just like Zheng He's voyages to the Western Ocean — the "cultures of the Grand Ming Dynasty" was the corporate mission, while the Holy Land Mecca was the ideal and value of enterprises. If the Chinese enterprises have the lofty ideals and values, they will not lose the direction just for the sake of the short-term interests. In addition, the Chinese enterprises need to build up the internal powers to forge a treasure ship. This "treasure ship" is the Chinese management mode in the era of globalization.

Since I first put forward the subject of "the Chinese management mode in the era of globalization" at the Chinese entrepreneurs summit in December 2006, it has aroused much debate; some people objected and some people agreed. However, I have recently found that more and more people are reaching consensus on this subject. Over the past thirty years since China's reform and opening up, why have so many enterprises succeeded? Why have they been persistently successful? In reality, management has played its role, while management innovation has also functioned. The unique Chinese management mode was created.

2. Review of 30 Years of Chinese Management and Fledgling Chinese Management Mode

By reviewing the reform and open-door policies endorsed by China in the past 30 years, we can divide this time span into five stages.

Stage I: 1978–1984, Period of Management Enlightenment,
Stage II: 1985–1993, Period of System Innovation,
Stage III: 1994–2000, Period of Chinese-Western Fusion,
Stage IV: 2001–2004, Period of Compliance with International Practices, and
Stage V: 2005–2008, Budding Period of Chinese Management Mode.

2.1. *Stage I: 1978–1984, period of management enlightenment*

Before the endorsement of the reform and open-door policies, China adopted the state-owned planned economic system. In this system, state-owned enterprises are merely production and processing units in the state-planned economy system. They do not have actual business operation decision-making power, not to mention real enterprise management.

On 11 October 1978, Deng Xiaoping presented a speech on the opening ceremony of the Ninth National Representative Conference of the All China Federation of Trade Unions. He proposed the following points: "To improve the currently backward productivity drastically, we have to change, in different ways, the production relationship, the superstructure, and the management modes of industrial and agricultural enterprises and the management modes of those enterprises by the state so that they fit in with the modern macro economy" (Deng, 2001).

The line is a profound one. It specifies that the reason of the backward economy of China lies in the backward production relationship and superstructure. Additionally, it specifies directly that the root cause is the backward "management mode".

In December 1978, the Third Plenary Session of the 11th Central Committee of the Communist Party of China (CPC) uplifted the curtain of reform and started the new exploration for management mode by Chinese enterprises. At that time, the focus of exploration lied in the system level. The main tasks were to change the over centralization of the power of state-owned enterprises and help them transit toward economic entities of "self-responsibility for profit and loss, self-run business operation, self-constraint, and self-development". The exploration for enterprise management mode was sparse.

Given that, the exploration nurtured a number of world-class enterprises in later times, such as Lenovo, Haier, and ZTE Corporation. These three enterprises share two common characteristics: firstly, they were all founded in 1984; secondly, they were brand new modern enterprises that were born from state-owned enterprises. The founding of a whole generation of modern enterprises with the three enterprises mentioned above marked that the Chinese enterprise management had completed the historic mission of the Period of Management Enlightenment.

2.2. Stage II: 1985–1993, period of system innovation

In this period, Chinese enterprises management showed two major characteristics. Firstly, the government boosted with state policies system innovation, creating an enterprise growth environment in the modern macro economy. Secondly, enterprises actively changed the business operation system at the business management level, stimulating innovative energy within enterprises. The healthy interaction between the government and enterprises helped Chinese enterprises overcome the difficulties in market-oriented reconstruction. Chinese enterprises became real enterprises that could participate in international competition.

For example, the government decreed in June 1986, Outline of Modernization of Enterprise Management; in February 1988, Regulations on Contract-based Projects; and in April 1988, Law of the People's Republic of China on Industrial Enterprises Owned by the Whole People. Enterprises management embarked on the orbit of legal operation through the decree and enactment of the laws and regulations. By the early 1990s, the Shanghai Stock Exchange and the Shenzhen Stock Exchange were established one by one. Stock, a kind of value securities that represent enterprise ownership, entered market circulation, which formally announced that ownership reconstruction achieved material breakthroughs.

While those management systems and management modes with obvious "capitalist" characteristics occurred rapidly, different objecting voices were heard here and there. The pace of enterprise management innovation in China slowed down. In 1992, the speech of Deng Xiaoping on his inspection trip to South China recognized the reform direction and behaviors, removing mental barriers of people.

At the level of enterprises, with the expansion of self-run business operation, Chinese enterprises were rejuvenated, exploring continuously for advanced management modes. A large number of foreign enterprises vied to get into China through sole funding, joint funding, technical cooperation, and even foreign trade. They provided references and examples to management innovation of Chinese enterprises. Meanwhile, Chinese enterprises walked out of China one by one, learning and introducing advanced management of foreign enterprises. They performed management innovation during the actual application of the learned advanced management. For example, the "fully loaded work method" of Shijiazhuang Plastic No. 1 Factory, the "OEC method" of Haier Refrigerator Factory, the "Wanfeng Mode" of Shajing, Shenzhen, and the "Shekou Mode" of Shenzhen Shekou Industrial Zone were all noticeable exploration. China Merchants Bank, the first financial organization run by an enterprise in China, was founded in 1987 in Shekou, Shenzhen.

In 1993, a number of modern enterprises with a modern management awareness and relatively high management performance occurred. As mentioned above, Haier was listed in the Shanghai Stock Exchange in November 1993; Lenovo was listed in Hong Kong Exchanges and Clearing Limited in February 1994; Zhongxin New Communications, predecessor of ZTE Corporation, completed the business operation system transition of "state-owned, private-owned, and self-run operations", boosting the enterprise on a healthy and fast-developing road and providing a "Zhongxin model" with high reference value to the reform of state-owned management system; China Merchants Bank moved its headquarters from Shekou to downtown, Shenzhen, starting a fast developing new stage of a real enterprise bank.

2.3. Stage III: 1994–2000, period of Chinese-Western fusion

In the previous stage, the size of Chinese enterprises was commonly small. Though they created some unique operation management method, the methods, for example, "full workload work method" and "OEC method", were in essence summary of personal experiences.

In 1994, the 1994 version ISO9000 standards were released. A large number of foreign enterprises passed the ISO9000 certification. ISO9000 as an international management standard was quickly promoted and became popular in China. Chinese enterprises have got into contact with a management world standard for the first time ever. At the same time, with the development computer technologies, accounting computerization gained more and more attention from Chinese enterprises, which adopted it. After 1997, the IT revolution brought about the Internet-enabled Chinese enterprises to capture quickly the international frontiers of management thinking, technology, and methodology. For example, business process reengineering (BPR) was proposed in 1990 by American management sage Michael Hammer and was known by Chinese enterprises after 1997. Once it was known by Chinese enterprises, BPR had a sweeping popularity in China. At that time, BPR became a synonym of enterprise management in China.

The most representative enterprise in this period was doubtlessly Huawei.

Huawei was founded in 1988. In 1995, Ren Zhengfei, president of Huawei, realized that the management that relied on the instincts and experiences of entrepreneurs could not adapt to Huawei's development. As a result, management experts and professors of Renmin University of China were invited to compile Huawei Basic Law. Compared with the "full workload method" and "OEC management method", Huawei Basic Law was a more systematic, scientific management methodology of Chinese enterprises. Based on the experiences of Huawei, it borrowed heavily from Western management thinking and theories. Huawei President Ren Zhengfei pointed out that Huawei Basic Law condensed our 10 years of valuable and painful accumulation and exploration and achieved further improvement by absorbing the optimum thinking and methodology in the industry. It became our theoretical basis for further advancement. It helped us to avoid empiricism. That was the basic standpoint of our compiling the Huawei Basic Law (Huang and Liu, 1999). In 1998 when Ren Zhengfei discovered the integrated product development (IPD) of IBM, he introduced it decisively in an all-round manner to Huawei. To remove the worries of employees, Ren Zhengfei proposed such project implementation principles of "fit the Chinese feet into American shoes" and "first stabilize it, then fix it, and eventually optimize it". The case of Huawei from the Huawei Basic Law to IPD lively reflected the characteristic of "Chinese-Western fusion" in the management of Chinese enterprises in this period.

In this period, by quickly, substantively introducing international management standards, thinking, methods, and tools, a large number of competitive enterprises, for example, Huawei, Lenovo, Changhong, Haier, TCL, Kongka, China Merchants Bank, and New Hope Group, were created.

In this period, the management of Chinese enterprises gained international attention. For example, the case that the Haier culture activated the shocked fish was formally written into the textbook of Harvard University. In January 2000, Zhang Ruimin, president of Haier, was finalized by the UK version Harvard Business Review as one of the "top 30 most reputed entrepreneurs in the world". It was the first time that a Chinese entrepreneur has gained the attention of the world. It also marked the huge success of the "Chinese-Western Fusion" of Chinese enterprises, which was of important historic significance.

2.4. Stage IV: 2001–2004, period of compliance with international practices

From 2000 onwards, in the globalization wave across the world, the management of Chinese enterprises started to comply with international practices.

After the 2000 version ISO9000 Standards was released, ZTE Corporation and other seven trial enterprises passed the new standard certification in 2000. Later on, those which had passed the certification of the 1994 version ISO9000 Standards took the certification of the 2000 version ISO9000 Standards. The 2000 version ISO9000 Standards integrated the latest thinking and methods of quality management. By passing the certification, Chinese enterprises quickly complied with international advanced management.

In other words, since 2000, a large number of international management standards, most advanced international management methods and tools, and management terminology, for example, KPI < ERP, CMMI, IPD, Six Sigma, balanced score card, project management, and supply chain became the daily terms of Chinese enterprises.

In this period, Chinese management research and management teaching were developed rapidly. MBA and EMBA courses were popular, showing a rapidly developing trend. The popularity of MBA teaching trained a large number of business operation talents and researchers with international management thinking, and helped Chinese management to become more systematic and quickly comply with international practices.

The compliance with international practices improved significantly the management performance of Chinese enterprises. Their international competitiveness increased. A large number of enterprises, for example, Huawei, ZTE, TCL, Gree, and Lenovo, started to walk into the overseas markets. A few Chinese enterprises of international fame went into the horizon of the world.

In 2004, the supplier certification experts of BT believed, after their all-round inspection of Huawei, that "Huawei is an American enterprise in China". In the same year, ZTE Corporation, major rival of Huawei, secured the order of digital communication devices for the Athens Olympic Games, winning huge international reputation for Chinese enterprises. In June of the same year, TCL acquired French company Thomson. Half a year afterwards, Lenovo acquired the global desktop and notebook business of IBM at the price of USD 1.25 billion.

The period from 1978, when Deng Xiaoping proposed the change of "management mode", to 2004, when Chinese enterprises galloped in the international market, fully shows that the Chinese government and enterprises had made initially the dream of modernization and internationalization of enterprise management after 26 years of tough exploration.

2.5. Stage V: 2005–2008, budding period of Chinese management mode

In this period, domestic research on enterprise management showed a new characteristic: more summary, introduction and promotion of management practice, and theory and methodology of Chinese enterprises. For example, loads of books about the management practice of local Chinese enterprises such as Haier, Huawei, ZTE, Mengniu, Wanke, TCL, Gree, and Netease cropped up in the market. The books showed the unique experiences and methodologies of Chinese enterprises.

Many theorists started to look at the management theory with Chinese characteristics in the perspective of local culture, for example, *G Management Mode* by Guo Hangang, *Dao-Oriented Management* by Qi Shanhong, *Learn Management from PLA* by Zhang Jianhua, and *Chinese Management* by Zeng Shiqiang. Particularly, *Dao-Oriented Management* by Qi Shanhong won the "Award for Excellent Management Works" by the International Management Institute (IMI) in December 2007.

Some excellent entrepreneurs summarized theories while running their businesses. By combining practice and theory, they constructed the management methodology and system that could fit in with the characteristics of their enterprises. Some of them also wrote books, spreading their thinking and methodology to society. For example, Deng Shimin, former president of China Everbright Bank, wrote *Our Road — Exploration of Management Mode of Chinese Enterprises*. By integrating over a decade of management experiences, the author focuses on the exploration of the enterprise management mode and characteristics that are suitable for the particular situation of China.

In the same period, a number of excellent Chinese enterprises, for example, Lenovo, Huawei, Haier, Gree, CIMC Group, and China Merchants Bank, started to march onto positions of world leaders. People, foreigners and Chinese alike, started to recognize the influence of China on the world. They started to discuss such topics as how Chinese enterprises would become world market leaders, and how China's GDP would exceed that of the United States.

3. Content of the Chinese Management Mode in the Era of Globalization

Many experts and scholars in the world provided different theoretical explanation to how China's economy and Chinese enterprises could develop in a high speed continuously. As China develops rapidly, such theories of China Threat and China Collapse occurred one by one. However, the peaceful rise of China neither bring any threat to the world nor experience any collapse. Those theories were broke one after another. Today, people suspect whether China can maintain the fast development and why Chinese enterprises can become future global market leaders. Those questions were the concerns of this annual conference.

What are the root causes for the continuous development of China's economy and Chinese enterprises? We believe that Chinese enterprises have strived to build the "Treasure Ship" of Zheng He in the era of globalization. The "Treasure Ship" is based on the five thousand years of traditional culture of China and also absorbs the most advanced management thinking and enterprise best practice of the modern times. In that regard, the "Treasure Ship" is brand new and has never been met in Western society before. The "Treasure Ship" is the Chinese Management Mode.

In the era of globalization, the Chinese management mode includes three aspects: modern Chinese ethical philosophy, modern management thinking, and successful management practice, as shown in Fig. 1.

3.1. Reconstruction of modern Chinese ethical philosophy

The Chinese has a unique ethical value system and philosophical system, which is the kernel of the Chinese culture and the valuable wealth our

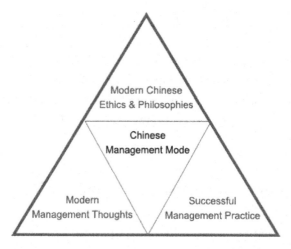

Fig. 1. The Chinese management mode in the era of globalization.

ancestors left to us. However, our culture originated from an agricultural society and petty farmer economy. Concerning ethical value, we stress the idea of hierarchy and blood and geographical relationships, for example, family relationship, friendship, fellow countrymen relationship, and emperor and official relationships. We regard such ethics "private merits". This ethics benefited the maintenance of the state control order and family order based on the petty farmer economy. In Western countries, their civilization originated from commercial economy due to their geographical locations close to oceans. The civilization focused more on the public order that maintained the fair trade in the commercial economy. We call it "public merit". The ethics based on "public merits" encouraged people to make full use of their innovative and adventurous spirits, and eventually urged the rise of Western industrial civilization and created the global leading positions of Western society.

In the first four periods of Chinese management development, we were imitating the West and had little efforts in fusing it with local culture. As a result, a social morale of worshipping foreign things, blindly copying foreign things, and lacking innovation was formed. Regarding basic theory or systematic management practice, Chinese enterprise management lacked originality. In the fifth period, the budding period of Chinese management, the social morale changed. However, there is a trend of exaggerating the effect of Chinese ethics and overly lessening Western ethics.

The correct path for us should be this: we take a fair, scientific attitude in comparing and analyzing the Chinese and Western ethics, combining "public merits" and "private merits", removing coarse and false parts, and saving essential and true parts. By doing so, we created a new Chinese ethical philosophy with Chinese cultural characteristics and orientation to the era of globalization.

It is a process of management innovation. In addition, it is a process of cultural innovation. It is the historic mission that the entrepreneurs have to shoulder. In that way, our economy and society can grow healthily, rapidly, and continuously. There will not be cases such as the melamine-tainted milk. There will not be people who criticized China with the so-called "China Threat".

3.2. Introducing, digesting, and creating innovatively modern management thinking

With the exchanges of Eastern thinking and Western thinking, Chinese entrepreneurs and management experts have realized the difference between them. The difference is that Eastern thinking is a kind of dialectic, systematic, and strategic thinking, whereas Western thinking is a kind of logical, analytical, and tactical thinking. For example, the ancient classic *The Art of War* by Sun Zi (or Sun Tzu) applies a dialectic, systematic, and macro perspective to think about the nature of war, and ended up with the strategic principle of "defeating the enemy without ever fighting" (Sun, 2006).

Currently, the mainstream thinking systems in the world came chiefly from Westerners. They were founded on the basis of Western logical thinking. Westerners apply logical thinking and such scientific means as logical reasoning, statistical analysis, and experiment and research to construct a precise, complicated management model, for example, ISO9000, ERP, and CMM. For Westerners who are used to think logically and analytically, it is all too natural, or even inherent, to use and follow the models and relevant programs. If they are required to work without them, it would result in confusing logic and work failure. Contrarily, the Chinese who are used to think dialectically and systematically are not used to the precise work brought about by the models. They cannot stand the endless, tedious details. It is the difference of thinking that resulted in lack of patience and seriousness when they introduced Western management modes. Ultimately, they ended up in a kind of ritualism and became perfunctory with such work. That is why the ISO9000 International Standards were almost decorative in a large number of Chinese enterprises.

However, Eastern thinking has its huge strengths. The use of the Eastern dialectic and systematic thinking will not get you easily in the whirlpool of details. As a result, you can notice the trend of changes in advance, follow the changes, or even create changes. Such strength is valuable for the rapidly developing information era.

In that regard, the problem left in front of Chinese entrepreneurs is to fuse Eastern and Western thinking, absorb the strengths of one thinking to reinforce the weaknesses of the other thinking, and create the management thinking that best suits Chinese enterprises in their global endeavors.

At this point, some practices of Japanese enterprises can be borrowed. For example, the Japanese developed corporate culture management on the basis of scientific management. They developed the TQM management method on the basis of the PDCA cycle, and the famous Toyota mode on the basis of IE.

3.3. Creating successful management practice of Chinese enterprises

In the era of globalization, Chinese enterprises and Western enterprises are at the same starting line. The difficulties that we meet are the same difficulties that Western enterprises meet. We will not find ready-made management practice and solutions from Western enterprises. We do not have teachers any more. What are we going to do?

The problem is to solve with the collaboration and cooperation of experts, scholars, consulting firms, and even governments. We need to solve the practical problems of enterprises innovatively and create the management practice of Chinese enterprises. Particularly, enterprises are the main entities of creation. Experts, scholars, and consulting firms summarize the best practice bit by bit, forming theoretical, systematic, and best practice model and spreading it to more Chinese enterprises. For example, Kingdee now has over 600,000 customers who created substantive best practices. Kingdee encourages internally that all ERP implementation consultants, management consultants, and product planners share information, extract and summarize the best practice models in different management domains, integrate them into our software products, and promote them in Chinese enterprises.

We hope that more Chinese enterprises and management experts can join this endeavor, creating the successful management practice for Chinese enterprises in the era of globalization.

In that way, our enterprises, especially some medium and small businesses, do not need to travel all the long ways to America or Japan. They can learn successful management practices that suit their needs from successful Chinese enterprises.

The previous three points are the content of the Chinese management mode in the era of globalization we summarize. It is obvious that the Chinese management mode is profound and meaning-laden. It needs our joint efforts.

4. Successful Management Practice System

What is the architecture of successful management practice? What are the basic elements it contains? During our services provisioning to a large array of Chinese enterprises, we summarize and extract a successful management practice system with a number of basic elements (see Fig. 2).

Firstly, culture is the base and the DNA of an enterprise. Cultures vary. Even in the same industry, the same market, and the same place corporate cultures are different.

Secondly, cultural atmosphere decides the behavioral criteria, organization structure, and legal person governance structure inside an organization. For example, in a culture of strict personal hierarchy, there will be more emphasis on the criteria and standard of behaviors. The organization will see clear-cut responsibility division and a relatively large number of layers.

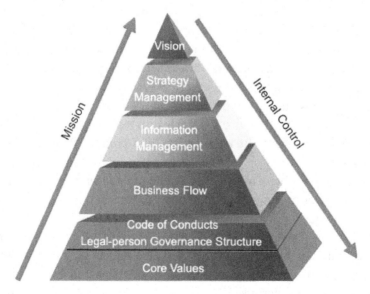

Fig. 2. Architecture of basic elements of a successful management practice system.

In a culture of equality and respect, there will be more emphasis on team work and mutual support. The organization structure is flat. The horizontal and vertical team collaboration is close.

Thirdly, service processes are laid over the organization. Like a needle with a string, service process stitches the enterprise resources distributed on different parts of the organization into a chain that can create value and provide value to customers in the processes.

Fourthly, to improve the operation efficiency and quality of service processes, and reduce the operation cost of service processes, we need to adopt IT to optimize and fix the service processes. In the era of globalization, IT should not be confined inside enterprises. Enterprises break the barriers of service processes with IT, achieving consolidation of supply chain.

Fifthly, it is strategic management. Strategy is the decisions made for the future business operation and behaviors on the basis of prediction of future environment changes by the enterprises. Strategic management is the systematic thinking and strategic thinking capability that business runners should have.

Sixthly, it is the corporate vision. Though corporate vision is a Western management phrase, it came in fact from oriental system thinking. Peter M. Senge, author of *The Fifth Discipline* and management master, valued the philosophy of Lao Zi (Lao Tzu) a lot. The five disciplines he raised are closely related to the thinking of Confucius, Taoism, and Buddhism (Peter, 2002). In his book, he raised five disciplines to address the systematic issues of enterprise management. One of the disciplines is to "establish a common vision".

If we can sort out the management modes of different industries with the systematic, scientific, and successful management model systems, we can form the Chinese management system. Of course, the Chinese culture has the spirit of harmony and accommodation. Our management mode must be accommodating and diverse. It will accommodate the advanced management practices of America, Europe, Japan, and other countries.

5. Cases of Chinese Management Mode

Many excellent Chinese enterprises have practiced or are practicing the Chinese management mode.

5.1. The "harmonious and different" organization management and control mode of China Merchants Holdings (Hong Kong) Limited

Hong Kong-based China Merchants Group is a prime example. As a large group operating in diverse industries with a history of 136 years, the Group has survived the century-long great changes in China's modern time and the Asian financial crisis. The secret is its good management and the scientific and rigorous modern enterprise management system. In the past, China Merchants Group (Hong Kong) had a diverse assortment of business. Later on, it simplified itself into three "core business sectors": shipping, transportation, and construction of relevant infrastructure and services, financial investment and management, and real estate development and operation. Regarding concentration and division of power, Qin Xiao, Chair of Board of Directors, innovatively created the "harmonious and different" organization management and control thinking. By "harmonious", he did not mean "harmony" in the form. Instead, he meant a smooth internal communication atmosphere. In this atmosphere, many persons with independent thinking capability can achieve conceptual, spiritual "harmony" after sufficient communication, and long-term interaction. Meanwhile, he also crated innovatively a full set of successful management practice for the functional positioning of the headquarters of modern enterprises, which is called "substitution model". By applying this management practice, China Merchants Group properly solved the problem of functional positioning of the headquarters.

5.2. "Gree Standards" of Gree Air-Conditioners

The slogan "Gree Makes Good Air-Conditioners" is well known to all. Yet if you have not met Dong Mingzhu and have not visited Gree Electric Appliances, Inc. of Zhuhai, it is hard for you to understand the deep meaning of the slogan. When I visited her at the year beginning, she showed me around the exhibition hall, the workshops, the laboratory, the staff dormitory, and other places of Zhuhai Gree Group. On the way, the word she mentioned most frequently to me was the "Gree Standards", which is the strictest and the highest standard in China's electrical appliance industry and also the standard in compliance with the international community.

Dong Mingzhu is too strict to repudiate all of her relatives, and all the suppliers that do business with Gree are all afraid of being related to Dong Mingzhu, because that will not benefit them. On my way home from Gree, I read the book *Move without Regret* by Dong Mingzhu carefully. In the end, I realized why Gree can make good air-conditioners. The answer is the "Gree Standards" of Dong Mingzhu.

Many emerging enterprises in the service industry, for example, Lianhua Supermarket that is known to be the "Chinese Wal-Mart", Press HR, CTRIP, and Little Sheep, capture the characteristics of Chinese enterprises and create their brand new service mode and management mode.

6. Sharing the Secrets of the Chinese Management Mode

We can see that Chinese enterprises created the Chinese management mode due to the differences of Eastern and Western cultures and thinking. The Chinese management mode is by no means a backward concept. It is a brand new creation based on the Western management by Chinese enterprises. We believe that six forces, government, entrepreneurs, management scholars, management consulting firms, social organization, and media, are pushing the creation of Chinese enterprise management. In the era of globalization, if we keep trying and working hard, the Chinese management mode will be certainly a success and go into the world. After learning Western management with all the heart for 30 years, Chinese enterprises will contribute the secrets of Chinese management to the world — the Chinese management mode.

References

Deng, X. 2001. *Selected Works of Deng Xiaoping* (2nd Volume), The People's Press.

Huang, W. and Liu, C. 1999. *Walking Out of Confusion*, People's Post and Telecommunication Press.

Peter, M.S. (translated by Guo Jinlong), 2002. *The Fifth Discipline*, Shanghai Joint Publishing.

Sun, T. 2006. *The Art of War*, Guangming Daily Press.

Global Competency Leadership and an Empirical Study of Chinese Managers*

Shuming Zhao

School of Business, Nanjing University,
Nanjing 210093, China
zhaosm@nju.edu.cn

The shortage of global competency leaders is an immense challenge for the internationalization of corporations. It is a crucial issue to cultivate and develop global competency leaders during the internationalization of companies, which needs further study in China. On the basis of a literature review on global competency leadership at home and abroad, this paper first proposes a five-level global competency leadership model incorporating a set of basic characteristics. Next, it analyzes the present situation and major problems of global competency leadership development in the internationalization of Chinese corporations. Finally, some measures for global competency leadership development of Chinese corporations are presented.

Keywords: Global competency leadership; Chinese companies; Internationalization; Human resource management and development.

1. Introduction

With the further development of China's reform and opening-up and the more stable establishment and improvement of the socialist market economic system, especially since China's entry into the WTO eight years ago, Chinese enterprises have already encountered international market

*This research is supported by Natural Science Foundation of China (70732002 and 70572048), "333 Project" of Jiangsu Province, and the Ministry of Education of China project on "Human Resource Management in Economic Transition and Development".

competition. More than 400 of the World's top 500 companies have invested in China, and most of them have set up managerial headquarters, manufacturing bases, and R&D centers or engineering centers in China (Zhao, 2005). In the industrial parks and economic development zones of the Yangtze River Delta, Pearl River Delta, Beijing-Tianjin-Tangshan, and the Bohai Sea Area, R&D and manufacturing have both realized global synchronization. With the rapid input of international capital and technology, many industries in China simultaneously face "international competition domestically and domestic competition internationally". Increasingly Chinese enterprises are involved directly in international markets and are adopting the "going-outside" policy. With the faster progress of internationalization, those enterprises are recognizing the need for more leaders with global competencies.

One research study conducted in the United States on the "global best enterprises in leadership development", surveyed 300 established global companies about their leadership. The study revealed that in order to deal with the increasingly diversified and competitive markets and to ensure the sustainable development of the companies, global excellent companies are doing their best to develop sufficient high-quality leaders, so as to make up for the shortage of global leaders (Ren, 2006). While in Asia, particularly in China, with the fast economic growth, there are countless enterprises emerging and growing rapidly. As a result, we need to face an issue deserving attention and alertness — the deficiency of global competency leaders. In an era of economic globalization, information networks, knowledge socialization, population urbanization, and e-currency, China is in urgent need to develop managerial professionals with global vision and cross-cultural leadership. Therefore, developing and managing global competency leadership will become the main task of human resource management and development in today's context.

2. What Is Global Competency Leadership?

Global competency leadership has been the focus of academia and enterprises. Global competency leadership refers to the leadership that can determine the future of business organization during its process of internationalization and globalization (Clark and Matze, 1999). Peter Drucker, the management guru, pointed out that there are two types of managers in the 21st century: one is the manager with global vision and the other is the laid-off type (Drucker, 1998, 1999). According to a Fortune 500 survey, 85% of the CEOs do not think that their companies have enough leaders with global competency, while global competency leadership is the key to success for global companies (Javidan and House, 2001). What competencies should global leaders have? This has been an important question for both academia and enterprises. Several researchers have contributed to our understanding of global competency leadership.

In the academic field, Brake (1997) proposed a global leadership model including three competencies: relationship management, business acumen, and personal effectiveness. Conner (2000) suggested six skills and capabilities of global leaders: to have business savvy, to know how to use personal influence, to bring a global perspective, to have strong character, to know how to motivate people, and to act like entrepreneurs. Liu (2002) specified that global leaders must have six characteristics including: plentiful work experience and leadership practice, deep understanding of global markets, ability to motivate employees, effective use of personal influence, emotional intelligence, and capability for cultural integration. Morrison (2000) conceptualized global competency leadership into three levels: the concept of global competency leadership, the characteristics that global competency leadership should have, and the competencies included in each characteristic. The above descriptive studies discussed the competencies that global competency leaders should have for high performance, but there are some limitations in these studies in terms of the generalizability and application of the findings due to the lack of empirical tests (Yu et al., 2003).

More systematically, Moran and Riesenberger (1994) identified 12 different competencies associated with the implementation of global strategies. The competencies were organized into four categories or characteristics: attitudes, leadership, interaction, and cultural understanding. Each category or characteristic contains three competencies, making 12 competencies in total. The three global leadership competencies included the ability to facilitate organizational change, to create learning systems, and to motivate employees to excellence. Also, the research of Black and colleagues (1999) on global multinational companies' leaders identified four major context-specific factors that impacted idiosyncratic characteristics: company affiliation, managerial position, country affiliation, and functional responsibility, each of which influences the types of characteristics required for effective global leadership. In addition to those idiosyncratic competencies, the authors also identified three distinct characteristics of effective global leaders: demonstrating savvy, exhibiting character, and embracing duality, each of which is relevant to leaders regardless of the company they work for, the position they hold, their country of origin, or their functional orientation. Based on their studies on 18,000 managers from 62 countries, House and colleagues (1999) developed a global competency leadership model of culturally endorsed implicit leadership theories (CLT). The model includes six dimensions: charismatic/value base, self-protective, humane-oriented, team-oriented, participative, and autonomous. Their studies found that cultural factors could influence global leadership competency, and different cultural backgrounds require different global leadership competencies. Their studies contributed to the cultural generalization and specialization of global leadership competency (Yu *et al.*, 2003). It is suggested, therefore, that in order to improve the managers' global business capability, their cultural sensitivity must be improved first (Javidan and House, 2001).

In practice, multinational companies have seen the biggest demand for global competency leaders, and at the same time have fostered a large number of talented leaders with global competencies. Jack Welch, the former CEO and Chairman of General Electric Company (GE), remarked, "The Jack Welch of the future cannot be me. I spent my entire career in the United States. The next head of GE will be somebody who spent time in Mumbai, Hong Kong, or Argentina. We have to send our best and brightest overseas and make sure they have the training that will allow them to be the global leaders who will make GE flourish in the future" (Javidan and House, 2002). A successful company cannot only provide high-quality products and services, but also must cultivate numerous excellent leaders. As is well known, GE is one of the best at cultivating excellent leaders. According to statistics, among the world top 500 companies, 173 CEOs are former GE senior managers. GE spends approximately US$1 billion annually on training and education. Each year about 6,000 GE executives travel from different GE business units all over the world to Crotonville for training at the Welch Leadership Center. Among the mentors at Crotonville, about 50% are senior executives from GE, including former Chairman of the Board and CEO Jack Welch and the incumbent Chairman of the Board and CEO Jeffrey R. Immelt (GM Model, 2007).

The key global issue for General Motors Corporation is how to transform the organization internally to become more globally competitive. Even for employees who may never go overseas, it is necessary to constantly sensitize everyone to the fact that they are in a global business (Roberts *et al.*, 1998). In another example, 3M Company has developed a model of global leadership competencies that consists of three categories of twelve competencies (Alldredge and Nilan, 2000). The first category is referred to as fundamental leadership competencies including ethics and integrity, intellectual capacity, maturity, and judgment, which should be possessed by new employees at the time of hire. The second category is the essential leadership competencies including customer orientation, developing people, inspiring others, business health, and effect, which is expected to develop, as employees become responsible for a function or department. The third category is the visionary leadership competencies including global perspective, vision and strategy, nurturing innovation, building alliances, and organizational agility.

To summarize, I argue that those who qualify as global competency leaders are persons who can communicate in international language, understand the operating rules of global markets, have global vision and operation ability, and achieve good results. Accordingly, global competency leaders should have four basic competency characteristics: first, to explore and innovate with internationalized vision; second, to have internationalized knowledge structure and be familiar with international conventions; third, to have international communication capability and meet the needs of international economic competition; fourth, to have strong national self-confidence and sense of social responsibility. A global competency leadership model includes five levels: the first level is the basic or core global competency, which is shown as no bias, open-mindedness, tolerance with ambiguity, world unity, personal interaction, emotional sensitivity, behavioral agility, inquiring mind, optimism, self-confidence, self-recognition, positive emotion, pressure management, interest diversity, self-consciousness, and relation interest. The second level is the inter-personal skills. In the globalization context, leaders need inter-personal skills to conduct deep-seated communication, dialog, and negotiation. They must also know quite well about different cultures, rites, values, and ways of thinking, so as to build teams with mutual trust. The third level is the competency to break through the boundaries of enterprises and build harmonious relations among the stakeholders of enterprises. The fourth level is the ability to make decisions ethically (Zhao, 2001, 2004). While considering the maximization of profit, decision makers should take it as a prerequisite not to violate social ethics and social responsibilities. The fifth level is the leaders' systematic skills. Leaders should make long-term strategies with a systematic perspective because of the complexity of the enterprise itself and the stakeholders.

Based on the five-level global competency leadership model, enterprises can offer human resource policies, plans, and practices, such as leveraging reverse expatriates, delivery of in-country training, and new overseas assignment, to develop competent global leaders (Mendenhall and Stahl, 2000; Mendenhall, 2007).

3. The Internationalization of Chinese Enterprises and the Development of Global Competency Leadership

The wave of globalization has swept each corner of the commercial world. For growth, companies have to consider competing and expanding in the world markets. The globalization means companies have to think globally while act locally. To achieve the dual goals of global strategy and local market reaction, companies need not only to form the organizational structures and strategic targets that adapt to the changeable external environments, but also to develop global leaders that can effectively implement strategies and corresponding corporate cultures (Wu, 2006). It is the latter, success at developing global leaders, which determines the success or failure of the internationalization of companies.

3.1. *The challenges facing Chinese companies going global*

According to a survey by McKinsey & Company, China will require 75,000 top-level executives with global experience by 2010, but at present China has only 7,000 such top-level executives. It is also found that companies in many parts of Asia are affected by the insufficiency of qualified executives. The percentage of companies facing a shortage of top-level executives with appropriate global experience in Asia is as follows: in Mainland China, 45.1%; in Hong Kong, 10%; in Taiwan, 14.3%; in South Korea, 8.3%, respectively. The percentages of companies facing the turnover of executives: in Mainland China, 43%; in Singapore, 5%; in Malaysia, 4.5%, respectively. Apparently, Chinese companies are now facing the urgent challenge of insufficiency of global competency leaders (Ding, 2006). This challenge is evident in three key aspects. The first aspect is the competences gap. In today's world, as the connection and communication between countries are continuously deepening and the clash and blend of different cultures are increasingly common, the process of globalization has demanded more competences for executives. The incumbent leaders of most companies in China lack strategic thinking ability, global vision, the ability to do business globally, and cross-cultural operating ability. The second aspect is the insufficiency of knowledge and skills. Most leaders, even the executives of some well-known listed companies, have mastered only a specific field of specialty knowledge, without professional management knowledge in finance, securities, insurance, accounting, or law. The third aspect is the deficient leadership team. In many companies, there are too many low-level managers but not enough competent middle-level managers and senior-level executives. Such companies with challenges in these three key aspects are in great need of leadership talent who can understand the WTO rules, conduct international negotiations, and do business globally.

3.2. The key issues in the development of global competency leaders for Chinese companies

The unprecedented competition for globalization talent, especially the shortage of global leaders, has imposed severe challenges for Chinese companies. The globalization of Chinese companies will inevitably require the globalization of leaders. In addition to having a good understanding of the different languages and different customs, those leaders with global competency will have to understand the distinct ways of thinking, different management styles, and corporate cultures in other countries.

For the internationalization of companies, the training and development of global competency leadership is a critical issue that needs to be researched and explored within the context of China. Several questions should be addressed. For example, we need to know what kinds of competencies are needed in the Chinese cultural circumstances. What influences will Chinese culture have on the growth of global competency leaders of Chinese companies? How do companies help leaders who are weak at certain characteristics to become more globally competent? (Yu *et al.*, 2003). Such questions should be answered in the internationalization of companies and be the research focus for Chinese scholars, as they study global competency leadership.

4. Research Questions and Analysis

The research of competences is an important content in global leadership. The building and evaluation of competences model is the basis and core of the development of global leadership research. It is an important theoretic principle for verifying the relationship between leadership and performance and for constituting specialized standard of professionalization. This paper builds a competences model of Chinese managers and verifies the differences of managers' competences on different levels, functions, industries, and regions and also proves their positive relationship with performances based on it.

4.1. Methods

We use empirical research method to build and testify this competences model of Chinese managers. First, we did a very detailed literature review to find a suitable construction method. Second, based on the first step, we conducted interview and BEI as the main method to build our competences model, and got almost the same results with the literature review. Third, we built a competences model and named each items according to the data collection and BEI analysis and also verified its validity and reliability using CFA. Fourth, we verified the differences of managers' competences on different levels, functions, industries, and regions using variance analysis and also proved their positive relationship with performances using regression analysis.

4.2. Data

Almost 30 managers joined our interview and answered structured questions according to the outlines we designed ahead of time. The time of each interview is about one hour and the contents of each interview include 8,000 words on average. Questionnaires were totally sent to about 2,000 managers all around China from different management levels, functions, industries, ownership, and scales. The age of managers is between 25 and 55 and their educational levels are junior colleges, undergraduates, masters, and doctors. The regions involved are Nanjing and Wuxi in Jiangsu Province, Zhuhai and Puning in Guangdong Province, Xiamen and Quanzhou in Fujian Province, and Qingdao in Shandong Province. Completed questionnaires were received from 1,122 individuals, a response rate of 56%.

4.3. Procedure

We took a variety of steps to insure that both the task and experimental manipulations were as realistic as possible. Figure 1 reports the detailed procedures of our research. We had four steps in this framework. First is the aims of strategies. Second is the collection and analysis of data. We collected all sorts of data of managers' competences, confirmed a professional group or work unit, chose 6–10 important competences, and depicted behavior index for each competence. Third, building of competences model. We named all the competences, endowed with practical definitions, listed typical behavior of each competence, and listed all the knowledge and skills needed. Fourth, creation of culture based on competences and evaluation of the performance on the each field of human resource practices.

4.4. Measures

We designed a questionnaire based on the literature review and the competences model we built. The questionnaire includes three parts, which measures different variables according to the research demands separately. The first part is the investigation of individual information, which includes name, gender, educational level, management level, management function, the scale and the ownership of the company, and so on. All the items were used as control variables during the data analysis. The second part is the measurement of managers' competences, which includes 11 competences and measures the ability extent that leaders possess objectively. Each competence item has relevant questions that can depict leaders' abilities on this dimension. Table 1 reports the 11 specific items on this part and their validity and reliability results. The third part is the measurement of

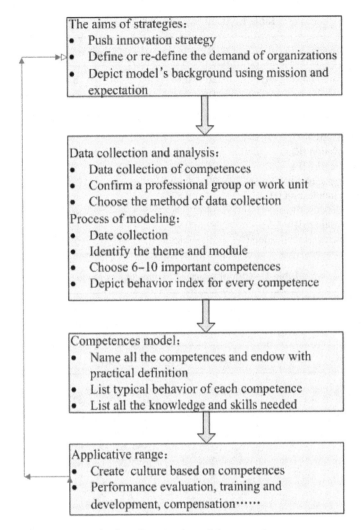

Fig. 1.   The procedure of the research.

managers' performance that concludes 20 questions, which measures both financial performance and behavior performance of each leader.

4.5. *Analysis*

CFA methods were used to verify the validity and reliability of managers' competences model. Table 2 and Fig. 2 show the fit index and CFA

Table 1. Items, validity, and reliability.

Competences	N	α	Γ	Variance explained (%)
Decision making (A)	20	0.85		53.39
EQ (B)	16	0.88		61.96
Self-efficiency (C)	11	0.82		62.67
Achievement	10	0.78	0.97	64.56
Motivation (D)				
Innovation (E)	12	0.76	0.96	52.77
Sociability (F)	16	0.90		58.91
Learning ability (G)	20	0.90		57.26
Communication (H)	14	0.87		59.43
Leadership (I)	14	0.90		63.76
Innovation (J)	19	0.90		62.02
Knowledge application (K)	15	0.85		59.41

Table 2. CFA of managers' competences model.

		Fit index		
NFI	IFI	NNFI	CFI	RMSEA
CFA 0.96	0.97	0.96	0.97	0.09

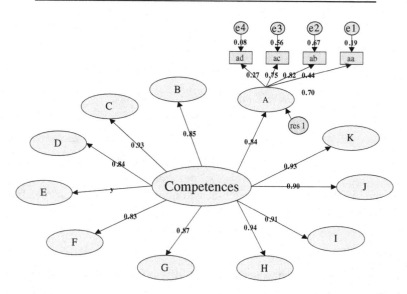

Fig. 2. CFA of competences model.

Table 3. Items, validity and reliability of performance.

Performance	Items	α	Variance explained (%)
Senior	15	0.83	68.47
Middle-level	8	0.81	60.06
Junior	5	0.88	67.31

Table 4. Regression analysis of managers' competences and performance.

Model	R^2	Adjust R^2	F	Beta
Senior	0.290	0.274	18.24**	0.47***, −0.35**,
J, H, G	(0.216, 0.024, 0.051)			0.35**
Middle-level	0.274	0.264	27.28**	0.26***,0.25**,
I, K, D, F	(0.199, 0.036, 0.021, 0.018)			−0.19**, 0.17**
Junior J	0.248	0.245	78.22**	0.50**

Table 5. CFA of managers' competences and performance.

CFA	Fit index				
	NFI	IFI	NNFI	CFI	RMSEA
Senior	0.91	0.93	0.91	0.93	0.08
Middle-level	0.98	0.98	0.97	0.98	0.09

model of managers' competences, and Table 3 shows the validity and reliability of managers' performance measurement. All the results prove the questionnaires this research used are effective.

Tables 4 and 5 are the results of regression analysis and relevant fit index. We can see from the data that managers' competences have significant relationship with their performance, and some competences are positively related to performance, while the others are negatively related to performance.

4.6. Results

4.6.1. The comparisons of differences among managers

Management Levels According to the data analysis, the management functions, age, enterprises' ownership, industries, regions, and performance of senior, middle-level, and junior managers have significant influences on their competences.

Management Functions   There are significant differences among and within management functions. Managers' levels, education levels, gender, age, enterprises' scales, ownership, industries, and regions have significant influences on their competences.

Industries   There are significant differences among and within industries. Managers' levels, functions, education levels, gender, age, enterprises' scales, ownership, and regions have significant influences on their competences.

Regions   There are significant differences among regions. In one region, managers' levels, functions, education levels, gender, age, enterprises' scales, ownership, and industries have significant influences on their competences.

From the analysis above, we get some conclusions on the characteristics of managers' competences, which will be significant to create and develop managers' competences in the future research and practices. First, competences' diversities among different management levels request that each manager should possess his or her relevant competences. Second, different functions need distinct knowledge and skills that have differences and diversification. Third, all kinds of factors within organizations and industries will affect the composing, development, and cultivation of managers' competences. Fourth, the differences of predominance and endowment among regions, economy level, and managing mode lead to the differences of managers' competences.

4.7. The relationship between managers' performances and competences

The results show managers' competences from different levels have significant effects on their performance. First, learning ability and innovation ability are positively related to senior managers' performance, while communication ability is negatively related to senior managers' performance. Second, sociability, leadership, and knowledge application are positively related to middle-level managers' performance, while achievement motivation is negatively related to senior managers' performance. Third, innovation ability is positively related to junior managers' performance.

5. The Practice of Global Competency Leadership Development

Different from the training in common skills and specialty knowledge, the development of global competency leadership cannot be achieved instantly. It takes time to develop the global leadership competence; it is a process, not just a singular training activity. The development of global competence requires ultimate change of people; only by putting people into situations, we can provide relevant activators to make this change happen (Mendenhall, 2007).

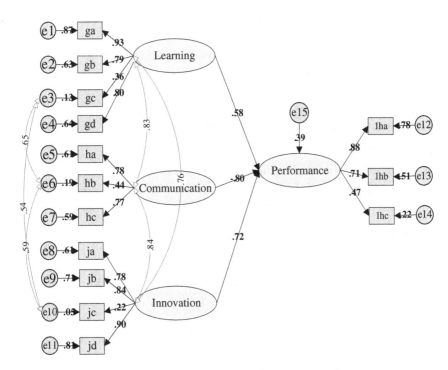

Fig. 3. CFA model of competences and performance — senior managers.

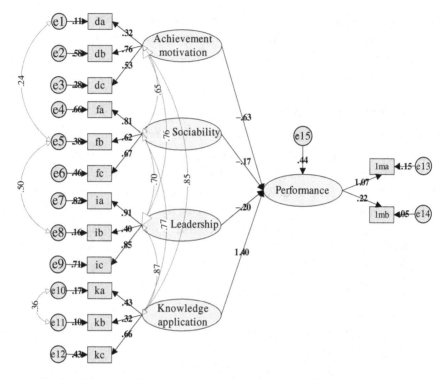

Fig. 4. CFA model of competences and performance — middle-level managers.

5.1. The approaches of developing global competency leadership

As for the means of developing global leaders, global teams and short-term overseas managerial training or business trips are considered effective (Maznevski and Distefano, 2000; Oddou *et al.*, 2000). Global teams are teams of managers from different parts of a multinational organizations working together to achieve a team-specific goal that is global in its scope. There are three processes in global team development: mapping, bridging, and integrating. Mapping refers to understanding the team members' compositional differences and accordingly recognizing their importance to build mutual relationships. Bridging is the communication across those differences to ensure that each member understands the others. Integrating refers to bringing the different perspectives and preferences together, resolving differences among them, and generating innovative, high-quality approaches to the task. Short-term overseas training or business travel can help leaders accept or appreciate the concept of doing things in different ways, and provide opportunities for leaders to observe the verbal and non-verbal behaviors of individuals in the host country. Besides, such travels can also help leaders learn to build trust with people in an open and modest way in new environments. Therefore, business trips and non-business learning can enrich global leaders' knowledge and improve their abilities.

As for Chinese companies, another effective training method is to let company leaders "go abroad". The accumulation of working experience abroad can help global leaders have a better understanding about modern international business, which in turn will help them find the suitable ways for their companies to enter international markets. "Going abroad" also helps leaders to understand the differences in management and technology between their own companies and international competitors as well as the impact of cultural difference on companies, and ultimately, may facilitate the companies to make effective international business strategy. "Going abroad" is one process to encourage that they understand and learn the advanced foreign technology and management practices.

Another effective approach for some companies would be to send their expatriate managers and project managers to EMBA, IMBA, MBA, and EDP programs in universities both at home and abroad. For example, the EMBA program of Nanjing University School of Business in cooperation with the Johnson Graduate School of Cornell University offers students many such opportunities. First, they attend classes taught by both Chinese and American professors at Nanjing University, and then the students go to Cornell University to finish three courses and visit American multinational companies to communicate with entrepreneurs and executives. The dual-degree IMBA program jointly runs by Nanjing University and the University of Missouri-St. Louis has provided meaningful experiences for students. They take the first year's courses at Nanjing University and the second year's courses at the University of Missouri–St. Louis. Afterwards they will get a paid internship in multinational companies in the United States for three months, and then they return to Nanjing University to finish their MBA thesis. Such IMBA program enables students to learn not only Chinese management but also Western management, and offers them the opportunity to work as an intern in prominent multinational companies.

Another recommendation is for Chinese companies to send executives to attend some international economic or managerial forums, which can broaden their horizon and develop their international strategic thinking ability. For example, the author was honored to be invited to deliver a speech at the Global Forum, with more than 100 CEOs participating, held in Tokyo, Japan on 21 February 2007. The speakers at the forum were from China, the United States, and Japan. The participants were from multinational corporations in Japan and the neighboring countries. The author talked about the strategic management of global enterprises, the managerial differences between Chinese enterprises and foreign enterprises, the international business environments and rules, as well as the development of global competency leadership. By participating in forums like this, leaders can benefit significantly to improve their global managerial skills.

In addition, as an alternative to cultivate backup talent, internationalized companies can send managers who have been identified as having high potential for development into key future leadership roles in their organizations to overseas companies as on-site interns who will participate in project negotiation and operation, improve cross-cultural communication, and improve problem-solving ability. Through job rotation, more interdisciplinary talents and professional talents mastering professional knowledge and foreign languages and familiar with international business practices will be developed.

5.2. The main contents of global competency leadership development

In order to build high-performance organizations and to achieve high performance, an effective global competency leader must have global vision, internationalized knowledge structure, be familiar with international conventions, and master international communication ability. Therefore, global competency leaders should be developed in such aspects as language, professional ability, culture, and vision through educational programs and firsthand experiential learning experiences that cultivate and emphasize these qualities.

5.2.1. Language ability training

Language ability is the prerequisite for global leaders to communicate smoothly with foreign counterparts. The training of language ability can take the means of short-term spoken language improvement (having native speakers as teachers) and/or IMBA programs (using English as the teaching language).

5.2.2. Professional ability training

Global competency leaders must have strategic thinking ability, advanced managerial philosophy, abundant relevant experience, systematic thinking, and ability to do things right and to do right things. Global competency leaders also must learn how to cooperate with colleagues, get knowledge from interpersonal communications, and spread such knowledge swiftly and effectively through their own networks. A global competency leader must have a strong desire for learning, and the skill to learn fast and continuously.

5.2.3. Cross-cultural training

Global competency leaders need to understand not only Chinese local cultures but also foreign cultures, customs, and rituals, so that they do their jobs with skill and ease. The training in cultural consciousness can promote the global competency leaders' awareness and appreciation of different national cultures, so that they behave properly and manage global managerial teams appropriately and effectively. Therefore, the training in social cultural sensitivity, such as the differences between eastern and western cultures and the foreign-related business etiquette, is an important focus in the training of global competency leaders.

5.2.4. Global vision training

With global vision, global competency leaders are able to appreciate the opportunity to work anywhere in the world. Companies cannot run in isolation. Benefiting from opportunities to learn the best practices from excellent overseas companies, the leaders of Chinese companies can advance their global competence in a relatively fast and easy way.

The effective global vision training approaches include internships in overseas companies, visits to overseas companies, and other short-term overseas learning experiences.

6. Conclusion

"The world is flat (Friedman, 2005)!" A leader with global competency is the favored person in the era of globalization that emphasizes a knowledge economy. The development of global competency leadership should focus on the global vision and cultural training of leaders with potential, help them expand beyond narrow-mindedness, change their singular viewpoint and local ideology, and develop a global mindset. For global leaders, to experience in other countries in person is an important way to learn global competence and be exposed to best global leadership practices of excellent companies. In doing so, global leaders can improve their ability to grasp global commercial opportunities and lead their companies in the progress toward internationalization.

References

Alldredge, M.E. and Nilan J.K., 2000. 3M's leadership competency model: an internally developed solution. *Human Resource Management*, 39 (summer/fall), 133–145.

Black, S., Morrison, A., and Gregersen, H., 1999. *Global Explorers: The Next Generation of Leaders*. Routledge, New York.

Brake, T., 1997. *The Global Leader: Critical Factors for Creating the World Class Organization*. Irwin Professional Publishing, Chicago.

Clark, B.D. and Matze, M.G.A., 1999. A core of global leadership: relational competence. In: Mobley, W.H. (eds.), *Advances in Global Leadership*, V1. Jai Press, Inc., Stamford, CT, pp. 127–161.

Conner, J., 2000. Developing the global leaders of tomorrow, *Human Resource Management*, 39 (summer/fall), 147–157.

Ding, M., 2006. Implement the priority of talents developing strategy to solve the problem of manager insufficiency. *Jiangsu Corporate Management*, 10, 8–9 (in Chinese).

Drucker, F.P., 1998. *Peter Drucker on the Profession of Management*. Harvard Business School Press, Boston.

Drucker, F.P., 1999. *Management Challenges for the 21st Century*. Collins Publishers, Inc.

Friedman, T.L., 2005. *The World Is Flat: A Brief History of the Twenty-First Century.* Farrar, Straus, and Giroux, New York.

GM Model, 2007. *Enterprise Management*, 5, 57 (in Chinese).

House, R.J., Hanges, P.J., and Ruiz-Quintanilla, S.A., 1999. Cultural influences on leadership and organizations: project globe. In: Mobley, W.H. (eds.), *Advances in Global Leadership.* Jai Press, Inc., Stamford, CT, US, pp. 171–233.

Javidan, M. and House, R., 2002. Leadership and cultures around the world: findings from GLOBE: an introduction to the special issue. *Journal of World Business*, 37(1), 1–2.

Javidan, M. and House, R.J., 2001. Cultural acumen for the global manager: lessons from project GLOBE. *Organizational Dynamics*, 29(4), 280–305.

Liu, M. and Liu, H., 2002. Global leader development strategy. *Chinese Human Resource Development*, 2, 19–21 (in Chinese).

Maznevski, M.L. and Distefano, J.J., 2000. Global leaders are team players: developing global leaders through membership on global teams. *Human Resource Management*, 39 (summer/fall), 195–208.

Mendenhall, M.E. and Stahl G.K., 2000. Expatriate training and development: where do we go from here? *Human Resource Management*, 39(2–3), 251–265.

Mendenhall, M.E., 2007. *Speech at Global Forum* in Tokyo on 21 February.

Moran, R. and Riesenberger, J., 1994. *The Global Challenge: Building the New Worldwide Enterprise.* McGraw-Hill, New York.

Morrison, A.J., 2000. Developing a global leadership model. *Human Resource Management*, 39 (summer/fall), 117–131.

Oddou, G., Mendenhall, M.E., and Rithie, J.B., 2000. Leveraging travel as a tool for global leadership development. *Human Resource Management*, 39 (summer/fall), 159–172.

Ren, J., 2006. Developing competence leadership based on corporate strategy. *Contemporary Managers*, 10 (in Chinese).

Roberts, K., Kossek, E.E., and Ozeki, C., 1998. Managing the global workforce: challenges and strategies. *The Academy of Management Executive*, 12(4), 93–106.

Welch, J. and Byrne, J.A., 2001. *Jack: Straight from the Gut.* Warner Business Books, New York.

Wu, S., 2006. Development and selection strategy of corporate internationalized managerial talent. *Chinese and Foreign Entrepreneurs*, 5 (in Chinese).

Yu, H., Fang, L. and Ling, W., 2003. Characteristics and training of the global leaders, *Advances in Psychological Science*, 11(4), 446–451 (in Chinese).

Zhao, H., 2005. *Economic Development Report of Chinese Headquarters in 2006.* Social Science Literature Publishing House, Beijing (in Chinese).

Zhao, S., 2008. A study on the "development of global competency leadership". In: Tan, T.-K. and Fu, X. (eds.), *Proceedings of the International Conference on*

Chinese Enterprise Research, 2007. World Science Publishing Co. Pte. Ltd., Singapore, pp. 31–43.

Zhao, S., 2008. *A Study of Professional Competence of Chinese Managers.* Beijing University Press, Beijng (in Chinese).

Zhao, S., 2004. On manager's professionalization, marketization and internationalization. In: Lin, Z. (eds.), *Chinese Human Resource Development Report.* Chinese Labor Social Security Press, Beijing (in Chinese).

Zhao, S., 2001. *Research on Human Resource Management.* China Renmin University Press, Beijing (in Chinese).

Enhance Government Public Management by Learning from US Successful Experiences

Chuanhong Wang

No. 2, Bingcaogang Street, East District of Panzhihua City,
Sichuan 61700, China
tchuan@sina.com

Enhancement of government public management plays a significant role in transforming government functions and maximizing government potential in macro-economic management. The US government's successful experiences in combination with our local actualities are discussed so as to explore a specific and workable solution to government public management, which is consistent with people-oriented philosophy, beneficial to improve administrative efficiency to make scientific decisions.

Keywords: Learning; Government; Public management; Innovation; Efficiency.

1. Introduction

With the tendency of economic globalization, informatization, and marketization, governments around the world are now engaged in deep reform in which public management has become a universal task. It is definitely necessary to keep track of the new practices exercised by foreign developed countries so as to innovate our public management. Reasonable elements inside their theories, methods, and approaches should be particularly learnt and referred. From August to December 2006, I took part in the "Public Policy and Public Management Training Program for the Young and Middle-aged Leaders from the Central State Organs and Local Government Institutions", offered by Duke University, USA. During that time, I learnt about fundamental theories and methods regarding public policy and public management of the United States, which deepened my understanding of the structure and mechanism of the US government and its public management. The philosophy, policies, methods, and approaches learnt from such a developed country give me a lot of insight into public management in our own country. In this paper, the solution to enhancing government public management in our country is explored based on analysis of the advanced conceptions and methods by the US government.

2. Essential Experiences in the US Government Public Management

2.1. Priority given to the "people-oriented" conception (cunshan)

In the United States, the municipal government is managed by the mayors elected by citizens or the managers employed by the municipal administrative committee elected by citizens. There is neither superior-inferior nor direct relation between the municipal government and the state government. The citizens have the right to impeach a government leader. Therefore, during administration of a local government, full consideration should be given to the wishes of the electorate or the public. The "people-oriented" conception is reflected in every detail of social administration. Besides creating a good environment for economic development, providing services, and dealing with public affairs, the US government makes particular efforts to address practical concerns of the people, such as granting loans to college students, offering agricultural product price subsidies, having medical fees paid by medical insurance programs for the aged, and public service organizations instituted for the mentally or physically disabled. Mass financial investment is directed to public services, especially unprofitable infrastructure and social welfare programs. In the past few years, the expenditure of the US federal government on welfare programs such as social insurance and public health has amounted to about half of the total government fiscal expenditure.

2.2. Active role in macro management

The major functions of the US government include making economic policies, imposing taxes, providing social securities (relief, welfare, insurance, etc.), promoting social justice, offering public products, managing national defense, handling foreign affairs, and maintaining public security. In the government hierarchy, the federal, state, and local governments perform their own duties strictly under their designated authorities. From the perspective of social management, the government assumes limited responsibility pursuant to law. For example, when a dispute rises between the public and a business group, the government stands neutral with no interference into the matter which shall be resolved by the judicial system. Such is a typical "limited responsibility government", which not only contributes to the inner constraint of the national public management system, thus preventing certain officials from having too much power and cutting shady deals, but also effectively relieves government overburden in administrative affairs and social disputes, so that the government can concentrate on economic and social development by using macro management.

2.3. Scientific public affairs management

The US government advocates specialized, professional, scientific, and modern management approaches, which produce the world highest efficiency in regional public affairs management. Thus a huge amount of social and financial resources can be saved. Firstly, they introduce the efficient mechanism to the public affairs management, restructure the existing operating mechanism aiming to build an "entrepreneur government", and cut administration costs. Secondly, they quantitatively analyze the decision-making cost and profit of public policies by making use of economic rationales and decision approaches to ensure that all policies proposed are appropriate; all decisions are made based on data, implemented and evaluated based on facts. Thirdly, they provide high priority to public participation, allowing independent consulting firms to be involved directly or indirectly in decision making of public affairs. Fourthly, they cultivate non-governmental organizations responsible for more social management and services.

2.4. Scientific innovation — source of development

Science and technology is the source of US economic prosperity. Strong ability in scientific innovation has not only built the US knowledge economy leading the world, but consolidated the United States' position as the greatest economic power in the world as well. The Research Triangle Park, which is supported by Duke University, North Carolina University, and North Carolina State University, is reputed as the "New Silicon Valley" of the United States. Along with the Silicon Valley in California and the High-Tech Park in Boston, it is considered one of the three most important contributors to the growth of US economy. Since its foundation, the Research Triangle Park has been standing at the front of high-techs and spear-heading in world science and technology development. In 1990s, the emergence of Internet and biotechnology brought the Research Triangle Park dozens of network and biotech R&D institutions. The 21st century has witnessed an unprecedented rise of the biotechnology, which becomes a hot topic in the Research Triangle Park. It not only creates wonders in scientific innovation, but provides a good platform where high-tech product development is strongly backed by higher learning institutions.

2.5. Emphasis on government efficiency

With great importance attached to administration efficiency, the US government has been striving to provide efficient and convenient services to enterprises and citizens in economic development. This is displayed in two aspects: One is the popularization of e-administration. In the 1990s, the Clinton Administration proposed a plan to build "information super high-way", then a plan was initiated to develop e-government. At present, almost all institutions of the federal, state, municipal, and county governments have launched their own websites. Up to 14,000 service items can be applied online and over 300 million applications and reports from enterprises and citizens are received from Internet by the government every year. The other is the wide implementation of government performance evaluation. As early as in 1940s, the US government established a framework system to evaluate government performance. Then in 1993, it approved the Government Performance and Results Act, which helped to regulate and standardize government performance evaluation. Today, almost all departments of the federal government and most local governments have established performance evaluation systems and put them into operation.

3. Enlightenments on Government Public Management

3.1. Transform government functions and build a "limited responsibility government"

Great efforts must be made to accelerate government function transformation, address the problems arising from the old system, readjust government structure and responsibility, and aiming to establish a new government function system that is tailored to the socialism market economy. The conception "service is the bounden duty of government" should be always borne in mind. Meanwhile, government administration and service should be steered to transform the "controlling government", "almighty government" into "service-oriented government" (Min, 2006), and "limited responsibility government". The government should back out not only from product market but also from factor market, so as to let the market and social elements play a greater role. Where the market works, the government should not undertake; and where an enterprise is supposed to decide, the government should not interfere. Instead, the government should focus on economic adjustment, market supervision, social management, and public service delivery. In brief, the government should be transformed to the provider of public products, the creator of a good market environment, and the protector of civil rights.

3.2. Stick to the "people-oriented" conception and pay close attention to people's livelihood

The people-oriented conception is the nature and core of the scientific development philosophy. In our work, we should always keep it in mind that "development is for the people, by the people, and the fruits should be shared among the people". As a result, more efforts should be made to improve people livelihood and promote social harmony. Welfare programs for the people should be implemented; the utmost, immediate, and specific concerns to the people, such as employment, social insurance, environmental protection, education, and medical care, should be preferentially addressed. The income distribution system should be gradually optimized aiming to increase income of the low-income group, expand proportion of the medium-income group, and effectively adjust income of the high-income group, thus narrowing the income gap between social members, which is regarded as the "core" problem of social justice. The government should make overall plans in which all factors are taken into consideration, develop all social undertakings in a coordinative manner so as to let the people fairly and equitably enjoy public products and social services such as culture, public health, and education. Complaints about livelihood should be highly thought of and conflicts should be envisaged and solved positively in order to promote social harmony.

3.3. Improve decision-making mechanism based on scientific process

As the decision maker, organizer, and executants of economic development and social affairs, the government shoulders important responsibility for making overall plans and coordinating all related parties. Therefore, a scientific and democratic mechanism should be built to improve decision-making quality. Further efforts shall be made to establish a complete inspection system so as to regulate official business discussions and claim responsibility for mistaken decisions. Thus, a decision-making mechanism can be formed which will go deep among the people, reflect their will, pool their wisdom, and value their resources. In addition, think tank or brain trust shall be more invested and better managed in a way that investigators, experts, scholars, and consultants can play active roles in decision-making process. The decision-making contents should be open to wider public opinions, allowing the people to know about, involve in, and supervise scientific and democratic decision-making process.

3.4. Encourage independent innovation and increase competitiveness

Untiring efforts should be made to implement the strategy of rejuvenating China through science and education and revitalizing China through talented persons, accelerate infrastructure construction required to develop science and technology, cultivate qualified innovative technical talents, foster national innovative spirit, activate innovative potential of all social members and build a healthy and harmonious innovation environment. The ability to innovate, inherit, introduce, digest, absorb, and re-innovate technologies should be improved. The primary purpose is to develop high technologies essential for economic and social development, address bottlenecking problems to generate a number of technologies, products, and standards with independent intellectual property rights and take the initiative in competition. We must press ahead to deepen sci-tech structural reform, consolidate enterprise's leading role in innovation, cultivate high-tech parks (bases) and establish a market-oriented and enterprise-dominated system for technological innovation to integrate all efforts of enterprises, universities, and research institutes, accelerate transformation from technological achievements into real productivity, and promote core competitiveness of enterprises.

3.5. Improve management methods and administrative efficiency

Firstly, management methods should be continuously improved by further standardizing working procedures and strictly observing rules and regulations to avoid administrative irregularities. Secondly, administrative costs should be substantially cut by improving public product supply, controlling public servants post-related consumption, reducing meetings, simplifying government institutions and staff, and constructing administrative service centers to achieve maximum profit with minimum cost. Thirdly, e-administration should be promoted and popularized by learning successful experiences from developed countries to build a public-oriented e-administration system supplying interactive and convenient public services. Fourthly, government performance evaluation shall be gradually implemented. The experience and practice in foreign countries should be used in combination with local actualities to establish a complete performance evaluation system that is consistent with the scientific development philosophy. Furthermore, evaluation rules and regulations shall be formulated so as to improve government performance.

4. Conclusions

Our country is at the critical moment when reform and opening up is being deepened and economic structure is being optimized. It is particularly imperative to enhance government public management and provide more and better public products and services tailored to economic and social development. Only by accelerating transformation of government functions, giving priority to people's livelihood, enhancing independent innovation, improving decision-making quality and administrative efficiency, can a local government, as the provider of fundamental public services and products, be geared to international standards and move forward with economic and social reform based on optimization of public management.

References

Cunshan, L., The Confucian people-oriented thoughts and democracy, *Chinese Book Review Monthly*, 12, 8.

Min, J. (2006). *Theory and Practice in Building a Service-Oriented Government*, University Press, Beijing.

Shangquan, G. (2006). Power rent-seeking corruption should be prevented, http://theory.people.com.cn/GB/49150/49152/4894361.html, 10–09.

Wenqiao, L. (2003). Transformation of government functions: Only with limited responsibility can efficiency be achieved, *Nanfang Daily*, 4–10.

Yajun, S. and Fei, L. (2004). Reflection on "post-bureaucracy system" with reference to "entrepreneur government", *Chinese Public Management*, 9, 11–14.

Research on the Earnings Management of Chinese Listed Companies Based on Cognitive Reference Points

Yanxi Li* and Youhui Zhang[†]

*School of Management,
Dalian University of Technology, Dalian, China
* mrliyx@dlut.edu.cn
[†] tangzimo@gmail.com*

Previous studies show that because of cognitive reference points, managers tend to conduct a particular kind of earnings management to affect the cognition of users of financial information. In order to examine whether this kind of earnings management exists in Chinese companies, this paper used Benford's law, which is used increasingly frequently in financial statistics, and conducted a survey on the related financial data of 1,443 listed companies in Chinese A-share market, and studied the current situation of earnings management in Chinese listed companies. The results show that this earnings management based on cognitive reference points also exists in Chinese companies. This paper explains the motive of earnings management from the perspective of cognitive psychology and provides a new method for the recognition and measurement of earnings management.

Keywords: Cognitive reference points; Earnings management; Benford's law.

1. Introduction

Earnings management occurs when managers use judgment in financial reporting and in structuring transactions to alter financial reports to either mislead some stakeholders about the underlying economic performance of the company or to influence contractual outcomes that depend on reported accounting numbers (Healy & Wahlen, 1999). Excessive earnings management may lead to such behaviors as profit manipulation and disclosure of false information, which impact the normal development of capital markets and harm investors' interests.

Typically, the following motives have been proved to cause earnings management. The early empirical research showed that firms tend to report a smooth income to give the shareholders and lenders the impression that they are low-risk firms (Beidleman, 1973). Later, the contracting view of the positive accounting theory provides more specific hypotheses for the occurrence and direction of earnings management in certain contexts. Firms' contracts are either explicitly or implicitly. Explicit contracts examined in accounting literature include management compensation (Healy, 1985), debt covenants (Defond & Jiambalvo, 1994), and taxation (Guenther, 1994). Implicit accounting-based contracts that have been researched include, for example, management buyouts (DeAngels, 1986) and labor union contract negotiations (Liberty & Zimmerman, 1986).

Other than these, however, some researchers pointed out another particular kind of earnings management, which is based on cognitive reference points (Carslaw, 1988; Thomas, 1989; Niskanen & Keloharju, 2000; Caneghem, 2002). They found that because cognitive reference points greatly affect human's cognitive process, managers tend to round up reported earnings, in a way to just increase the first digit, when they notice a high digit in the second-from-the-left position of the earnings. After this relatively small adjustment, these earnings can be significantly enhanced in the mind of users of financial report. This type of earnings management called the "earnings round-up behavior" will leave more low numbers and fewer high numbers in the second position, so it can be detected through relevant statistics of financial data. The earnings round-up behavior has been found in several countries.

Our study finds that a similar behavior exists in Chinese listed companies and that it is even statistically greater than in other countries.

The remainder of this paper is organized as follows. In Sec. 2, we give a brief overview of the previous relevant studies. The specific design of our research is discussed in Sec. 3. In Sec. 4, the empirical results are provided. Conclusions are presented in Sec. 5.

2. Literature Review

This study is sponsored by National Natural Science Foundation of China (70772087).

2.1. Cognitive reference points

Rosch, Gabor, and Granger found that cognitive reference points greatly influence human's perception (Rosch, 1975; Gabor & Granger, 1966). A reference point is defined as "(…) a stimulus (…) which other stimuli are seen in relation to (Rosch, 1975)". Rosch pointed out that the closest $N * 10^k$ is a reference point in human's perception of numbers. That is to say, when people perceive a certain number, they try to use the closest $N * 10^k$ to help with the perception. For example, people use 200 to perceive both 199 and 201.

But this reference point cannot help explain the existence of the well-known "$1.99" phenomenon in the marketing field. "$1.99" phenomenon means that the price of $1.99 is perceived to be lower than a price of $2.00. However, according to the reference point suggested by Rosch, people should recognize such two prices almost as the same. For this phenomenon, Brenner and Brenner suggested that the first-from-the-left digit is a more important reference point than the closest $N * 10^k$. They held that because of the biological constraint that human beings only have a limited amount of memory, causes memory is primarily used to store the most important bits of information (Brenner & Brenner, 1982). Therefore, when people perceive a number, they place the most emphasis on the first digit, then less on the second digit, and so on progressively through the number. Thus, people tend to round down numbers rather round up numbers, because the process of rounding up is a more complex process than rounding down. For example, people are prone to round 199 to 190 or even 100, rather than to 200, the more rational number. This theory perfectly explains the "$1.99" phenomenon. Relevant evidence has also been provided by Georgoff (1972) and Lambert (1975). The first digit is also the key reference point discussed in this paper.

2.2. Previous researches on earnings management based on cognitive reference points

Researchers suggest that the above-mentioned cognitive reference point, the first digit of a number, can be used to recognize earnings management (Carslaw, 1988; Thomas, 1989; Niskanen & Keloharju, 2000; Caneghem, 2002). According to them, when the second digit of an income number is a high number, managers often adjust the number to a small degree by increasing the first digit. This is because the change in the reference point can significantly change humans' cognition. So users of financial information will perceive the number abnormally greater. This type of earnings management is called the "earnings round-up behavior". This behavior will inevitably change the distribution of numbers in the second position of reported earnings: there will be more low numbers and fewer high numbers.

Carslaw was the first to investigate whether managers round up their reported earnings. Carslaw found an abnormally high frequency of the number zero and an abnormally low occurrence of the number nine in ordinary income and net income of financial statements of New Zealand firms. Moreover, the higher frequency of zero is consistent with the compensatively lower frequency of nine. This demonstrates that managers tend to round up income numbers to the reference points of $N * 10^k$. The sample for this study did not include companies reporting a negative income, because Carslaw did not expect that the perception of negatives is affected by the same reference points as that of positives.

Thomas extended Carslaw's study in several ways: (1) he used a sample of US data; (2) he did not eliminate loss observations; (3) he also performed the analysis on quarterly earnings; and (4) furthermore, he studied on reported EPS. Although some difference existed, Thomas found similar earnings round-up behavior in both earnings before extraordinary items and discontinued operations and EPS. Specially, results based on negative earnings showed an inverse pattern: for example, a statistically significant higher (lower) than expected occurrence of nines (zeros) in the second position. The results apply to both annual and quarterly earnings.

Niskanen and Keloharju then found earnings round-up behavior in net income of Finnish companies. Unlike the two earlier researchers, Niskanen and Keloharju found significantly fewer sixes and sevens, rather than eights and nines, as the second digit, and significantly higher incidence of both zeros and ones as the second digit. The results showed that Finnish companies go even further when engaging in round-up behavior, a phenomenon that might be explained by the liberal Finnish accounting law.

Caneghem's research suggested that managers of UK-listed companies tend to round up reported pre-tax income, in a way that increases the first digit by one when they are faced with a nine in the second position for this particular earnings measure. This study contributed to researches of this kind mainly in that it introduces in the research discretionary accruals, which were estimated by both Jones model and modified Jones model. The results showed that discretionary accruals are used by managers rounding-up reported earnings figures.

2.3. Expected frequencies of numbers in a certain position

Intuitively, most people might suppose that the frequency of any number occurring in a certain position of a number is one-ninth for the first digit and one-tenth for the other digits. However, this is not the case. Instead, such frequency complies with Benford's law. According to National Institute of Standards and Technology (NIST), the Benford's law is defined that "on a wide variety of statistical data, the first digit is d with the probability

$$\log_{10}(1 + 1/d) \tag{1}$$

(NIST, 2005)". From this definition, it can be concluded that the second digit is d_2 with the probability

$$\sum_{d_1=1}^{9} \log_{10}\left(1 + \frac{1}{10d_1 + d_2}\right), \tag{2}$$

and the third digit is d_3 with the probability

$$\sum_{d_1=1}^{9} \sum_{d_2=0}^{9} \log_{10}\left(1 + \frac{1}{100d_1 + 10d_2 + d_3}\right) \tag{3}$$

(Zhu $et\ al.$, 2007).

This law describes the fact that the frequencies of numbers, from zero to nine, in a certain position in a number diminish progressively. Simon Newcomb first discovered such phenomenon for the first digit in a large variety of numbers in 1881. It went unnoticed until Frank Benford, apparently unaware of Newcomb's paper, concluded the same law and published it in 1938, supported by huge amounts of data (NIST, 2005). Benford pointed out the equations for frequencies of numbers in the first digit (the results are shown in Fig. 1). From then on, researchers have found various types of numbers, which conform to Benford's law, including numbers in census, stock indexes, geography, the study of infectious diseases, and accounting (Wang *et al.*, 2007).

Specially, it had been proved by the following scholars that a large sample of financial data conform to this law, which is the reason why all the earlier researches on earnings management based on cognitive reference points used Benford's law. Using central limit similarity theory, Hill proved that if a sample of numbers are radix-unbiased and proportional unbiased, they conform to Benford's law (Hill, 1995a,b). Moreover, Raimi and Boyle suggested that if a sample of numbers consist of numbers from different sources or are calculated through addition, subtraction, multiplication, or division, they conform to this law (Raimi, 1969a,b; Boyle, 1994). Besides,

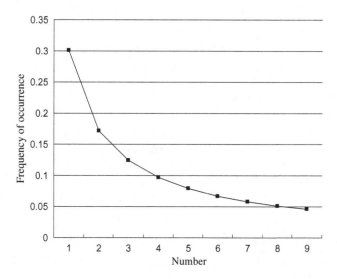

Fig. 1.   Frequency of occurrence of numbers as the first digit based on Benford's law.

using Benford's law, Nigrini and Mittermaier managed to detect several frauds in taxation and accounting, also demonstrating the application of this law in financial domain (Nigrini & Mittermaier, 1997).

3. Research Design

3.1. Hypotheses development

Our goal is to examine whether earnings round-up behavior exists in Chinese companies. According to earlier researches, if a higher (lower) than expected incidence of low (high) numbers as the second digit of reported earnings can be detected and the extent of such two anomalies is approximately the same, it is safe to say that the earnings round-up behavior exists. We thus test the following hypothesis:

Hypothesis 1: There will be significantly more low numbers and compensatively fewer high numbers as the second digit of reported earnings than expected by Benford's law.

What is more, it is not likely that managers conducting earnings management will only adjust the first two digits of income numbers, so earnings round-up behavior can also result in abnormal distribution of numbers in other positions. The key purpose of this behavior is to increase the first digit of an income number through minimum adjustment. As a result, unlike earlier researchers, we hold that managers conducting earnings round-up behavior also tend to put a low number in the third position. However, the anomalies in the third position might be less significant than those in the second, because according to the theory of cognitive reference points, the third digit is even less important than the second in the cognitive process. Yet this also lends support to the existence of earnings round-up behavior. Thus we also test the hypothesis as follows.

Hypothesis 2: There will be more low numbers and compensatively fewer high numbers as the third digit of reported earnings than expected by Benford's law.

3.2. Selection of sample and accounting title

All the financial data used in this paper were gathered from the database of GTA Research Service Center. We selected all the non-financial companies in Chinese A-share market listed before 31 December 2006 and studied on net income and EPS in annual financial reports of selected companies between 2001 and 2006. We eliminated the companies reporting a negative income, because not enough evidence had proved that the cognitive process of negatives follows the same way as that of positives.

3.3. Hypotheses testing method

Similar to previous researchers, to test whether the observed distribution of numbers differs from the distribution based on Benford's law, we used the normalized Z-statistic. That is:

$$Z = \frac{|p - p_0| - \frac{1}{2n}}{\sqrt{\frac{p_0(1-p_0)}{n}}}, \qquad (4)$$

where p and p_0 are the observed and expected proportions, respectively, and n is the sample size. The second term in the numerator is a continuity correction to bring normal and binomial probability curves into closer agreement, and should be applied only when it is numerically smaller than $|p - p_0|$.

4. Results

4.1. Frequencies of the second digits

The statistical results of the frequencies of second digits are shown in Tables 1 and 2.

Table 1 clearly indicates statistically significant anomalies in the second position of the reported net income. The three most conspicuous anomalies are higher than expected incidence of zeros and lower incidence of sixes and nines. In addition, the "percentage deviation from expected frequency" column manifests that the deviation of zero is approximately equivalent to the sum of deviation of six, seven, and nine, the three relatively high numbers.

Table 2 shows similar anomalies of reported EPS. Still, the incidence of zeros is significantly higher, and yet the obviously lower incidence of eights and nines is observed. The deviation of zero also nearly equals the sum of deviation of eight and nine.

Table 1. The frequency of the second digits of Chinese listed companies' net income.

Digit	Observed frequency	Percentage of all observations	Expected percentage of all observations	Percentage deviation from expected frequency	Z-value
0	951	0.14411	0.11968	0.02443	6.09581**
1	764	0.11578	0.11389	0.00189	0.46267
2	693	0.10502	0.10882	−0.0038	0.97256
3	698	0.10577	0.10433	0.00144	0.36349
4	634	0.09608	0.10031	−0.00423	1.12465
5	651	0.09865	0.09668	0.00197	0.52105
6	557	0.08441	0.09337	−0.00896	2.48142*
7	563	0.08532	0.09035	−0.00503	1.40497
8	578	0.08759	0.08757	0.00002	0.01631
9	510	0.07728	0.08500	−0.00772	2.22536*

Note: *Statistically significant at the 5% level, **Statistically significant at the 1% level.

Table 2. The frequency of the second digits of Chinese listed companies' EPS.

Digit	Observed frequency	Percentage of all observations	Expected percentage of all observations	Percentage deviation from expected frequency	Z-value
0	934	0.14154	0.11968	0.02186	5.45108**
1	788	0.11941	0.11389	0.00552	1.39268
2	711	0.10774	0.10882	−0.00108	0.26102
3	686	0.10396	0.10433	−0.00037	0.07948
4	616	0.09335	0.10031	−0.00696	1.86224
5	644	0.09759	0.09668	0.00091	0.22947
6	609	0.09229	0.09337	−0.00108	0.28130
7	607	0.09198	0.09035	0.00163	0.44144
8	512	0.07759	0.08757	−0.00998	2.84703**
9	492	0.07456	0.08500	−0.01044	3.01990**

Note: *Statistically significant at the 5% level, **Statistically significant at the 1% level.

Such results are consistent with Hypothesis 1.

It is worth noticing that the Z-values in previous studies are mainly between 2 and 4, and the maximal value is only 4.78, appearing in Carslaw's study. However, the Z-values of zero in Tables 1 and 2 are 6.09581 and 5.45108 respectively, both significantly greater than 4.78, the maximal

Z-value in previous studies. From this point of view, earnings round-up behavior in Chinese companies is more serious than the companies in other countries.

4.2. *Frequencies of the third digits*

Tables 3 and 4 show the statistical results of the frequencies of third digits. As can be seen in Table 3, similar abnormalities also exist in the third position of reported net income. The five most obvious anomalies are higher than expected incidence of zeros, ones, and twos and lower incidence of eights and nines. And the sum of deviation of zero, one, and two is about equivalent to the sum of deviation of six, seven, eight, and nine. Table 4 indicates analogous abnormities in reported EPS. Higher incidence of zeros and ones can be found apparently. Statistically, the incidence of high numbers is not significantly abnormal, but it is easy to find that such incidence is all lower than expected. And the sum of deviation of zero and one still equals approximately the sum of deviation of high numbers.

Therefore, the above results are consistent with Hypothesis 2. As far as the Z-values are concerned, the anomalies for the third digit are less evident than those for the second. This can be explained by the less importance of the third digit in the cognitive process.

Table 3. The frequency of the third digits of Chinese listed companies' net income.

Digit	Observed frequency	Percentage of all observations	Expected percentage of all observations	Percentage deviation from expected frequency	Z-value
0	753	0.11411	0.10178	0.01233	3.29184**
1	757	0.11471	0.10138	0.01333	3.56839**
2	720	0.10911	0.10097	0.00814	2.17361*
3	679	0.10289	0.10057	0.00232	0.60734
4	622	0.09426	0.10018	−0.00592	1.58213
5	678	0.10274	0.09979	0.00295	0.77978
6	630	0.09547	0.09940	−0.00393	1.04672
7	609	0.09229	0.09902	−0.00673	1.81064
8	581	0.08804	0.09864	−0.01060	2.86618**
9	570	0.08638	0.09827	−0.01189	3.22490**

Note: *Statistically significant at the 5% level, **Statistically significant at the 1% level.

Table 4. The frequency of the third digits of Chinese listed companies' EPS.

Digit	Observed frequency	Percentage of all observations	Expected percentage of all observations	Percentage deviation from expected frequency	Z-value
0	768	0.11638	0.10178	0.01460	3.90254**
1	727	0.11017	0.10138	0.00879	2.34485*
2	666	0.10092	0.10097	−0.00005	0.00813
3	677	0.10259	0.10057	0.00202	0.52548
4	626	0.09486	0.10018	−0.00532	1.41813
5	639	0.09683	0.09979	−0.00296	0.78095
6	638	0.09668	0.09940	−0.00272	0.71757
7	619	0.09380	0.09902	−0.00522	1.39850
8	609	0.09229	0.09864	−0.00635	1.71022
9	630	0.09547	0.09827	−0.00280	0.74369

Note: *Statistically significant at the 5% level, **Statistically significant at the 1% level.

5. Conclusions

The main conclusions and contributions of this paper can be summarized as follows. First, we examine the anomalies in the third digit of reported earnings in addition to merely the second. This contributes to researches of this kind in that it extends the application of the theory of cognitive reference points and provides new evidence for earnings round-up behavior. Second, we find that earnings roundup behavior exists in Chinese listed companies. Managers of Chinese listed companies tend to round up reported net income and EPS and to leave low numbers in the second and third positions of such numbers. Finally, as can be seen in the Z-values, earnings roundup behavior is more serious in Chinese companies than companies in other countries.

References

Beidleman, C.R., 1973. Income smoothing: the role of management. *Accounting Review*, 48(4), 653–667.

Boyle, J., 1994. An application of fourier series to most significant digit problem. *The American Mathematical Monthly*, 101, 879–886.

Brenner, G.A. and Brenner, R., 1982. Memory and markets, or why are you paying $2.99 for a widget. *The Journal of Business*, 147–158.

Caneghem, T.V., 2002. Earnings management induced by cognitive reference points. *British Accounting Review*, 34(2), 167–178.

Carslaw, C.A.P.N., 1988. Anomalies in income numbers: evidence of goal oriented behavior. *Accounting Review*, 63(2), 321–327.

DeAngelo, L.E., 1986. Accounting numbers as market valuation substitutes: a study of management buyouts of public stockholders. *Accounting Review*, 61(3), 400–420.

DeFond, M.L. and Jiambalvo, J., 1994. Debt covenant violation and manipulation of accruals. *Journal of Accounting and Economics*, 20, 145–176.

Gabor, A. and Granger, C.W.J., 1966. Price as an indicator of quality: report on an enquiry. 43–70.

Georgoff, D.M., 1972. *Odd-Even Retail Price Endings*. Michigan State University Press.

Guenther, D.A., 1994. Earnings management in response to corporate tax rate change: evidence from the 1986 tax reform act. *Accounting Review*, 69(1), 230–243.

Healy, P.M. and Wahlen, J.M., 1999. A review of the earnings management literature and its implications for standards setting. *Accounting Horizons*, 13(4), 365–383.

Healy, P.M., 1985. The effect of bonus schemes on accounting decisions. *Journal of Accounting and Economics*, 11(1), 85–107.

Hill, T., 1995a. Base-invariance implies Benford's law. *Proceedings of the American Mathematical Society*, 123(3), 887–895.

Hill, T., 1995b. A statistical derivation of the significant-digit law. *Statistical Science*, 10(4), 354–362.

Lambert, Z.V., 1975. Perceived prices as related to odd and even price endings. *Journal of Retailing*, 51, 13–22.

Liberty, S.E. and Zimmerman, J.L., 1986. Labor union contract negotiations and accounting choices. *Accounting Review*, 61(4), 692–712.

National Institute of Standards and Technology, 2005. Benford's Law. http://www.nist.gov/dads/HTML/benfordslaw.html.

Nigrini, M.J. and Mittermaier, L.J., 1997. The use of Benford's law as an aid in analytical procedures. *Auditing: A Journal of Practice and Theory*, (16), 52–67.

Niskanen, J. and Keloharju, M., 2000. Earnings cosmetics in a tax-driven accounting environment: evidence from finnish public firms. *The European Accounting Review*, 9(3), 443–452.

Raimi, R., 1969a. Mathematical support for Benford's law using banach and other scale invariant measures. *The American Mathematical Monthly*, 76, 342–348.

Raimi, R., 1969b. The peculiar distribution of first digits. *Scientific American*, 109–120.

Rosch, E., 1975. Cognitive reference points. *Cognitive Psychology*, 7(4), 532–547.

Thomas, J.K., 1989. Unusual patterns in reported earnings. *Accounting Review*, 64(4), 773–787.

Wang, F., Li, X., and Sun, X., 2007. Research on Benford's law and its application in audit. *Communication of Finance and Accounting* (comprehension version), (3), 13–16.

Zhu, W., Wang, H., and Chen, W., 2007. Detecting fraud using Benford's law. *Application of Statistics and Management*, 26(1), 41–46.

Part 3

Globalization of Chinese Enterprises

Study of the Life Cycle of Small- and Medium-Sized Enterprises Based on External Environmental Perspective

Xiaohong Chen* and Yu Cao

*School of Business, Central South University,
Changsha, Hunan 410083, China
cxh@mail.csu.edu.cn*

Based on the research of small- and medium-sized enterprises' (SMEs) life cycle, plus the data and information that was acquired from bankrupt SMEs in five metropolises including Shenzhen, Guangzhou, Changsha, Zhengzhou, and Chengdu during period 2000–2007, the relationship between the life cycle of SMEs in the five metropolises and their external environment is evaluated and comparatively analyzed. The results show that the external environment has positive impact on SMEs' lifecycle; the economic environment, technological environment, and human resources environment have prominent influences on SMEs' lifecycle, but the influences of political environment, socioculture environment, and natural resources environment on SMEs' lifecycle are inconspicuous. Furthermore, the reason for the results above is analyzed and the countermeasures on how to prolong the life cycle of SMEs in China from the perspectives of both government and corporation are proposed.

Keywords: Empirical research; External environment; Life cycle; SMEs.

1. Introduction

Since the 1980s, along with the development of small- and medium-sized enterprises (SMEs) that has been playing an increasingly prominent role in

---

*Corresponding author: Xiaohong Chen, School of Business, CSU, Changsha 410083, China. cxh@mail.csu.edu.cn.

the national economy, governments and academia have paid more attention to the survival and development of SMEs. In the aspects of stimulating economic growth promoting competition in the industry, and promoting industrial innovation, increasing state tax revenue, creating employment opportunities, absorbing surplus labor, and other aspects, SMEs have played an irreplaceable role compared with large enterprises.

However, while SMEs create great value in the development of the national economy, they are facing a series of problems. National SMEs development experience and research results indicate that the difficulties of SMEs in the developmental process are far greater than those encountered in large enterprises, which is the cause of the slow development of SMEs and accelerates the death of SMEs. SME researchers have reached consensus on SMEs having shorter life cycle generally, which is stirring up almost all the scholars studying the issue of the survival of SMEs crazily. Overseas research shows that SMEs are of very high mortality rate. In the United States, only about 68 percent of all SMEs can survive for five years, 19 percent of enterprises for 6 to 10 years, only 13 percent of the enterprises survive for more than 10 years, while in France, more than 50 percent of new businesses have demised in five years. However, the living conditions of China's SMEs and causal study are seldom involved domestically. The paper reveals the inherent mechanism of the life cycle and provides reference for the government and SMEs themselves to take measures to extend the life cycle by analyzing the life cycle of SMEs in Shenzhen, Guangzhou, Changsha, Zhengzhou, and Chengdu.

2. Literature Review

There are few studies on the business survival and influence factors that are domestically present, but foreign scholars have studied on this issue from different perspectives. From the viewpoint of financial experts, the enterprises' survival and death are related to the credit risk of the enterprises, and a large number of models and documentation have been produced from this point of view. Traditional credit risk models mainly from the company's financial rate, predict and discriminate the enterprise bankruptcy possibility, which mainly include Altman's Z-score and Zeta model, neural network model, etc. (Altman, 1968, 1983). Modern methods use more complex mathematical tools and models, and its main purpose lies in the measurement of the enterprises' credit risk and making an early warning in financial crisis. The factors that affect the enterprise life cycle and survival are very extensive. Brüderl and colleagues (1992) divided the factors into three areas, which are individual entrepreneurs, enterprises, and environmental factors (such as industry, geographic cycle, economic cycles, etc.). Personal factors of entrepreneurs have an impact on the life cycle and the survival of enterprises, such as entrepreneurs' gender, age, occupational background, educational attainment, etc., and the lack of information on entrepreneurs personal characteristics restricted the study of the relationship between the entrepreneurs personal characteristics and the life cycle of the enterprises, as a result, there are few empirical studies about the impact of entrepreneurs' personal characteristics on the business survival. Rofik and colleagues (2004) make an empirical study using the data from the French National Statistics and the Bureau of Economic Research.

From the factors of enterprise perspective, the foreign scholars mainly study the influence of the age and the size of the enterprise on the enterprise survival and life cycle. On the influence of the age to the enterprises survival, different foreign scholars have different views; Carroll and Hannan (2000), Nelson and Winter (1982), and Stinchcombe (1965) think that with the growth of enterprises' age, it would possible to gradually adapt the circumstances, form a unique culture and processes, and establish a relationship of trust with other enterprises in the market, so the elderly enterprises have higher survival rates than new enterprises; Brüderl and Schussler (1990), Fichman and Levinthal (1991), Mahmood (2000), and other studies have suggested that the risk of enterprises' death is not the monotonous decreasing growth by their age. At the beginning of the enterprises, the business risk of death reaches to its pole when the enterprise seed capital depleted is increasing as the business seed capital consumes constantly. Subsequently, the business risk of death decreases with the age increasing of enterprises. Therefore, the relationship of enterprises risk of death and age is similar to an inverted "U"-type. Baum (1989) and Hannan (1998) think the behavior of elderly enterprises is even more rigid than the young corporate. Thus they cannot be better adapted to the dramatic changes in the competitive environment. So when companies reach a certain age, enterprises risk of death will increase again. From the size of business, foreign scholars' view is fairly unanimous. In their opinion, the smaller the size of the business is, the bigger its distance from the smallest effective size is, so it will have a greater risk of death than those of the larger enterprises.

From environmental factors, foreign scholars do the research mainly from the perspective of industries, regions, and the economic cycle. The main idea from the industry perspective is to study factors affecting the survival of the enterprises such as the minimum effective size, growth rate of industry, entering rate of the industry, etc. These studies show that if the minimum effective size of the industry is larger, the enterprises risk of death is greater, as the enterprises to be more difficult to achieve the minimum requirement as defined by the industry's effectivity scale. If the enterprise is in a high-growth industry, its risk of death is smaller, as facing better demand conditions. Mata and Portugal (1994) and Audretch (1995a,b) did empirical researches for it. But Gort and Steven (1982) raised a contrary view. They believe that high-growth industries tend to be in the early stages of the industries life cycle and it demands highly that enterprises must adapt to the changing environment, which leads to that the enterprises in a high-growth industries face higher risk of death. The higher the entering rate of the industry is the fiercer competition in the industry is. The high rate of entering means the high rate of withdrawal. So the enterprises in the industry of a high rate of entering faced a greater risk of death.

Regarding the geographical impact on the survival of SMEs, studies have shown that regional concentration of business has both positive and negative effects to the enterprises survival. But Georgios and Helen (2000) do the empirical study through the enterprise data of Athens and other regions in Greece and the results show that SMEs in the high regional concentration have better prospects for survival. Positive results also show that the economic cycle will have a significant impact on the enterprises survival. The businesses in the economic recession are facing greater risk of death than that in the economic prosperity.

Because of the restrictions of data access, domestic and foreign scholars' study on the impact of environment to enterprise survival was limited to easy-to-measure and statistical environment variables. And the corporate external environment is very broad, covering not only trade and regional characteristics of the above variables but also including numerous factors such as economic, political, technical, social, cultural, human resources, and natural resources etc. Scholars at home and abroad have not started theoretical and empirical studies over the external environmental factors impact on the survival of enterprises.

In addition, domestic and foreign scholars' researches on relationship between the external environment and the organizations have produced a large number of theoretical schools, such as population ecology school, the system school. However, these studies focused primarily on the relationship between organizational environment and the organizational strategy. The research paradigm of "environment-strategy-performance" mainly discussed the relationship between the environment, strategy and performance of enterprises, rather than on the impact of external environment of enterprises to their survival. Some domestic scholars studied the relationship between the enterprises external environement and the enterprises' life cycle from the qualitative perspective. For example, Su and Li (2004) studied the impact of Chinese family business enterprises' external environment to their life cycles qualitatively. In their opinion, it is prone to yield a negative impact to the survival and development of an enterprise if the reponse of the family business to the changes of external environment is too large or too small. External factors sometimes can also play a decisive role in the survival and development of Chinese family business. However, there is lack of relevant empirical research.

On the problem of the factors impacting the business survival, foreign scholars use data of different countries and regions to do empirical research. But currently there is no domestic relevant empirical research in this area.

This paper starts with the relevant empirical research using China's five metropolises' data of SMEs life cycle (Shenzhen, Guangzhou, Changsha, Chengdu, and Zhengzhou), and through the establishment of the external environment evaluation index system of China's SMEs. It studies the impact of the above five metropolises on the economic environment, political environment, technology environment, social cultural environment, human resource environment, and natural resources environment for the life cycle of SMEs, thus avoids the inadequacy that many foreign scholars only study on the impact of the environment "label variables" for the survival of enterprises. This is the major theoretical contribution and innovation of this paper.

3. The Comparative Analysis of the Life Cycle of SMEs' Status Quo in Five Chinese Metropolises

From December 2006 to August 2007, we went deep into the industrial and commercial bureau of Shenzhen, Guangzhou, Changsha, Zhengzhou, and Chengdu, the five metropolises, investigated a number of enterprises, and collected the data of enterprises' life cycle. The data collected from each city during 2000 to 2007 of this survey mainly focused on SMEs' founded time, cancelled time, registered capital, its industry information, etc.

In order to ensure the reliability of the result by statistical analysis, we screened the data provided by the industrial and commercial bureaus of each city at first. As the informational process of each industrial and commercial bureau is different and the standard of each city's adjusting its enterprise information database is different, the resulted phenomenon in which the number of yearly cancelled enterprises in each city's enterprises' information database is imbalance or even the number of cancelled enterprises in one day (or a few days) is much higher than the average level (for instance, the average number of cancelled enterprises is only a few hundred in a city each month; however, surprisingly sometimes, the number in one day may reach thousands). We think this is an anomaly that results from the informational process in each city and the data must be deleted. Therefore, this paper firstly got the statistical number of cancelled enterprises each year in each city and then we deleted the data of some month or dates which had a higher level of the average cancelled enterprises' number. This guaranteed the reliability of our result. Secondly, this paper distinguished and eliminated types of enterprises; Honjo (2000) and Rofik and colleagues (2004) removed filial or branch offices of existed companies in their study. Referring to their principle, we removed these type of enterprises in our study too, such as filial and local branches of other enterprises, local offices of foreign-invested enterprises, local agencies of foreign (regional) enterprises, and so on. Finally, given that our country is in the transition process from planned economic to market economic system, a large number of aged state-owned enterprises and collective enterprises under the original planned economic system may influence the outcome, so we deleted the type of enterprises which are state-owned or collective enterprises at last. Finally, we got the number of cancelled enterprises samples in 2000–2007 of

Table 1.   Yearly distribution of the five metropolises' cancelled enterprises.

City	2000	2001	2002	2003	2004	2005	2006	2007	Total
Shenzhen	938	1,063	751	953	1,671	1,014	1,302	602	8,294
Guangzhou	13,010	19,315	17,461	8,031	6,064	4,180	4,448	2,091	74,600
Changsha	845	833	480	447	435	588	662	247	4,537
Chengdu	—	—	483	545	497	513	578	—	2,616
Zhengzhou	450	477	539	547	618	547	521	—	3,699
Total	15,243	21,688	19,231	9,978	9,285	6,842	7,511	2,940	92,638

Note: The date of 2007 is before the survey date, it is the same below.

each city which is shown in Table 1 and the statistical analysis of the life cycle of five metropolises' SMEs is shown in Table 2.

By analyzing the sample data of the five metropolises' SMEs' life cycle, we arrived the result that the average life cycle of the five metropolises' cancelled enterprises is 4.32 years, where the enterprises with a life cycle below three years is 44.31%, with a life cycle between three and five years is 25.66%, with a life cycle between 5 and 10 years is 23.08%, and with a life cycle more than 10 years is 6.95% of all enterprises. Specifically, the above five metropolises' died SMEs' average life cycles are all below five years, the longest life cycle is Guangzhou which is 4.67 years and the shortest life cycle is Shenzhen which is only 2.55 years. The life cycle of Changsha, Chengdu, and Zhengzhou is between them, which are 3.80, 3.14, and 2.74 years respectively. The specific circumstances of each city's died SMEs' life cycle are listed in Table 2.

4. The Model Fitting of the Status of the Five Metropolises' SMEs' Life Cycle

In survival analysis, scholars at home and abroad usually used to describe the distribution of the life cycle with normal distribution, exponential distribution, gamma distribution, Weibull distribution, and log-logistic distribution. Therefore, we fitted and tested the distribution of data of died SMEs' life cycle in 2000–2007 of the five metropolises including Shenzhen. The software of Minitab is used here to test whether the distribution of the date of the five metropolises' SMEs' life cycle obeys normal distribution, log-normal distribution, exponential distribution, gamma distribution,

Table 2. Statistical analysis of the bankrupt five metropolises' SMEs' life cycle.

		2000	2001	2002	2003	2004	2005	2006	2007	Total
Shenzhen	Number	938	1,063	751	953	1,671	1,014	1,302	602	8,294
	Average	2.21	2.45	2.56	2.32	1.92	1.81	2.31	2.69	2.55
	Below 3	62.74%	61.14%	62.65%	69.56%	60.31%	60.48%	66.50%	67.11%	63.45%
	3–5	20.00%	20.54%	25.25%	20.22%	29.63%	27.36%	26.67%	21.60%	24.57%
	5–10	17.04%	18.32%	12.10%	20.00%	10.00%	12.17%	16.84%	21.30%	11.92%
	Above 10	0.21%	0.00%	0.00%	0.22%	0.06%	0.00%	0.00%	0.00%	0.06%
Guangzhou	Number	13,010	19,315	17,461	8,031	6,064	4,180	4,448	2,091	74,600
	Average	4.64	4.71	4.87	4.02	4.10	5.16	5.10	5.23	4.67
	Below 3	38.45%	37.93%	31.08%	48.89%	52.42%	43.23%	42.04%	43.19%	39.47%
	3–5	26.95%	27.68%	34.13%	23.38%	19.29%	19.31%	20.84%	20.42%	26.84%
	5–10	27.82%	26.87%	27.92%	21.54%	19.44%	23.78%	24.37%	22.62%	25.66%
	Above 10	6.78%	7.51%	6.87%	6.19%	8.84%	13.68%	12.75%	13.77%	8.03%
Changsha	Number	845	833	480	447	435	588	662	247	4,537
	Average	3.74	3.82	3.57	3.98	3.36	3.94	3.92	4.16	3.80
	Below 3	45.23%	45.48%	47.50%	41.16%	43.67%	45.37%	46.25%	42.67%	44.99%
	3–5	26.39%	34.70%	20.00%	21.70%	17.70%	20.06%	18.88%	20.65%	23.72%
	5–10	18.56%	16.10%	26.05%	28.18%	27.08%	23.80%	27.04%	22.78%	22.81%
	Above 10	9.82%	3.72%	6.46%	8.94%	11.55%	10.75%	7.83%	13.89%	8.48%

(Continued)

Table 2. (*Continued*)

		2000	2001	2002	2003	2004	2005	2006	2007	Total
Chengdu	Number	—	—	483	545	497	513	578	—	2,616
	Average	—	—	2.95	3.31	2.97	3.42	3.05	—	3.14
	Below 3	—	—	53.45%	54.68%	60.58%	54.58%	58.47%	—	56.39%
	3–5	—	—	24.38%	27.55%	21.76%	20.27%	25.41%	—	23.96%
	5–10	—	—	21.73%	17.77%	17.64%	25.15%	15.55%	—	19.43%
	Above 10	—	—	0.43%	0.00%	0.00%	0.00%	0.56%	—	0.36%
Zhengzhou	Number	450	477	539	547	618	547	521	—	3,699
	Average	2.94	2.39	2.86	3.13	2.76	2.67	2.41	—	2.74
	Below 3	55.34%	60.72%	56.52%	57.83%	60.97%	59.60%	67.97%	—	56.16%
	3–5	28.46%	24.69%	31.13%	31.98%	25.40%	24.86%	20.23%	—	28.66%
	5–10	15.32%	14.60%	12.36%	10.20%	13.46%	15.53%	11.21%	—	13.37%
	Above 10	0.88%	0.00%	0.00%	0.00%	0.16%	0.00%	0.57%	—	1.81%

Table 3. Test results of whether the distribution of the date of the five metropolises' SMEs' life cycle obeys normal distribution, log-normal distribution, and exponential distribution.

	Normal			Log-normal			Exponential	
	Mean	SD	p	Loc	Scale	p	Mean	p
Shenzhen	2.552	1.481	<0.005	0.1561	1.131	<0.005	2.552	<0.003
Guangzhou	4.674	3.741	<0.005	1.462	1.097	<0.005	4.674	<0.003
Changsha	3.799	2.680	<0.005	1.444	0.8840	<0.005	3.799	<0.003
Chengdu	3.143	2.033	<0.005	0.7896	1.092	<0.005	3.143	<0.003
Zhengzhou	2.743	2.058	<0.005	0.5502	1.231	<0.005	2.743	<0.003

Table 4. Test results of whether the distribution of the date of the five metropolises' SMEs' life cycle obeys gamma distribution, Weibull distribution, and log-logistic distribution.

	Gamma			Weibull			Log-logistic		
	Shape	Scale	p	Shape	Scale	p	Loc	Scale	p
Shenzhen	1.337	1.329	<0.005	1.242	1.898	<0.010	0.2907	0.5839	<0.005
Guangzhou	1.443	4.392	<0.005	1.235	6.793	<0.010	2.199	0.3903	<0.005
Changsha	1.910	2.947	<0.005	1.532	6.233	<0.010	1.542	0.4677	<0.005
Chengdu	1.545	2.308	<0.005	1.436	3.432	<0.010	0.9553	0.5335	<0.005
Zhengzhou	1.229	2.232	<0.005	1.212	2.906	<0.010	0.7212	0.6286	<0.005

Weibull distribution, and log-logistic distribution. The testing result is shown in Tables 3 and 4. The frequency distribution and the probability density function of this distribution are shown in Figs. 1 to 5.

For the situation depicted in Tables 3 and 4, it is observed that as the discussed six kinds of probability distribution, the proven statistical result of SMEs' life cycle data of five metropolises during 2000–2007 period, p, are all below the level of 0.01. Therefore, we rejected the null assumptions that SMEs' life cycle submits aforesaid distribution. In addition, from Figs. 1 to 5, the image of probability distribution obtained by fitting is much discrepant with the frequency diagram depicted on the base of the swatches, which the intuition behind is a witness to the discussed proven. The SMEs' life cycle of our country does not correspond with the usual distribution in the exist-analyses. In this case, we can get the further estimate of the SMEs'

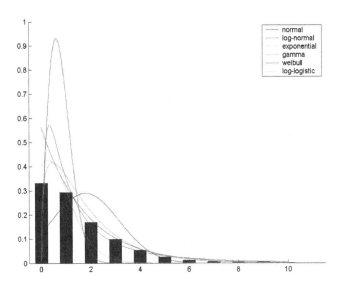

Fig. 1. Test result of the distribution of the SMEs' life cycle data in Shenzhen.

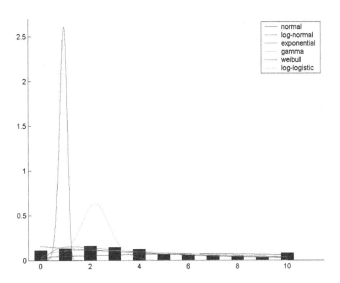

Fig. 2. Test result of the distribution of the SMEs' life cycle data in Guangzhou.

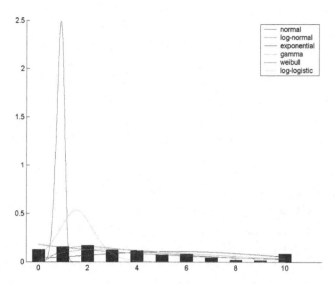

Fig. 3. Test result of the distribution of the SMEs' life cycle data in Changsha.

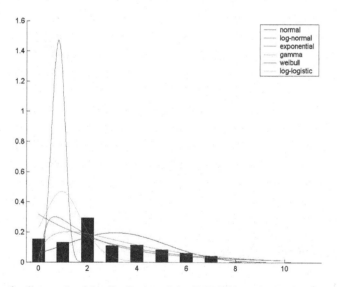

Fig. 4. Test result of the distribution of the SMEs' life cycle data in Chengdu.

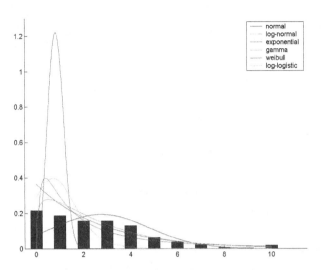

Fig. 5. Test result of the distribution of the SMEs' life cycle data in Zhengzhou.

life cycle data distribution of the country by means of the kernel function.[1] Owing to the difficulty to present explicit analysis formula by this means, this paper would not keep on estimating life cycle data of five metropolises by means of the kernel function.

5. The Empirical Research of SMEs' Life Cycle and External Environment Relation

In order to take further steps to study the relation between the SMEs' life cycle and the external environment, we send out over 12,000 questionnaires to survey about the exterior living environment of enterprises located in the above-mentioned five metropolises through Guangdong, Zhejiang, Shanghai, Jiangsu, Beijing, Hubei, Henan, Sichuan, Chongqing, Hunan in Jun, 2007. By using the constitutive equations model, we obtain enterprise's external environment evaluating indicator system and the score and rank of the external environment and sub-environment of the discussed urban enterprise as Table 5.

---

[1] The kernel function method refers to an infinite series of various kernel functions to generate the most appropriate distribution function, but the method is very difficult to give the distribution's explicit expressions.

Table 5. The external environment score (rank) and SMEs' life cycle of the five metropolises discussed.

City	The holistic external environment of enterprises		Economic environment		Political environment		Technological environment		Socioculture environment		Human resources environment		Natural resources environment		The average life cycle of enterprises	
	Score	Rank	Score	Rank	Score	Rank	Score	Rank	Score	Rank	Score	Rank	Score	Rank	Ensemble average	Rank
Guangzhou	3.577	1	3.708	1	3.419	1	3.670	1	3.716	1	3.425	2	3.254	5	4.67	1
Shenzhen	3.415	2	3.539	4	3.325	2	3.651	2	3.220	5	3.484	1	3.509	1	2.55	5
Changsha	3.414	3	3.598	2	3.191	4	3.466	3	3.689	2	3.132	3	3.395	4	3.80	2
Chengdu	3.398	4	3.513	5	3.264	3	3.410	4	3.688	3	3.103	4	3.457	2	3.14	3
Zhengzhou	3.311	5	3.544	3	3.088	5	3.289	5	3.553	4	2.939	5	3.405	3	2.74	4

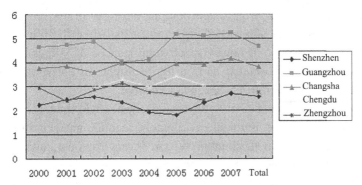

Fig. 6. The comparison of typical value of enterprise life cycle of each year in five metropolises.

As noted in the Literature Review, the external environment of enterprise should have an influence on the life cycle, but how the influence take place under heaven is still awaited the ulterior empirical test. As depicted in Fig. 6, it is a summarization of typical values of SMEs' life cycle of each year in five metropolises from 2000 to 2007. The rank of the status of SMEs' life cycle in the other four metropolises is Guangzhou, Changsha, Chengdu, and Zhengzhou, except Shenzhen, which is practical unanimity with the rank of external environment in noted five metropolises in Table 5. Wherefore, we can assume that:

Assumption 1: the better the enterprise external environment will be the longer the enterprises' life cycle.

Each sub-district of external environment of enterprise is a dimension composed of the external environment, thereinto economic environment including six dimensions that are market, client, competitor, financial institution, business cycle, and agency; political environment including four dimensions that are government, law, policy, and politics event; technological environment including two dimensions that are technology transfer and diffusion environment and technical feature of enterprise; socioculture environment including three dimensions that are cultural context, social public opinion, and community relation; human resources environment including two dimension that are acquirability of qualified person and growth degree of the human resources market; natural resources environment including seven dimensions that are space-time resource, natural resources, energy source, geography and climate, basic facilities, environmental protection, and extent of injury during disasters. It is foreseen that while supra each subdivided environment is better, the life cycle of enterprises is longer too; however, the significances of influence which each subdivided environment had on the life cycle of enterprises show some differences. Therefore, we can assume that:

Assumptions 2–7: the better the total external environment, including economic environment, political environment, technological environment, socioculture environment, human resources environment, and natural resources environment, the longer the enterprise life cycle spreads.

Due to the restrictions of sample number, this paper adopts simple regression analysis to verify the above-mentioned assumptions, the consequences of regression analysis is the situation depicted in Table 6.

It is observed that the external holistic environment of SMEs and each subdivided environment have a positive influence on the life cycle of SMEs (Table 6), but these influencing degrees present distinct differences, which demonstrate that above-mentioned assumptions 1–7 come into existence. Economic environment, technological environment, and human resources environment have prominent influences on SMEs' life cycle, and the regression coefficient of each subdivided environment of which all come to the confidence level of 95%, and adjusted rate of return values totally come to the level of 0.5. However, the influences of political environment, socioculture environment, and natural resources environment on SMEs' life cycle are inconspicuous. We conclude that what influence SMEs' life cycle are mainly economic environment, technological environment, and human resources environment.

According to the evaluating indicator system of SMEs' external living environment established above, we interpret the significant differences of the influences which each subdivided environment has on SMEs' life cycle as following: economic environment contains market, clients, competitors, financial institutions, intermediaries, and other factors, which reflect the enterprise market prospects in the industry, the degree of competition, the conditions of corporate financing, the service of intermediaries, etc. Technological environment reflects the difficulty of the enterprises to adopt advanced technology to upgrade the competitiveness, and for the competitiveness of enterprises is ultimately a competition of talents, the human resources environment decide the ease of all kinds of personnel access to the enterprise, so as to determine the company's human resources costs

Table 6. The regression analysis consequence of SMEs' life cycle based on their external subdivided environment.

	Economic environment	Political environment	Technological environment	Socioculture environment	Human resources environment	Natural resources environment	The holistic external environment of enterprises
α	−29.479*	−13.219*	−14.460*	−29.168	−9.089*	−32.602	−21.523*
	(−3.333)	(−1.837)	(−6.166)	(−1.565)	(−3.703)	(−1.105)	(−4.418)
β	9.209*	5.186	5.218*	8.946	4.024*	10.516	7.332*
	(3.739)	(1.316)	(7.701)	(1.758)	(5.173)	(1.227)	(5.157)
R^2	0.875	0.464	0.967	0.607	0.930	0.429	0.930
Adjusted R^2	0.812	0.398	0.951	0.411	0.896	0.144	0.895
F	13.983	3.732	59.310	3.091	26.756	1.505	26.594

Note: *Stand for prominent below the level of significance of 5%.

and the level of technical management levels, which all have a more direct impact on enterprises. Owing to the mobility of SMEs, the foundations of SMEs are usually conjunct with local socioculture environment and natural resources conditions. Since the expansion of markets, local SMEs by the impact of social and cultural environment are not confined to the local limited scope; for single SME, as the consumption of resources is limited, the access of natural resources to SMEs face less restrictions compared to large enterprises in short term, so it does not constitute a significant impact to the SMEs survival. Considering all above, toward to the factors of external living environment that influences SMEs' life cycle in our country, the major factors influencing SMEs' life cycle are economic environment, technological environment, and human resources environment in our country. While political environment, socioculture environment, and natural resources environment do not have prominent influences on SMEs' life cycle.

6. Conclusion

1. This article analyzes the data of SMEs that cancelled by industrial and commercial bureau in Shenzhen, Guangzhou, Changsha, Zhengzhou, Chengdu, and so on from 2000 to 2007, and concludes that the average life cycle of the dead SMEs in these five metropolises is 4.32 years. Among them, the average life cycle of 44.31% the dead SMEs is less than three years, the average life cycle of 25.66% the dead SMEs is three to five years, and the average life cycle of 23.08% the dead SMEs is 5 to 10 years. This shows from one aspect that the average life cycle of our country is short. There is an urgent need for improvement.

2. Through the test of the distribution of the data about the dead SMEs in these five metropolises, we find that the data about life cycle of SMEs in our country does not obey the log-normal distribution, exponential distribution, gamma distribution, Weibull distribution, and log-logistic distribution, which are usually used in the survival analysis, perhaps it is caused by that we only get the data of life cycle about the cancelled SMEs, and ignored the effect of the existing enterprises to the integral distribution about life cycle of SMEs in our country.

3. According to the analysis of the relationship of the life cycle of SMEs in five metropolises and their external survival environment, this article

finds that there is a high positive correlation between external survival environment of SMEs in some areas and the life cycle of SMEs there, the better the external environment is, the longer the life cycle of SMEs is. Looking from every environment, economic environment, technology environment, and human resources environment are effect much more to the life cycle of SMEs. This paper explains and analyzes about it, so we can know the effect and measures of government and enterprise to prolong the life cycle of SMEs.

In the stand of our government, it is urgent to create a good external environment for the survival and development of the SMEs. Because economic environment, technology environment, and human resources environment influence much more on the life cycle of SMEs, so the government must pay attention to these environment factors firstly. The government can promote reform of financial institutions to improve the credit guarantee system, and solve the problem about financing difficulty of SMEs, improve the condition of export service, organize different kinds of business trade meeting to sale, promote the production of local SMEs to domestic, open the market, and create conditions to establish the popularity of the production.

Secondly, the government must improve local technology serve, advocate technology innovation, encourage the enterprise introducing advanced technology to improve competitiveness, and promote the technology cooperation between SMEs and universities, scientific research institution, and other enterprises. Thirdly, the government should enhance talent training, universalize basic education, develop higher education, encourage the establishment of professional skill training institutions, improve the talent market, improve population fluidity, and create good residential environment, so as to attract and retain talent. At the same time, the government must enhance and improve its construction, perfect the reflecting laws, make great efforts to create healthy, civilized, and harmony social cultural environment, enhance credibility construction, and develop local characteristics industrial cluster combined with local customs.

As for the enterprises, solving self survival problem is the basic of development and grandness, the entrepreneur should improve self-quality, learn advanced management concept, operate enterprise with the scientific ways, and enhance their abilities to adapt to the change of environment. The entrepreneurs of SMEs should have sharp market olfaction and must make great efforts to exploit new market; they should also have susceptibility to technology, introduce new technology to strengthen the technical cooperation with other enterprises and universities and scientific research institutions, improve self technology, urge industrial upgrading, at the same time, pay attention to talent training, attract high-quality talent to join in, enhance the strength of talent in the enterprises continuously, and decrease the death risk of enterprises.

4. This paper preliminarily makes an empirical research on life cycle of SMEs and its influence factors, but there are still some limitations. If we define that registering cancelled by industrial and commercial bureau means the death of enterprise, as well as conclude that the enterprise is dead, but in fact, there are differences between voluntary cancellation and involuntary cancellation when enterprises are cancelled in industrial and commercial bureau, the enterprises which are voluntary cancel is not because of the survival difficult all the time, therefore, strictly speaking, only the enterprises which are involuntary cancel can be defined as dead. In addition, this article only makes statistic of the registering time and cancelled time of enterprises cancelled by industrial and commercial bureau, not including the number and time of establishment of SMEs that still alive, so we cannot analyze the life cycle of SMEs with the hazard ratio model which is generally used internationally, causing some errors in the result. Secondly, because of the difficulties in the research, we only get the data of the dead SMEs in five metropolises just like Shenzhen; the number of samples is a little less. When analyzing the effect of the external environment to the SMEs, just use the simple univariate regression analysis. Therefore, the relationship between the life cycle of SMEs and external environment should verify with the data of some other metropolises. These limitations will be improved in our future research.

References

Altman, E.I., 1983. Exploring the road to bankruptcy. *The Journal of Business Strategy*, 4(2), 36–41.

Altman, E.I., 1968. Financial ratios, discriminant analysis and the prediction of the corporate bankruptcy. *The Journal of Finance*, 23(4), 589–609.

Audretsch, D.B. and Vivarelli, M.V., 1995. New firm formation in Italy: a first report. *Economic Letters*, 48(1), 77–81.

Audretsch, D.B. and Mahmood, T., 1995. New firm survival: new results using a hazard function. *The Review of Economics and Statistics*, 77(1), 97–103.

Audretsch, D.B., 1995a. *Innovation and Industry Evolution*. MIT Press, Cambridge, MA.

Audretsch, D.B., 1995. Innovation, growth and survival. *The Review of Economics and Statistics*, 13(4), 441–457.

Baum, J.A.C., 1989. Liabilities of newness, adolescence, and obsolescence: exploring age dependence in the dissolution of organizational relationships and organizations. *Proceedings of the Administrative Science Association of Canada*, 10, 1–10.

Brüderl, J. and Schussler, R., 1990. Organizational mortality: the liabilities of newness and adolescence. *Administrative Science Quarterly*, 35, 530–547.

Brüderl, J., Preisendörfer, P., and Ziegler, R., 1992. Survival chances of newly founded business organizations. *American Sociological Review*, 57, 227–242.

Carroll, G. and Hannan, M., 2000. *The Demography of Corporations and Industries*. Princeton University Press, Princeton, New Jersey.

Chen, X. and Wang, F., 2008. A Chinese SMEs' external surviving environment evaluation index system research based on SEM. *Journal of Business Economics*, (10), 42–47.

Elena, C. and Orietta, M., 2006. Survivor: the role of innovation in firms' survival. *Research Policy*, 35, 626–641.

Fichman, M. and Levinthal, D., 1991. Honeymoons and the liability of adolescence: a new perspective on duration dependence in social and organizational relationships. *Academy of Management Review*, 16, 442–468.

Georgios, F. and Helen, L., 2000. Location and survival of new entry. *Small Business Economics*, 14, 311–321.

Gerlach, K. and Wagner, J., 1994. Regional differences in small firm entry in manufacturing industries. Lower Saxony, 1979–1997. *Entrepreneurship & Regional Development*, 6, 63–80.

Gort, M. and Steven, K., 1982. Time paths in the diffusion of product innovations. *The Economic Journal*, 92(3), 630–653.

Hannan, M., 1998. Rethinking age dependence in organizational mortality: logical formulizations. *American Journal of Sociology*, 104, 126–164.

Honjo, Y., 2000. Business failure of new firms: an empirical analysis using a multiplicative hazards model. *International Journal of Industrial Organization*, 18, 557–574.

Mahmood, T., 1992. Does the hazard rate for new plants vary between low- and high-tech-industries? *Small Business Economics*, 4(3), 201–209.

Mata, J. and Portugal, P., 1994. Life duration of new firms. *Journal of Industrial Economics*, 42, 227–246.

Mohmood, T., 2000. Survival of newly founded business: a log-logistic model approach. *Small Business Economics*, 14, 223–237.

Nelson, R. and Winter, S., 1982. *An Evolutionary Theory of Economic Change.* Harvard University Press, Cambridge, MA.

Rofik, A., Jean, B., and Nicolas, L.P., 2004. An explanation of the life span of new French firms. *Small Business Economics*, 23, 237–254.

Silviano, E.-P. and Juan, A., 2006. Manez-Castillejo. The resource-based theory of the firm and firm survival. *Small Business Economics*.

Stinchcombe, F., 1965. Social structure and organizations. *Handbook of Organizations*. Rand McNally, Chicago.

Su, Q. and Li, X., 2004. The interior government, external environment and the life cycle of Chinese family business (Chinese). *Management World*, (10), 85–96.

Study on Identification of Product Life Cycle Based on Fuzzy Diagnosis Model*

Hong Zhao, Zheng-Yang Zhao and Yuan Jiang

*Management School of Graduate University,
Chinese Academy of Sciences, Beijing 100190, China*

A product life cycle refers to the entire evolving process of a product from it entering the market to its seceding. Only by accurately analyzing the life cycles of the products can an enterprise successfully set up conductive marketing target and relevant strategies. Based on the fuzzy recognition theory, this article builds the fuzzy membership function through the division of life cycle and discussion of recognition index. The result of the recognition model was discussed and analyzed, and then the application of this method was illustrated.

Keywords: Product life cycle; Identification models; Fuzzy recognition and analysis.

1. Introduction

The concept of a product's life cycle first appeared in the field of economic management, proposed by Dean (1950) and Levir (1965), and the purpose is to examine the product marketing strategy. At that time, the product life cycle is divided in accordance with the market evolution process of the products into introduction, growth, maturity, and decline phases (Rinde and Swanj, 1979). After decades of development, product life cycle concept and content are constantly evolving, continuously expanding the application

---

Correspondence: Hong Zhao, Professor of Management School of Graduate University, Chinese Academy of Sciences, Beijing 100190, China, zhaohong@gucas.ac.cn.
*Project of National Natural Science Foundation of China (70872103).

areas, but mainly applied in the areas of products research or marketing strategy.

Chinese scholars have had a lot of in-depth studies on the product life cycle, mainly focusing on qualitative research, which is more focused on the selection of product life cycle indicators and description of product life cycle theory. However, scholars have begun to explore in this regard. In recent years, Chinese scholars have proposed using fuzzy math theory in fuzzy identification of product life cycle.

This article is a brief review of the development of product life cycle theory, and has summarized and analyzed the current division method of product life cycle stages. Then, it discussed the prerequisites for the selection of the key indicators used in product life cycle identification, and selected product sales and market share as a Generally Applicable Indicator for product life cycle identification. Then, a fuzzy recognition model was built according to the theory of fuzzy math, and the results of identification models were analyzed and discussed. Finally, an example was used to illustrate the application of fuzzy identification evaluation method.

2. Overview of Product Life Cycle Literature

2.1. *Product life cycle and its stage divisions*

The term of product life cycle has different meanings and contents in the works from both at home and abroad. According to its proposal and formation time, it mainly includes the following three types:

Professor Raymond Vernon from Harvard University (1966) put forward the "product cycle" theory with international investment and international trade involved. He divided the product cycle into three stages, namely, innovative stage, sophisticated stage, and standardized stage from the perspective of the US manufacturing industry. Product life cycle is described as the product which because of comparative advantage and competitive conditions at the three stages of changes that have taken place in the United States to a large extent determine the enterprise's external direct investment flows to the motivation and time in the international market.

Booz and colleagues (1968) from the United States proposed that the product life cycles changed according to their time of entering the market. The life cycle of a product can be divided into the introduction period, growing period, maturing period, and receding period. A new type of product life cycle theory was formed in which a period where the product was determined through the sales and competitiveness of the product. During the late 1980s to the early 1990s, marketing theory had new development, green marketing concept emerged. People gradually begun to establish the new idea of production and operation in green marketing environment, sustainable development of the product life cycle came into being. This theory was focused on relationship of entire product life cycle with the environment, including the process of obtaining initial natural resources and energy from the nature, forming of the final products through design, exploring, smelting, processing and reprocessing and other processes such as product storage and transportation, sales, consumption and usage to the scrap and disposal of the products, thereby to constitute a material transformation life course (Huang and Fan, 2004).

In this article, the meaning of the life cycle belongs to the second theory, but the methods used in this article can serve as reference for other product life cycle theories. According to the description by Philip (2002) in *Marketing Management*, the product life cycle can generally be divided into the introduction period, growing period, maturing period, and receding period.

2.2. *Identification models and methods of the product life cycle*

Identification of the enterprise product life cycle stages is an important aspect of the enterprise product life cycle study. Only by accurately judging the enterprise product life cycle stage, enterprises can select consistent marketing objectives and marketing strategies with the product life cycle to ensure corporate survival and sustainable development.

A lot of identification methods can be used to confirm enterprise product life cycle stages. The current product life cycle identification method has basically two types: one experience identification (Hu, 1998), including sales growth ratio method, analog prediction method, penetration analysis, and prediction method. Experience identification is based mainly on past experience, for the already accumulated wealth of statistical data in a certain category of products or the use of a certain industry experience discrimination are very practical values, to be able to identify the product life cycle, there is a good guide role, but not enough empirical data to support those products or industries, the method shows a lot of limitations, the application of up naturally rather difficult. At the same time, because often only a single indicator of the product life cycle evaluation, the conclusions may be biased.

The other is the mathematical model method, mainly referring to curve fitting (Cai *et al.*, 1999; Cox, 1967) and fuzzy mathematics. Comperz curve method can be used in accordance with the typical product life cycle curve fitting; however, the product life cycle curve does not always follow such a curve and only a single indicator is considered, so this way is not generally adopted. Fuzzy math method deficiencies are mainly membership function set up to determine the parameters of the difficulties involved in the experience points, because one of the selection problems, which give the application of this approach, has brought some obstacles. Fuzzy math was proposed by Chen and Qiao (2001) and improved and developed by Weixi and Zhicheng (2003), Zhu (2005), Hao (2006), and others to improve and develop. Fuzzy math method is thought to select the first selection of product-related indicators, and then in accordance with the fuzzy math of the theory, these indicators were set up at different stages of the membership function, computing and various indicators at different fuzzy interval on the degree of membership. It is based on the maximum membership degree principle; identify enterprise product life cycle-stage approach.

In this article, we rebuild membership functions based on the work of our predecessors, while simplifying the parameters at the same time; we made the model more rigorous.

3. Indexes for Product Life Cycle Identification

3.1. Basic assumptions for identification of product life cycle

Product life cycle is influenced by many factors, so in the use of fuzzy comprehensive evaluation method, we simplify the complex situation to an ideal status to obtain more general conclusions. We make the following assumptions:

(1) Macroeconomic-maintaining stability and product life cycle free from the impact of the economic cycle.

Product life cycle is influenced by macroeconomy and industry life cycle. Macroeconomic trends have a great influence on product sales and profits. Similarly, as the law of development of the industry, life cycle of product of the industry has a great influence on development, which cannot be ignored. Under normal circumstances, the impacts of product life cycle are inseparable from the industry life cycle. The development of substitute products or alternative technologies will undoubtedly affect the product life cycle.

(2) The competitive environment of the product remains relatively stable.

The changes of product competing environment are the unity of quantitative and qualitative changes and are continuous, gradual processes instead of mutation ones. So we begin with simplifying the environment to draw more general conclusions.

3.2. Selections of indexes for product life cycle identification

As to the selections of indexes for product life cycle identification, the focuses of different scholars vary. In his famous book *Marketing Management*, Kotler described the various characteristics of stages of product life cycle mainly from the perspective of sales, profit margins. In China, Zhu adopted the product sales with its change rate and market share with its change rates and profitability of enterprise products with its change rate these three indexes to study the characteristics of the product life cycle.

Based on the principles: importance, concise, availability of the data, and maneuverability, we select product sales, product profit margin, and market share as the indicators for identification of product life cycle. Product sales and profit margins as the absolute amount can effectively reflect the characteristics of the product while market share as the relative indicators can effectively reflect the product itself and the environment changes.

3.3. Characteristics of product life cycle indicators at various stages

Although there are many indicators to reflect changes in the product life cycle, we can use product sales and profit margins as well as market share to describe this process. According to the analysis of Philip *et al.*, we can describe the change of these three indicators of product life cycle in four phases.

When a product first enters the market, the sales of products are under the breakeven point, and sales grow at a slow speed; when the product enters the growth period, the product sales grow rapidly across the breakeven point, the scale of the sales expand rapidly, and the growth rate is accelerating; when the products is in the mature stage, the product sales basically stay stable, sales grow at a slower pace; when the products enter the recession period, the sales shrink rapidly, and the sales are at a negative growth.

And the profit margins will correspondingly change with the different stages of product life cycle. In introduction period, the profit is negative; while in next stage profit margin, the decline of profit growth indicates the mature stage, and profit gradually disappears in recession period.

Similarly, the market share in introduction period is low, and expands gradually in growth period, but market share remains relatively constant in mature period because of fiercely competition, and in the recession period, market share declines rapidly.

4. Improved Fuzzy Evaluation Model for Product Life Cycle

The changes of product sales, market share and sales margins reflect the characteristic of product life cycle. In accordance with the relevant principles of Fuzzy math, first we set up membership function for these three indicators in the life cycle of four stages separately and calculate the various indicators at different fuzzy interval of membership, then according to the various fuzzy sets in various life cycle stages, we obtain membership degree of the product life cycle stage to each fuzzy set; lastly we analyze the results of the model based on the various fuzzy sets of membership.

4.1. *Model formulation*

We assume eigenvalue vector of product life cycle as $X = (x_1, x_2, x_3)$, x_1 represents product sales, x_2 represents market share, and x_3 represents profit margin. We divided the three evaluation indicators into four level "low" (L2), "relatively low" (L1), "relatively high" (H1), and "high" (H2), L2, L1, H1, and H2 are closed interval with both upper and lower limits. We construct each fuzzy set for each type of status and define the membership function with piecewise functions.

Membership functions are the upward convex function defined on fuzzy sets, when the values of product sales, product market share, and product sales margins are between beginning and ending boundaries, there are not significantly different, so we propose that the set L2 (as well as the L1, H1, and H2) obey uniform distribution, because of the fuzziness, the fuzzy sets of adjacent cross exists, therefore, the three indicators of the fuzzy set membership functions are symmetrical, uniform distribution trapezoidal with a cross.

For example, the membership function of index x_1 was shown in Fig. 1, segment $a_2a_3 = a_4a_5$, and $a_1a_2 = a_3a_4 = a_5a_6$, each parameter value and the relationships between them are described in the following formula.

The fuzzy sets that represent lower income from the product sales are defined as

$$u_{\tilde{s}_2}(x_1) = \begin{cases} 1 & 0 < x_1 \le a_1 \\ \dfrac{a_2 - x_1}{a_2 - a_1} & a_1 < x_1 \le a_2 \\ 0 & x_1 > a_2 \end{cases} .$$

a_1 and a_2 are given by the decision-makers. If a product sale is below a_1, then we think that product sale is low. a_2 represents the smallest income that can be considered as relatively small, here we have $a_2 > a_1$.

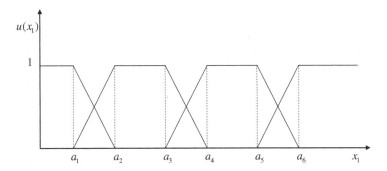

Fig. 1. Symmetric, uniformly distributed and crossed trapeziform membership function.

The fuzzy sets that represent relatively small income from product sales are defined as

$$
u_{\tilde{s}_2}(x_1) = \begin{cases}
0 & 0 < x_1 \le a_1 \\
\dfrac{x_1 - a_1}{a_2 - a_1} & a_1 < x_1 \le a_2 \\
1 & a_2 < x_1 \le a_3 \\
\dfrac{a_4 - x_1}{a_4 - a_3} & a_3 < x_1 \le a_4 \\
0 & x_1 > a_4
\end{cases} .
$$

We have $a_4 > a_3 > a_2$, and as stated, a_2 represents the smallest income that can be considered as relatively small, while a_5 represents the largest income that can be considered as relatively high, a_4 represents the smallest income that can be considered as relatively high, $a_4 = a_3 + (a_2 - a_1)$, $a_2 a_3$ indicates the boundary that can be considered as relatively low product sales.

The fuzzy sets that represent relatively high income from product sales are defined as

$$
u_{s_3}(x_1) = \begin{cases}
0 & 0 < x_1 \le a_3 \\
\dfrac{x_1 - a_3}{a_4 - a_3} & a_3 < x_1 \le a_4 \\
1 & a_4 < x_1 \le a_5 \\
\dfrac{a_6 - x_1}{a_6 - a_5} & a_5 < x_1 \le a_6 \\
0 & x_1 > a_6
\end{cases} .
$$

We have $a_6 > a_5 > a_4$, a_5 represents the largest income that can be considered as relatively high, $a_5 = a_4 + (a_3 - a_2)$, and a_6 represents the smallest income that can be considered as high, $a_6 = a_5 + (a_2 - a_1)$. $a_4 a_5$ indicates the boundary that can be considered as relatively high product sales.

The fuzzy sets that represent high income from product sales are defined as

$$
u_{\tilde{s}_4}(x_1) = \begin{cases}
0 & 0 < x_1 \le a_5 \\
\dfrac{x_1 - a_5}{a_6 - a_5} & a_5 < x_1 \le a_6 \\
1 & x_1 > a_6
\end{cases} .
$$

Similarly, as shown in Tables 1 and 2, we can get the membership functions of market share and profit margin.

At this point, we set up product life cycle indicators of the three membership functions.

4.2. Fuzzy diagnosis model of product life cycle

We use $\tilde{T}_1$, $\tilde{T}_2$, $\tilde{T}_3$, and $\tilde{T}_4$ to express the four stages of product life cycle, i.e., introduction period, growth period, mature period, and recession period.

Because of just entering the market, in introduction period, the product was not universally accepted and therefore there is little income from product sales, when compared with similar products the market share is also small; and because of the relatively high cost of product sales, so sales margins are relatively low, even negative. A fuzzy set to express this situation is $\tilde{T}_1 = (\tilde{s}_1 \cup \tilde{s}_2) \cap (\tilde{g}_1 \cup \tilde{g}_2) \cap (\tilde{p}_1 \cup \tilde{p}_2)$.

In growth period, product has been accepted by the market, consumers begin to buy. At this point, Product Sales revenue grows rapidly, market share accounting for similar products is also gradually increasing. So the cost of product sales is diluted, making a profit from product sales improved, the fuzzy set can be expressed as $\tilde{T}_2 = (\tilde{s}_3 \cup \tilde{s}_4) \cap (\tilde{g}_3 \cup \tilde{g}_4) \cap (\tilde{p}_3 \cup \tilde{p}_4)$.

In mature period, products have been recognized by the consumers, but the emergence of competitive products, making the market competitive. Although product sales revenue remained relatively high level, market share has stabilized at a higher level, profit margin declines because of the intense market competition, resulting in lower prices and marketing costs increased. The fuzzy set can be expressed as $\tilde{T}_3 = (\tilde{s}_2 \cup \tilde{s}_3) \cap (\tilde{g}_2 \cup \tilde{g}_3) \cap (\tilde{p}_2 \cup \tilde{p}_3)$.

Recession period refers to the period that products gradually exit market. The characteristic of this phase is that the alternative of the product continues to emerge, which can better meet consumer demand. Original Product Sales revenue and market share decline, and product prices are not falling, leading to declining margins. When the products profit margins do not exist, the products will gradually withdraw from the market.

One thing we must note is that because the recession period have the same numerical characteristics as introduction period, but the nature of them is totally different, we have $\text{Supp}(\tilde{T}_1 \cap \tilde{T}_4) = \emptyset$. So when analyzing the fuzzy set, we must discriminate recession period and introduction period.

Table 1. Membership function of market share.

Market share	Fuzzy set $\tilde{g}_i$ corresponding to membership function $u_{\tilde{g}_i}(x_2)$ ($i = 1, 2, 3, 4$)				
Fuzzy state					
$\tilde{g}_1$ that represents market share is low	$0 < x_2 \leq b_1$ 1	$b_1 < x_2 \leq b_2$ $\dfrac{b_2 - x_2}{b_2 - b_1}$	$x_2 > b_2$ 0	—	—
$\tilde{g}_2$ that represents market share is relatively low	$0 < x_2 \leq b_1$ 0	$b_1 < x_2 \leq b_2$ $\dfrac{x_2 - b_1}{b_2 - b_1}$	$b_2 < x_2 \leq b_3$ 1	$b_3 < x_2 \leq b_4$ $\dfrac{b_4 - x_2}{b_4 - b_3}$	$x_2 > b_4$ 0
$\tilde{g}_3$ that represents market share is relatively high	$0 < x_2 \leq b_3$ 0	$b_3 < x_2 \leq b_4$ $\dfrac{x_2 - b_3}{b_4 - b_3}$	$b_4 < x_2 \leq b_5$ 1	$b_5 < x_2 \leq b_6$ $\dfrac{b_6 - x_2}{b_6 - b_5}$	$x_2 > b_6$ 0
$\tilde{g}_4$ that represents market share is relatively high	$0 < x_2 \leq b_5$ 0	$b_5 < x_2 \leq b_6$ $\dfrac{x_2 - b_5}{b_6 - b_5}$	$x_2 > b_6$ 1	—	—

1. b_1, b_2, and b_3 are decided by decision makers according to prior experience. If product sales is under b_1, then we think that market share is low; b_2 represents the smallest rate that can be considered as market share is low, so we have $b_2 > b_1$.

2. $b_4 = b_3 + (b_2 - b_1)$, $b_5 = b_4 + (b_3 - b_2)$, $b_6 = b_5 + (b_2 - b_1)$.

Table 2. Membership function of profit margin.

Profit margin	Fuzzy set $\tilde{p}_i$ corresponding to membership function $u_{\tilde{p}_i}(x_3)$ ($i = 1, 2, 3, 4$)				
Fuzzy state					
$\tilde{p}_1$ that represents profit margin is low	$x_3 \le c_1$ 1	$c_1 < x_3 \le c_2$ $\dfrac{c_2 - x_3}{c_2 - c_1}$	$x_3 > c_2$ 0	— —	— —
$\tilde{p}_2$ that represents profit margin is relatively low	$x_3 \le c_1$ 0	$c_1 < x_3 \le c_2$ $\dfrac{x_3 - c_1}{c_2 - c_1}$	$c_2 < x_3 \le c_3$ 1	$c_3 < x_3 \le c_4$ $\dfrac{c_4 - x_3}{c_4 - c_3}$	$x_3 > c_4$ 0
$\tilde{p}_3$ that represents profit margin is relatively high	$x_3 \le c_3$ 0	$c_3 < x_3 \le c_4$ $\dfrac{x_3 - c_3}{c_4 - c_3}$	$c_4 < x_3 \le c_5$ 1	$c_5 < x_3 \le c_6$ $\dfrac{c_6 - x_3}{c_6 - c_5}$	$x_3 > c_6$ 0
$\tilde{p}_4$ that represents profit margin is relatively high	$x_3 \le c_5$ 0	$c_5 < x_3 \le c_6$ $\dfrac{x_3 - c_5}{c_6 - c_5}$	$x_3 > c_6$ 1	— —	— —

1. c_1, c_2, and c_3 are decided by decision makers according to prior experience. If product sales is under c_1, then we think that market share is low; c_3 represents the smallest rate that can be considered as market share is low, so we have $c_2 > c_1$.

2. $c_4 = c_3 + (c_2 - c_1)$, $c_5 = c_4 + (c_3 - c_2)$, $c_6 = c_5 + (c_2 - c_1)$.

Table 3. Fuzzy set and membership degree of lifecycle phases of products.

Life cycle of product y	Fuzzy set	Membership degree
Introduction period $\tilde{T}_1$	$(\tilde{s}_1 \cup \tilde{s}_2) \cap (\tilde{g}_1 \cup \tilde{g}_2) \cap (\tilde{p}_1 \cup \tilde{p}_2)$	$u_{\tilde{T}_1}(y)$
Growth period $\tilde{T}_2$	$(\tilde{s}_2 \cup \tilde{s}_3) \cap (\tilde{g}_2 \cup \tilde{g}_3) \cap (\tilde{p}_2 \cup \tilde{p}_3)$	$u_{\tilde{T}_2}(y)$
Mature period $\tilde{T}_3$	$(\tilde{s}_3 \cup \tilde{s}_4) \cap (\tilde{g}_3 \cup \tilde{g}_4) \cap (\tilde{p}_3 \cup \tilde{p}_4)$	$u_{\tilde{T}_3}(y)$
Recession period $\tilde{T}_4$	$(\tilde{s}_1 \cup \tilde{s}_2) \cap (\tilde{g}_1 \cup \tilde{g}_2) \cap (\tilde{p}_1 \cup \tilde{p}_2)$	$u_{\tilde{T}_4}(y)$

Based on the theory of fuzzy math, if both $\tilde{A}$ and $\tilde{B}$ are fuzzy sets, then $\tilde{C}_1 = \tilde{A} \cup \tilde{B}$ and $\tilde{C}_2 = \tilde{A} \cap \tilde{B}$ are both fuzzy sets, and the membership functions of them are as follows.

$$u_{\tilde{C}_1}(y) = \max\{u_{\tilde{A}}(y), u_{\tilde{B}}(y)\}$$

$$u_{\tilde{C}_2}(y) = \min\{u_{\tilde{A}}(y), u_{\tilde{B}}(y)\}.$$

The fuzzy sets and membership degrees of the various stages of product life cycle are shown in Table 3.

4.3. *Fuzzy identification and analysis*

Of a product, we can measure the membership degree $\tilde{T}_1(y)$, $\tilde{T}_2(y)$, $\tilde{T}_3(y)$, and $\tilde{T}_4(y)$ of current product life phase to the four stages of product life cycle according to their sales revenue, market share and product margins, and the definition of fuzzy set-style.

On the one hand, based on the maximum membership degree principle, we can determine the current position of product life cycle phases; on the other hand, we can also predict product life cycle development in accordance with degree of membership to guide the enterprise to take corresponding measures to deal with changes of product life cycle.

We can make the corresponding analysis to the different situations:

1. $\tilde{T}_1(y) = 1$, $\tilde{T}_2(y) = 0$, $\tilde{T}_3(y) = 0$, $\tilde{T}_4(y) = 0$. At this time, product is in introduction period. Companies should draw up appropriate marketing strategy mainly based on characteristics of product introduction period.
2. $\tilde{T}_1(y) > 0$, $\tilde{T}_2(y) > 0$, $\tilde{T}_3(y) = 0$, $\tilde{T}_4(y) = 0$ and $\tilde{T}_1(y) > \tilde{T}_2(y)$. According to principle of maximum membership degree, the product is

still in the import process, but has shown some of the characteristics of growth period. Companies should draw up some marketing tactics to reflect the characteristics of growth period.

3. $\tilde{T}_1(y) = 0$, $\tilde{T}_2(y) = 1$, $\tilde{T}_3(y) = 0$, $\tilde{T}_4(y) = 0$. At this time, product is in growth period. Companies should draw up appropriate marketing strategy mainly based on characteristics of product growth period.

4. $\tilde{T}_1(y) = 0$, $\tilde{T}_2(y) > 0$, $\tilde{T}_3(y) > 0$, $\tilde{T}_4(y) = 0$ and $\tilde{T}_2(y) > \tilde{T}_3(y)$. According to principle of maximum membership degree, the product is still in the import process, but in the final phase, there has been little room for growing, some characteristics of maturity can be seen. Companies should make adjustments in advance to gain maturity in the product competitive environment to achieve the competitive advantage.

5. $\tilde{T}_1(y) = 0$, $\tilde{T}_2(y) = 0$, $\tilde{T}_3(y) = 1$, $\tilde{T}_4(y) = 0$. At this time, product is in mature period. Companies should draw up appropriate marketing strategy based mainly on characteristics of product mature period.

6. $\tilde{T}_1(y) = 0$, $\tilde{T}_2(y) = 0$, $\tilde{T}_3(y) > 0$, $\tilde{T}_4(y) > 0$ and $\tilde{T}_2(y) > \tilde{T}_3(y)$. According to principle of maximum membership degree, the product is still in the mature stage, but there has been some signs of decline, the competitive advantage is gradually lost. On the one hand, enterprises should pay attention to adjust strategy to keep the products at maturity and harvest profits as long as possible; On the other hand new product development should be strengthened, pay attention to the introduction of new products to the market in order to prevent risks associated with period of recession.

7. $\tilde{T}_1(y) = 0$, $\tilde{T}_2(y) = 0$, $\tilde{T}_3(y) = 0$, $\tilde{T}_4(y) = 1$. At this time, product is in recession period. Companies should draw up appropriate marketing strategy mainly based on characteristics of product recession period.

5. Empirical Application

Assuming one company has two similar products y and z, its sales volume, market share and product profit information are shown in Table 4.

In order to calculate the degree of membership of fuzzy sets, parameter value of membership function corresponding to each fuzzy set must be given as shown in Table 5 below.

Table 4. Life cycle indexes of Products A and B.

Year	Sales volume	Market share (%)	Profit margin (%)
	Relevant information of Product A		
2005	600	4	−3
2006	1,150	9	5
2007	2,400	25	13
	Relevant Information of Product B		
2005	3,800	25	14
2006	4,850	32	19
2007	5,700	38	22

Table 5. Parameters relating to membership function.

a_1	a_2	a_3	a_4	a_5	a_6
1,000	2,500	3,500	5,000	6,000	7,500
b_1	b_2	b_3	b_4	b_5	b_6
10	17.5	25.5	33	41	48.5
c_1	c_2	c_3	c_4	c_5	c_6
3	7.5	10.5	15	18	22.5

Table 6. Membership degrees of Products A and B in different phases.

Year	$u_{T_1}(A)$	$u_{T_2}(A)$	$u_{T_3}(A)$	$u_{T_4}(A)$
	Membership of Product A to stages of product life cycle			
2005	1	0	0	0
2006	0.56	0.1	0	0
2007	0	0.33	0.67	0
	Membership of Product B to stages of product life cycle			
2005	0.22	0.78	0	0
2006	0	0.44	0.56	0
2007	0	0.11	0.89	0

We can calculate membership degree of the products y and z to the four stages of product life cycles under the fuzzy mathematical model, the result is shown in Table 6.

According to Table 6, we can analyze the stages of both product A and B.

For Product A, in 2005, the membership degree to introduction period is 1, the product is in introduction period; in 2006, the membership degree to introduction period is 0.56, according to the principle of maximum membership, the product is still in introduction period, but has some characteristics of growth period already; in 2007, the membership degree to growth period is 0.33, the membership degree to mature period is 0.67, the product is already in mature period, but some features of growth features exist.

For Product B, in 2005, the membership degree to introduction period is 0.22, the membership degree to growth period is 0.78, indicates that the product is in the transition from introduction to growth period, but we can think the product is in growth period already.

The product is in introduction period; in 2006, the membership degree to introduction period is 0.6, according to the principle of maximum membership, the product is still in introduction period, but has some characteristics of growth period already; in 2007, the membership degree to growth period is 0.11, the membership degree to mature period is 0.89, the product is already in mature period, but some features of growth features exist.

From the analysis of results of the model, we argue that the model can be used to identify the stages of product life cycles, but more importantly, the model can be used to predict the evolution path of the product life cycles, reflect the dynamic changes in the evolution of life cycle process, it can provide meaningful guideline for decision makers.

6. Limitation and Further Research

When recognizing the phase of the product life cycle, especially in the transition of two adjacent phases, it is very difficult to differentiate.

In this article, based on previous researches, we divide the product life cycle into introduction period, growth period, mature period and recession period, and select product sales, growth rate and profit margin as the identification indexes to describe the characteristics of various stages of product life cycle.

Then, according to theory of fuzzy math and fuzzy evaluation, we construct membership function of selected indexes and fuzzy set of various stages to evaluate the phase of product life cycles; still we analyze the possible outcomes of the model. Lastly, two sets of data were selected to verify the application of the model. The conclusions show that the set up of the product life cycle fuzzy recognition model can effectively identify the product life cycle, and has a certain value. The new research points of this article are included: Reconstruct the membership function, making it clearer and concise, while the parameters of the model shrink from 12 to 6; therefore, the model is more feasible. The possible outcomes of the model are concluded and analyzed.

There are the following limitations in this article and further research: first, the construction of membership functions involves the determining of the parameters, which depend on the experience of the decision makers or experts, with a certain degree of subjectivity; secondly, only two sets of data are selected for authentication, and the relevant case studies should be selected and analyzed.

References

Booz, Allen & Hamilton, 1968. *Management of New Products*. New York.

Cai, L., Mao, C., and Zhao, Y., 1999. Models of product life cycle. *Natural Science Journal of Jilin Industrial University*, (3), 48–52.

Chen, X. and Qiao, Z., 2001. Fuzzy identification of product life cycle. *Journal of China Agricultural University*, 6(4), 1–6.

Cox, W., 1967. Product life cycles as marketing models. *Journal of Business*.

Dean, J., 1950. Pricing policies for new products. *Harvard Business Review*, 28(6), 45–53.

Hao, Y. and Zhu, X., 2006. Fuzzy recognition of enterprise product life cycle stages. *Statistics and Decision-Making*, 10(2), 120–121.

Hu, J., 1998. Analysis and forecasting methods of product life cycle, *Beijing Statistics*, 11.

Huang, S. and Fan, Y., 2004. Review on product life cycle research. *Computer Integrated Manufacturing Systems*, 10(1), 1–9.

Liang, W. and Li, Z., 2003. Research on product life cycle simulation of the prototype system. *Journal of Huazhong University of Science and Technology*, 31(10), 99–101.

Levir, T., 1965. Exploit the product life cycle. *Harvard Business Review*, 43(6), 81–94.

Philip, K., 2002. *Marketing Management*, 11th edn., Prentice Hall.

Raymond, V., 1966. International investment and international trade in the product cycle, *Quarterly Journal of Economics*, 80(2).

Rinde, R. and Swanj, E., 1979. Product life cycle research: a literature review. *Journal of Business Research*, 7(3), 219–242.

Zhu, X., 2005. Study on identification methods based on fuzzy enterprise product life cycle. *Statistics Education*, 12(1), 21–24.

Mobile Communication Enterprises Competition Model and Strategies Analysis Considering Difference of Product Quality

Ze Ye, Zhen Zhou and Caihong Chang

School of Economics and Management,
Changsha University of Science and Technology,
Changsha, Hunan 410076, China
Yeze2003@263.net

There is a typical two oligarchies competition structure in China's mobile communication market. The actual operation status of enterprises indicates that competition issue of mobile communication enterprises cannot be explained by the classic Bertrand model. After seriously analyzing the characteristics of China's mobile communication market, this article establishes the Nash-equilibrium model for enterprises' competition, which considers difference of product quality. According to analysis on the Nash-equilibrium model, characteristics and strategies of enterprises' competition are proposed. At last, combined with the actual data and experience of enterprises' competition. This article analyzes and verifies the model, and competition strategies for enterprises are also studied, evaluated and proposed.

Keywords: Difference of product quality; Bertrand paradox; Nash-equilibrium; Competition strategy.

1. Introduction

After the establishment of China Mobile Communications Corporation (hereinafter referred to China Mobile) in 2000, China's mobile communication market has entered two oligarchies competition era of China Mobile and China Unicom Limited Corporation (hereinafter referred to China Unicom) (Wu *et al.*, 2002). This article uses industrial organization theory combined with operation business practice of China Mobile and China Unicom to establish and analyze Nash-equilibrium model of oligarchic competition in mobile communications market. And it focuses on the analysis of effects on mobile communication enterprises' competition behavior and operation performance caused by difference of product quality, so it can provide a theoretical basis for the development of competitive strategy of enterprises and government regulation policy.

As there is no problem of decision making in production, two oligarchies competition meet with Bertrand model in a relatively mature market of mobile communication services. Supposing the oligarchies enterprises' production costs of current mobile communication market are the same, the products have no difference in quality and consumers can switch between two different enterprises with no extra costs. In addition, the Government did not restrict competition provisions, so two oligarchies competition of our mobile communication market fits with Bertrand model. According to this model, the Nash-equilibrium strategies of China Mobile and China Unicom are to choose market price equivalent unit cost of the market price, and each received 50% of the market share and the two enterprises have zero profit.

2. Bertrand Paradox of China's Mobile Communication Market

According to Bertrand model, under certain conditions, only two companies' Oligopoly market is enough to achieve the complete competition results; the result is not only difficult to explain in theory, but also does not meet the fact, known as Bertrand Paradox (Jean, 1997). Based on the actual result of the market competition of China Mobile and China Unicom, there was a clear phenomenon of paradox Bertrand. Table 1 is China Mobile and China Unicom's change circumstances in subscribers of the two enterprises, market share, and average prices from 2001 to 2007. We can see that the price of China Unicom has been lower than the price of China Mobile and both of their market shares were no much change, maintained at a stable level respectively. Overall, there was no switching of consumer behavior as Bertrand model indicated.

Why did the actual results of two enterprises come to the different conclusion in market competition based on theoretical model? Generally, China's mobile communications market competition does not meet the

Table 1.   Subscribers, market share, price, and profit (2001–2007).

	2001	2002	2003	2004	2005	2006	2007
China Mobile: Subscribers (10 thousand)	10,382	11,770	14,160	20,421	24,660	30,120	38,660
China Unicom: Subscribers (10 thousand)	4,100	6,817	8,080	11,208	12,779	14,237	16,249
China Mobile: Market share (%)	71.69	63.32	63.67	64.56	65.87	67.90	70.41
China Unicom: Market share (%)	28.31	36.68	36.33	35.44	34.13	32.10	29.59
China Mobile: Average tariff (RMB/min)	0.60	0.56	0.41	0.31	0.28	0.24	—
China Unicom: Average tariff (RMB/min)	0.54	0.44	0.33	0.26	0.24	0.21	—
China Mobile: profit (million)	41,006	49,367	53,637	60,634	74,711	93,145	124,725
China Unicom: profit (million)	—	6,192	5,823	6,105	6,527	8,445	13,155

Sources: Consolidation on the relevant data.

conditions required by Bertrand model assumptions. For example, product cost and product quality of two companies are not the same (Li and Tang, 2006), or even in terms of price, competition is not very free, and there is still some regulation (Zhang, 2006). However, which factors affect the company's pricing strategy and consumer choice, and even operation performance? How deep is the impact? Even though two enterprises have different prices but the market share has always maintained at a basic stability in the proportion. That is, what is difference of assumption conditions between the actual market and Bertrand model? Which difference is the fundamental reason for the apparent inconsistency in actual result of the competition results and conclusions of theoretical calculations?

3. Reasons of Bertrand Paradox in China's Mobile Communication Market

The reasons why Bertrand paradox occurred are concluded and summarized in the following four main factors after the theoretical analysis: restriction of productive capacity, difference of unit costs, difference of product quality, and time dimension. If we take the China's characteristics of mobile communications market and the Government communication industrial policy into consideration, switching costs and regulation policy are other two factors. We analyze and evaluate impacts of these four aspects and determine the factors to be considered to modify the model as follows.

1) Whether capacity constraints exist? Bertrand model assumes that all enterprises can meet the needs of the market. In fact, because of this great state of the market uncertainty, in many markets of two oligarchies competition, an enterprise cannot meet all market demands with production capacity. Edgeworth is the first person using production capacity constraints to explain Bertrand Paradox (Jean, 1997), Compared with other markets, communication market including mobile communications market is an exception. As reasons such as foresight in infrastructure construction, universal service, and two oligarchies competition in China's mobile communication market, it is relatively reasonable for the assumption that an enterprise meets all market demand.

2) Assumption of the equal marginal cost is reasonable. After a long period of development, China's mobile communication business has entered a relatively stable period of development, especially after large-scale infrastructure investment. During this period, investment on infrastructure has decreased relatively, and enterprise development will focus on the formed production capacity and make full use of, continuously improve its product and service quality, access to the larger market, and achieve better economic returns. On the part of cost structure, it shows typical characteristics of relatively large in fixed cost and relatively low in variable cost and marginal cost. In the case of small marginal cost, it is reasonable to assume China Mobile and China Unicom have the same marginal cost. In fact, on competition issues in many mobile communications companies, marginal cost has been made assumption to zero. Because of the specialty of communications assets and other reasons, the fixed costs of communication companies have the nature of sunk cost. If we do not consider the sunk cost, we can reach the conclusion of equal unit cost on the assumption of equal marginal cost. Under such circumstances, marginal cost and average cost have the same economic meaning. Therefore, the assumption of equal marginal cost is not the reason that leads to Bertrand paradox of China's mobile communications market.

3) The assumption that switches cost equals to zero is reasonable. We assume that the switching cost of Bertrand model is equal to zero. That is, consumers choose different products produced by enterprises and their switching costs can be neglected. The survey and analysis of actual switching action of consumer show that consumer will have four kinds of switching cost in the process of re-select mobile communication service enterprise (Li and Tang, 2006): switching cost of procedure, switching cost of financial, switching cost of quality, and switching cost of relation.

The impact of switching cost to switching behavior of consumers is an objective existence, but its mechanism and the result are more complicated. Firstly, the impact of switching cost to switching action lies on the switching benefit. Actually, consumers' action depends on net switching cost. And net switching cost is equal to the difference made by the switching costs mentioned above and switching benefits by improving the quality of products. Any consumers' switching actions are the results of balancing the costs and benefits. Therefore, we cannot briefly consider the switching costs. For this reason, in some researches, switching costs and difference of product quality are always used alternatively. Secondly, in the aspect of value measurement, it is hard to measure value with certain benefits or losses of related switching action of consumers for it involved subjective judgments (Oz, 2002). On the other hand, we cannot have a uniform standard and threshold value because different consumers have different clients relationship, and also different switching costs and threshold value caused by switching actions. Finally, the size of switching actions is related with switching times. Supposing the expected switching actions will last for a long time when consumer made a decision to converse from the impact angle of switching actions, that means even though the one-time switching cost is large, the unit switching costs is small after long time consideration. Even the impact of decision making is relatively small. Under such circumstances, the switching cost can be neglected. That is to say, the assumption of switching costs in Bertrand model is reasonable. The survey and analysis of actual switching action of China's consumers also show consumer's switching action exists objectively, one of years' switching rate even reached 37.78%, and the main reasons for switching action are priced and others, even some relevant researches did not consider switching cost as a factor (Wang, 2006).

4) The assumption that the products have equal quality is reasonable. It is assumed that the products provided by enterprises have no difference in Bertrand model, but actually, there exist differences in products and service quality provided by different enterprises. Mobile communication service belongs to experience product. Communication service provided by different enterprises (network) exist differences in the degree of clear voice, rate of one time on connection, break rate, and so on. Therefore, competition model of mobile communications market should consider difference of product quality.

5) Time dimension is that we suppose the game between two oligarchies enterprises is one-off. The low price part will gain the whole market forever, and the lose part will do no action. This is obviously unpractical. If we think the lose part will also depreciate to take more market share, then the part firstly low the price cannot gain full benefit. Price war will appear after a long period competition. In addition, the anticipation of "price war" will lead to enterprises' collusion (Bezzina and Penard, 2000). The results of collusion are probably those two oligarchies enterprisers' fixed price are higher than marginal costs and then gain economic profits. According the above analysis, it is clear that competition between the China Mobile and China Unicom is not one-off, but repeated game of many times. Therefore, unreasonable assumption of time dimension is the important reason that made the inconsistency between the theoretical conclusion and actual result.

6) In the aspect of the assumption of free competition policy, one assumption has not put special stress but has implied in the Bertrand model is that free competition of market and no restrict competition-controlled strategy. Compared with other various industries, the mobile communication sector is an important part of country's basic industries. The national control policies may have an impact on the competitiveness of mobile communications enterprises. In theory, we have practiced strict control on the price of China's mobile communication industry. Take price as an example, China's mobile service charges implemented two-way charges, and practiced the policies of the government pricing and government guidance-based, supplemented with market price adjustment. Government has formulated relevant policies at various times, mobile communications companies have limited rights of independent pricing, so this has formed a very narrow band of prices by the policy of limited

upper and lower price. Therefore, it does not meet the conditions of free competition. However, there are some differences with regulation policies in the actual tariff standard, mobile communications services enterprises broke through the pricing policy restrictions in various forms and rates, such as discount package and so on. Therefore, they achieve the competition to some extent. As shown in Table 1, the average tariffs per minute are reduced by 60% from 2001 to 2006. For this reason, we hold that China's mobile communication market meet with free competition conditions.

Compared with six factors above, we can see that product quality, time dimension, and switching cost have a relatively large impact on the results of two oligarchies competition in China's mobile communication market. The main reason is probably the difference of product quality. To make a brief introduction and analysis on Bertrand paradox problem in mobile communication market, we establish the two oligarchies competition model considering the difference of product quality for China's mobile communication market; switching cost and time dimension are also considered on analysis, to explain the difference between the model conclusions and the actual results.

4. Model and Analysis of Two Oligarchies Competition Considering Difference of Product Quality

Consulted to relevant model (Valletti, 1999), two oligarchies competition model considering difference of product quality can be established (Jean, 1997), and we make calculations based on the model, then analysis that whether result of calculations can be consistent with the actual data.

5. Model of Two Oligarchies Competition for Mobile Communication Market Considering Difference of Product Quality

China Mobile and China Unicom are assumed operator No. 1 and No. 2, China Mobile as the first mover, chooses price p_1 and offers service product whose quality is q_1; China Unicom as the entrant, whose product price is p_2 with quality q_2; and the product quality of China Mobile is better than China Unicom's, namely, $q_1 > q_2$, that is $\Delta q = q_1 - q_2$. Consumers' preference is denoted by $U = \theta q - p$, where θ is the quality preference parameter for consumers, who is uniform distribution in population of consumers where between $\underline{\theta} \geq 0$ from $\bar{\theta} = \underline{\theta} + 1$ and the distribution destiny is 1. The costs for any quality of products of the two operators are assumed to be the same, namely, the production costs of both are c. At the same time, the whole market is covered completely by the products of two operators, a consumer has to buy one product from either of the two operators, and the consumer's switching cost of unit product s is ignored.

It is assumed that consumers with high parameter θ buy China Mobile's product and consumers with low parameter θ buy China Unicom's. High quality of product is in accordance with high price and vice versa, if and only if $\theta q_1 - p_1 = \theta q_2 - p_2$, namely, $\tilde{\theta} = \frac{p_1 - p_2}{\Delta q}$, the consumers with the parameter $\tilde{\theta}$ show no difference in the two operators' brands. Therefore, the demand function can be derived below[1]:

$$D_1(p_1, p_2) = \bar{\theta} - \frac{p_1 - p_2}{\Delta q}$$

$$D_2(p_1, p_2) = \frac{p_1 - p_2}{\Delta q} - \underline{\theta}$$

Operator i between the two pursues profit maximum by choosing p_i:

$$\Pi_i = (p_i - c)D_i(p_1, p_2)$$

Therefore, the reaction function is

$$p_1 = R_1(p_2) = (p_2 + c + \bar{\theta}\Delta q)/2$$

$$p_2 = R_2(p_1) = (p_1 + c - \underline{\theta}\Delta q)/2$$

Based on Nash-equilibrium:

$$p_1 = c + \frac{2\bar{\theta}\Delta q - \underline{\theta}\Delta q}{3} = c + \frac{2\bar{\theta} - \underline{\theta}}{3}\Delta q \qquad (1)$$

$$p_2 = c + \frac{\bar{\theta}\Delta q - 2\underline{\theta}\Delta q}{3} = c + \frac{\bar{\theta} - 2\underline{\theta}}{3}\Delta q \qquad (2)$$

---

[1] θ is uniform distribution from $\underline{\theta} \geq 0$ to $\bar{\theta} = \underline{\theta} + 1$, so the demand $D_1(p_1, p_2) = \Pr\{\tilde{\theta} \leq \theta \leq \bar{\theta}\} = \bar{\theta} - \frac{p_1 - p_2}{\Delta q}$. In the same way, $D_2(p_1, p_2) = \frac{p_1 - p_2}{\Delta q} - \underline{\theta}$.

Therefore, the demands are

$$D_1 = (2\bar{\theta} - \underline{\theta})/3 \tag{3}$$

$$D_2 = (\bar{\theta} - 2\underline{\theta})/3 \tag{4}$$

The profits are

$$\Pi_1(p_1, p_2) = (2\bar{\theta} - \underline{\theta})^2 \Delta q/9 + c(2\bar{\theta} - \underline{\theta})/3 \tag{5}$$

$$\Pi_2(p_1, p_2) = (\bar{\theta} - 2\underline{\theta})^2 \Delta q/9 + c(\bar{\theta} - 2\underline{\theta})/3 \tag{6}$$

6. Analysis of the Two Oligarchies Competition Model of Mobile Communication Market in China

Based on the result above, it is indicated that price, market demand, and profit are affected by the result of enterprises game equilibrium when considering difference of product quality. According to the model above, we will discuss changes of price, market demand, and profit respectively when considering difference of product quality of the two oligarchies, verify the model's rationality through comparing with the actual condition of mobile communication market in China.

6.1. Price change

Based on Eqs. (3) and (4), the following conclusions can be drawn:

Firstly, price depends on cost, coefficient of consumers' quality preference, and difference of product quality. The influences of quality preference θ and difference of product quality Δq on price are combined together. Secondly, $p_1 - p_2 = (2\underline{\theta} + 1)\Delta q/3$, $p_1 - p_2 > 0$ eternally when $\underline{\theta} \geq 0$, therefore, the price of China Mobile's product is always higher than the price of China Unicom's, which is inconsistent with the conclusion of the same price for two in the Bertrand model, however, consistent with the actual data of two operators prices. Thirdly, the proportion relation in quantitative terms of the two operators: $p_1/p_2 = (3c + (2\bar{\theta} - \underline{\theta})\Delta q)/(3c + (\bar{\theta} - 2\underline{\theta})\Delta q) = (3c + (\underline{\theta} + 2)\Delta q)/(3c + (1 - \underline{\theta})\Delta q)$, $p_1/p_2 = (3c + 2\Delta q)/(3c + \Delta q)$ when $\underline{\theta} = 0$. This result indicates that $\Delta q > 0$, so $p_1/p_2 > 1$ eternally, but the difference between them cannot be much, when assumed Δq equals to $2c$, namely, the effectiveness difference between China Mobile's and China

Unicom's is two times of their each unit cost, so $p_1/p_2 = 5/4 = 1.25$. This result is similar with actual data of two operators' prices shown in Table 1.

Fourthly, the two operators show difference when comparing price levels of unit cost. $2\bar{\theta} - \underline{\theta} = 2\underline{\theta} + 1$, whereas $\underline{\theta} \geq 0$, under this condition, the China Mobile's price p_1 is higher than cost definitely, namely, monopoly profit is obtained; the China Unicom's price p_2 may be higher or lower than the cost, which is mainly determined by the difference level of consumers' quality preference: when the difference level is high relatively, $\bar{\theta} - 2\underline{\theta} \geq 0$, namely, $\bar{\theta} \geq 2\underline{\theta}$, or $\underline{\theta} \leq 1$, price of China Unicom is higher than its cost, so China Unicom is profitable; however, when consumer's demand for quality of minimum consumption is low relatively, $\bar{\theta} - 2\underline{\theta} \leq 0$, namely, $\bar{\theta} \leq 2\underline{\theta}$, the China Unicom's price is lower than its cost based on model calculation, under this condition, its production will stop when price is lower than its unit cost. Certainly, in that way, price equals to unit cost and there is no profit.

6.2. Demand or market share change

Based on Eqs. (3) and (4), there are some conclusions as following:

Firstly, the demand only has relation with the coefficient of consumers' quality preference and no relation with other parameters such as quality difference. On the whole, $2\bar{\theta} - \underline{\theta}$ and $\bar{\theta} - 2\underline{\theta}$ represent difference of consumers' quality preference to some extent; therefore, the larger the difference of consumers' quality preference is, the more the market demand for the two operators. Secondly, if it is assumed $\underline{\theta} \geq 0$ and $\bar{\theta} = \underline{\theta} + 1$, market demands for two operators can change into $D_1 = (\underline{\theta} + 2)/3$ and $D_2 = (1 - \underline{\theta})/3$ that indicates the influences of the coefficient of consumers' minimum quality preference $\underline{\theta}$ on two operators' market demand is asymmetric, and no matter how much $\underline{\theta}$ is, the market demand for China Mobile is always greater than zero; whereas China Unicom has to face the fact that its market demand equals to zero when $\underline{\theta}$ is near to 1. Actually, China Mobile will obtain the whole market share in the mobile communication realistic market, there is no market share left for the other. The conclusion explains that an operator who offers low quality products will be expelled by fierce competition in price when the difference of consumers' quality preference is little relatively and the coefficient of consumers' preference on minimum quality is large relatively, namely, equals to 1. The low quality product offered by the entrant cannot compete with high one offered by the first mover. However, if the entrant decides to offer high quality products, it will evoke fierce competition in price which suppresses the increase of demand related with improvement in quality (Valletti, 1999). And it also indicates that there is a favorable condition for China Unicom when the difference of consumers' quality preference is large relatively and the coefficient of consumers' preference on minimum quality is little relatively. Thirdly, the proportion of market demand between the two operators $D_1/D_2 = ((\underline{\theta} + 2)/3)/((1 - \underline{\theta})/3) = (\underline{\theta} + 2)/(1 - \underline{\theta})$, $D_1/D_2 = 2$ when $\underline{\theta} = 0$ that shows the market demand for China Mobile is two times that of China Unicom's, or China Mobile takes 2/3 of the whole market share, whereas 1/3 is left for China Unicom. It is noteworthy that, as Table 1 indicated, the actual demand proportions of mobile communication market between China Mobile's and China Unicom's are very close to the result of model calculation.

6.3. *Profit change*

At last, based on the Eqs. (5) and (6), the following conclusions concerning profit can be drawn: 1) profit of enterprise is proportional to the difference of quality Δq, and is also positive correlation to square of the difference of quality preference. Namely, the larger the difference of product quality and the difference of consumers' quality preference, the more profitable for the two operators; moreover, the difference of consumers' quality preference has an amplification effect (when the value of the difference is greater than 1) or reduction effect (when value of the difference is less than 1). 2) Because $2\bar{\theta} - \underline{\theta} - (\bar{\theta} - 2\underline{\theta}) = \bar{\theta} + \underline{\theta} \geq 0$, the profit of China Mobile is always higher than China Unicom's. It can be concluded by further analysis: China Mobile can obtain profit definitely when $2\bar{\theta} - \underline{\theta} > 0$; whereas the profit of China Unicom depends on the difference level of consumer's quality preference. When the difference of consumer's quality preference is large relatively, namely, $\bar{\theta} - 2\underline{\theta} > 0$, or the coefficient of minimum quality preference $\underline{\theta} < 1$, China Unicom is profitable; However, when the difference is little relatively, namely, $\bar{\theta} - 2\underline{\theta} < 0$, market share of China Unicom equals to zero, its profit also equals to zero (without considering sunk cost and excluding price-below-cost possibility). In this way, China Mobile obtains the one unit market share totally and profit $\bar{\theta}\Delta q/2$.

3) It is assumed that the two operators' are both profitable (positive profit), and profits' proportion is related to the difference of consumers' quality preference. When the difference of consumers' quality preference is large relatively, namely, $\bar{\theta} - 2\underline{\theta} > 0$, profits' proportion between the two operators equals to $((2\bar{\theta}-\underline{\theta})/(\bar{\theta}-2\underline{\theta}))^2 = ((\underline{\theta}+2)/(1-\underline{\theta}))^2$, when $\underline{\theta} = 0$, the profits' proportion equals to 4. Namely China Mobile's profit is 4 times of China Unicom. If combined with the above proportion relation on market share, when $\underline{\theta} = 0$, 2 times of market share and 1.25 time of price, it should be 2.5 times of income, whereas 2.5 time of income is corresponding with 4 times of profit, that indicates product cost reduces sharply because of scale effect.

4) We discuss amplification effect of $\underline{\theta}$ on profit. According to calculation formula of profit proportion $((\underline{\theta} + 2)/(1 - \underline{\theta}))^2$, as the only parameter to determine the proportion value, $\underline{\theta}$ is plus subject in numerators, whereas minus subject in denominators, in this way, $\underline{\theta}$ change will amplify the change of profit proportion value. Due to square calculation on the numerator and denominator subject, amplification effect of $\underline{\theta}$ will double increase at product way. Amplification effect of $\underline{\theta}$ can be calculated by derivation on the formula of proportion relation, namely, $6(\underline{\theta}+2)/(1-\underline{\theta})^3$, let us call it the amplification coefficient of profit proportion. For instance, When $\underline{\theta} = 0$, profit proportion equals to 4, the amplification coefficient of profit proportion equals to 12; If $\underline{\theta} = 0.7$, the amplification coefficient of profit proportion equals to 600. The larger the $\underline{\theta}$ is, the more obvious the amplification effect.

6.4. Operation strategy change

The result of two oligarchies competition in Bertrand model leads to complete competition. Under this competition model's condition, the two enterprises cannot pursue profit maximum by choosing and adjusting some of variables, so there is no operation strategy in fact.

Based on the two oligarchies competition model after considering difference of product quality, there are operation strategies to realize more profit which can be adopted in enterprise' operation under the condition of game equilibrium. Supposing the two enterprises aiming at profit maximum, according to the Eqs. (5) and (6), an operator can adopt operation strategy which is shown in two parts: firstly, by enhancing the difference of product quality. Because quality difference is proportional to profit, the larger the difference of product quality, the more profitable the two enterprises; when $\Delta q = 0$, the profits of two equal to zero too. Therefore, when product quality of an enterprise is certain, the two can both obtain more profit through one of the operators enhancing or reducing its product's quality to increase the difference in quality. In this way, the game equilibrium result in product quality of two enterprises leads the two oligarchies competition model after considering difference of product quality into two-stage game, namely, there is competition in quality before price competition (Shaked and Sutton, 1982). It is assumed that there exists a quality interval $[\underline{q}, \bar{q}]$ which covers all consumers, and q_i must belong to the interval $[\underline{q}, \bar{q}]$, the initial states of quality of two are q_1 and q_2 respectively, and $q_2 \leq q_1$. At the first stage, Operator 1 chooses q_1 to make profit function $\Pi(q_1, q_2)$ maximum; Operator 2 adopts q_2 to make profit function $\Pi(q_1, q_2)$ maximum. Based on the profit function formula: the larger the difference of product quality, the more profitable for operators. Therefore, whatever the quality strategy adopted by the other, the optimal selection of Operator 1 is to enhance quality to the upper line $\bar{q}$. Correspondingly, the optimal selection of Operator 2 is to reduce the quality to the bottom limit $\underline{q}$. Therefore, there are two pure Nash-equilibriums of game in quality in theory, namely, $\{q_1^c = \bar{q}, q_2^c = \underline{q}\}$ and $\{q_1^c = \underline{q}, q_2^c = \bar{q}\}$. To analyze further, the profit obtained by offering high-quality product is always larger than that obtained by offering low-quality product, and it is assumed that there is a time difference in entering the market; therefore, the optimal selection for the first mover is to choose the product with high-quality $\bar{q}$, the second mover can only choose to offer the product with low quality $\underline{q}$. In this way, the only strategic combination of game equilibrium in quality is generated (Jean, 1997). Difference on quality can mitigate competition in price, so it makes operators more profitable. For mobile communication service products, they are asked for no defect for the basic communication functions; therefore, the subject that how operators could do to show difference in different quality service products to consumers and get their acceptance has different answers in different countries (Penard, 2002).

Secondly, the difference of consumers' quality preference is corresponding to the difference of enterprise's quality. According to profit function formula, the larger the difference of consumers' quality preference, the more profitable for enterprise, so in order to pursue profit maximum, enterprises must have operation strategy for consumers. Certainly, consumer's preference vary from person to person, however, enterprises still have many ways such as marketing to effect consumers and lead to generate more difference of consumers' quality preference. On the whole, different consumers' groups hold different quality preference, how to design corresponding service products that lead consumers to find value of difference in quality is an important subject that needs enterprise to deal with (Anckar and Incau, 2002). On the other hand, if the consumption of mobile communication service views as one of daily necessities, the whole level of consumers' quality preference on mobile communication service product will increase as the economic development, namely, the coefficient of minimum quality preference $\underline{\theta}$ will increase too, but quality difference may reduce, in other words, the whole trend of economic and society development will reduce the difference of quality preference on mobile communication service product and the profit of mobile communication enterprises. It is noteworthy that the influence of difference level of quality on enterprise is asymmetric, as what we discussed above: only when difference of consumers' quality preference exists, the enterprise which offers high-quality service product can always obtain positive profit; on the other hand, for enterprise which offers low-quality product, it can obtain positive profit only when difference of consumers' quality preference is enough large, namely, $\bar{\theta} - 2\underline{\theta} > 0$. Therefore, the enterprise which offers low-quality product has more reasons to pay more attention and resource to effect and enhance the difference of consumers' quality preference.

Thirdly, we discuss changes of price and output strategy. Different with the result of Bertrand model, the two oligarchies competition model considering the difference of product quality indicates the asymmetric Nash-equilibrium for price and output (demand). According to the calculation formula of equilibrium price and demand, the two strategies above which is beneficial to enterprise's profit maximum are also suitable for the strategies of price and output (demand): the larger the quality difference, the higher the equilibrium price of enterprise; the larger the difference of consumers' quality preference, the larger the market demand (output) of enterprise. However, to enhance the quality difference cannot be adopted as one of enterprise's pricing strategies, because increase of equilibrium price cannot account for price change; moreover, it leads to a series of changes in demand and price after considering the time dimension. Why we discuss about the strategy of price and output? Because it may help existed enterprises to review their price and output after multiple games, this paper does not make a further analysis on this subject.

6.5. Effects of switching cost and time dimension

After establishing the competition model considering difference of product quality and analyzing on calculation result based on the model, we make a brief analysis on possible changes of the model and conclusion when considering switching cost and time dimension, which can help to make the development on the model and the conclusions above.

When considering switching cost s, if and only if $\theta q_1 - p_1 = \theta q_2 - p_2 - s$, consumers show no difference on product or service that were offered by two enterprises. Based on the modeling mechanism above, we can consider to establish the two oligarchies competition model considering the product quality and switching cost, then get calculation result from corresponding game equilibrium. On the whole, the calculation formulas of equilibrium price, demand, and profit show no fundamental change after considering the switching cost. The equilibrium price of China Mobile is higher than China Unicom's, the two equilibrium prices increase or decrease the same $1/3 s$ comparing to the foundation of original price; the market demand for China Mobile is higher than China Unicom's, the two market demands increase or decrease the same $1/3 s \Delta q$. Because the price and demand of China Mobile are higher than China Unicom's after considering the switching cost, correspondingly, China Mobile's profit is also larger than China Unicom's after considering the switching cost. Certainly, it is beneficial to China Mobile which offers high-quality product after considering switching cost. Therefore, there are just some changes of quantity fluctuation for the calculation result above, and the conclusion above shows no fundamental change.

The effect of time dimension is very important, although time dimension does not introduce in the model, this article considers the result of dynamic game between the two operators in its analysis as possible. Product mix and price strategy are two important factors in the time dimension, and this article explains their change trends and interaction. Admittedly, the interaction between the two operators is very complicated, some researchers have analyzed on this field preliminarily (Chen, 2005; Ning et al., 2006).

7. Evaluation and Suggestions of Competition Strategy for Mobile Communication Enterprises

By combination with the actual data and experience of China Mobile and China Unicom, we analyze and verify the model above and rationality of the conclusion above, in this way, evaluation and suggestions for operation strategies of the two enterprises are put forward.

8. Evaluation of Competition Model and Strategy for Mobile Communication Enterprise

Combined with actual competition situation of mobile communication market domestic and overseas, many researchers have discussed enterprises' competition model, utilizing actual data to exam and explain their models (Valletti and Cave, 1998; Wen-Chueh et al., 2004). Based on the actual data of China's mobile communication market, this article makes Experimental analysis on the model and its calculation result, and then explains the actual data based on the model's calculation result.

8.1. Explanation on operation states of China Mobile and China Unicom based on the model above

As shown in Table 1, the data of price, market share, and profit of China Mobile and China Unicom are far away from the result of Bertrand model, but basically corresponding on the calculation result of the Eqs. (1)–(6).

Firstly, in the aspect of price, as data of Table 1 indicated, the average prices of China Mobile are always higher than China Unicom, which is consistent to the different value between the Eqs. (1) and (2). Although prices of the two have decreased, their size proportion relation shows

Table 2. Comparison between calculation and actual data on price.

Term	2001	2002	2003	2004	2005	2006	2007	Avg.
China Mobile: Average tariff (RMB/min)	0.60	0.56	0.41	0.31	0.28	0.24	—	0.40
China Unicom: Average tariff (RMB/min)	0.54	0.44	0.33	0.26	0.24	0.21	—	0.33
Proportion between actual tariffs	1.11	1.27	1.24	1.19	1.17	1.14	—	1.17
Calculation result based on model	1.21	1.21	1.21	1.21	1.21	1.21	—	1.21

no change. After making Rational Simplification and assumption for parameters, the proportional relation between calculation result and actual data can be listed and calculated as following:

During the term "Calculation result based on model" in Table 2, it is assumed that the coefficient of minimum consumer's preference $\theta = 0.2$. Because the quality difference of unit product Δq equals to the effectiveness difference between high-quality product and low quality one, the effectiveness of low-quality product is assumed to equal to its cost c, whereas the cost of high-quality product equals to c, but its effectiveness is 1.5 time of cost c, and $\Delta q = 1.5c - c = 0.5$, in this way, based on the above relation formula of price proportion, $P_1/P_2 = (3c + 2.3\Delta q)/(3c + 0.7\Delta q) = 1.21$. After comparing the calculation result based on the model to actual prices proportion and analyzing, it can be found that the actual prices proportion is very close to the calculation result based on the model, which demonstrates the model's explanatory power for practical case. Generally, consumer's evaluation value on the effectiveness of high-quality product and the coefficient of minimum consumption preference θ will rise gradually as economic and society development. According to calculation formula of proportion, changes of these two factors have totally opposite effects on proportion value; therefore, it is not easy to draw a conclusion.

Secondly, in the aspect of demand, we can get a conclusion based on the Eqs. (3) and (4) that the market demand for China Mobile is greater than zero, whereas the market demand for China Unicom is greater than zero with conditions. The market demand for China Unicom equals to zero when the difference of product quality preference is little relatively, namely, $\bar{\theta} - 2\underline{\theta} \leq 0$. When it is assumed that there are market share for the both operators, namely, $\bar{\theta} - 2\underline{\theta} > 0$, the proportion between calculation result and actual data is simple relatively, that is $(\underline{\theta} + 2)/(1 - \underline{\theta})$, if $\underline{\theta} = 0$, namely, there exist consumers who accept service at any quality level, so the proportion equals to 2, if $\underline{\theta} = 0.2$, namely, there exist consumers who accept service at minimum quality level, and the proportion is 2.75, as shown in Table 3 below.

Demand proportion of the two operators shows in the term 'Calculation result based on model' in Table 3 when $\underline{\theta} = 0.2$. Although there is little difference between actual data, it still holds explanation power. 1) A stable value exists in both calculation result based on model and actual data; consumers can choose operators when there is price difference or price difference has relative change; however, market demand proportion shows no obvious change and maintains a stable proportion at two times. 2) Effect of the value of $\underline{\theta}$ on market demand proportion is obvious, according to calculation formula, $\underline{\theta}$ is plus subject in numerators, whereas minus subject in denominators, in this way, $\underline{\theta}$'s change will evoke much more change on proportion. The smaller the $\underline{\theta}$ is, the more close between calculation result based on model and actual data. In Table 3, why actual figures from early years (such as 2001, 2002) and late years (such as 2006, 2007) are closer to calculation result based on model than the middle's? That may be relevant with changes of enterprise marketing's objects and consumers' value. If two operators both focus on developing low-end quality market such as rural and campus markets, coefficient of consumers' minimum quality preference will decrease; therefore, the proportion of market demands will be large. On the other hand, like other product markets, low-end quality product market depends on relative value. If consumers find the relative value of low-end quality communications product, the coefficient of quality preference may

Table 3. Comparison between calculation and actual data on market share.

Term	2001	2002	2003	2004	2005	2006	2007	Avg.
China Mobile (%):	71.69	63.32	63.67	64.56	65.87	67.90	70.41	66.77
China Unicom (%):	28.31	36.68	36.33	35.44	34.13	32.10	29.59	33.23
Proportion between actual market share	2.53	1.73	1.75	1.82	1.93	2.12	2.38	2.04
Calculation result based on model	2.75	2.75	2.75	2.75	2.75	2.75	2.75	2.75

be adjusted by them automatically, in this way, market demand proportion will increase.

3) In the aspect of profit, when the difference of consumers' quality preference is relatively large, namely, $\bar{\theta} - 2\underline{\theta} > 0$, as we mentioned above, according to calculation formula of profit proportion $((\underline{\theta} + 2)/(1 - \underline{\theta}))^2$, it shows that there is a stable relation on profit proportion of the two operators. As the only parameter to determine the proportion value, the amplification effect of $\underline{\theta}$ is very obvious, in other words, the value of profit proportion is sensitive to the change of coefficient $\underline{\theta}$. In order to using the same coefficient in all verifying analysis, the above table shows the profit proportion calculation result based on model when $\underline{\theta} = 0.2$. There is a difference between calculation result based on model and actual data.[a] However, it is not far away. In addition, the result in Table 4 is still reasonable when considering amplification effect or sensitiveness to profit of $\underline{\theta}$, and neglecting other factors' effect.

8.2. Operation strategy of the two enterprises in line with the conclusions of the model

Compared the analysis conclusion based on the model with the actual operation strategies of enterprises, there are two consistent points.

Table 4. Comparison between calculation and actual data on profit.

Term	2001	2002	2003	2004	2005	2006	2007	Avg.
China Mobile: Profit before tax (million RMB)	41,006	49,367	53,637	60,634	74,711	93,145	124,725	71,032
China Unicom: Profit before tax (million RMB)	—	6,192	5,823	6,105	6,527	8,445	13,155	7,708
Proportion between actual data	—	7.97	9.21	9.93	11.45	11.03	9.48	9.85
Calculation result based on model	7.56	7.56	7.56	7.56	7.56	7.56	7.56	7.56

Explanatory notes:
1. Lack of China Unicom's profit data in 2001.
2. Profit before tax data in Table 4 is consolidation on the two operators' annual financial reports.

1) In the aspect of choosing and combined state of product quality, the first mover has chosen to provide high-quality products, the entrant has provided low-quality products, the quality strategy combination of China Mobile and China Unicom is $[\bar{q}, \underline{q}]$, which is consistent with the analysis conclusion based on the model completely. China Mobile and China Unicom have entered the mobile communication market in 1987 and 1994 respectively, China Mobile as the first mover has given priority to the provision of high-quality product $\bar{q}$, while China Unicom mainly has had to provide low-end product $\underline{q}$, and thus the two have formed the significant difference of product quality Δq. The formation of such combination may not be the results strictly in accordance with the above model of a conscious action in the products' quality in China Mobile and China Unicom. However, as the result of long-run competition and development, the combination can certify the above conclusion based on the model.

2) The two enterprises are both interested in product differentiation. According to the model's analysis result, product differentiation can alleviate competition in price (Busse, 2000), providing profit to enterprise. Unlike the quality or vertical differentiation mentioned in the model, in the actual competition, the two enterprises have utilized not only vertical differentiation, but also horizontal differentiation, namely, varieties differentiation. Comparatively speaking, China Mobile focuses on vertical differentiation and China Unicom concentrates on horizontal differentiation. Take China Mobile for example, Under the corporate vision of "become the creators of excellent quality" and corporate brand of "China Mobile — mobile communications experts", China Mobile developed three large customers Products of the "GoTone," "M-Zone," "Easy-own" and other business products of "Mobile Monternet," "E-solution," etc. thus it has created a product portfolio in three dimensions with different series products. As a core product, the "GoTone" has gone through a process of from simple strategy to brand products, which is a process of continuously approaching the ceiling of the quality $\bar{q}$. In 1990s, China Mobile concentrated on intensive work of the "GoTone" brand and locates "GoTone" as "dependable." It also creates dependence on demand from the aspects of experts' quality, successful people's choice and support of the critical moment. In addition, China Mobile takes the appropriate

advertising strategy, highlighting its differences with the differences quality of competitors, and guides consumer's awareness of quality preference. For example, "Good signal, good mobile," "I can," etc. Those advertising languages indicated its feature of high quality completely.

9. Suggestions to the Competition Strategies in China's Mobile Communications Enterprises

From the analysis shown above, the operation status and strategies of China Mobile and China Unicom are rational as a whole. They have accorded with the model of two oligarchies competition considering the difference of product quality. However, these two enterprises have not consciously exercised their strategies as analyses and suggestions based on the model. There are analyses concerning operation strategy in the following aspects.

9.1. *Strategy adjustment in difference of product quality*

Firstly, China Mobile and China Unicom should make difference respectively in the aspect of high- and low-quality products. China Mobile need not expand low-end product, at the same time, China Unicom need not expand high-end product. This will mix up their quality difference, debase consumers' using evaluation of the difference in quality, namely, it will reduce the difference of product quality Δq and thereby reducing each benefit. If an enterprise wants to implement the product and quality differentiation strategy based on game equilibrium in clarity, the strategy value of differentiation should be realized from competition advantage, price accordance, etc., (Manuel *et al.*, 2006). Compared to high-quality service of China Mobile, China Unicom has not concentrated on providing service for low-end market intentionally. China Unicom may have a misconception that the quality of their own is not as better as competitor; it will damage its benefits in guiding and developing the consumer's preferences in the difference of quality. Actually, comparative value of product is what consumers accept with. Like there are different quality product markets in automobile market obviously, and low-quality products may achieve greater success than high one, low-quality is just a operational strategy.

Secondly, the product's difference should give priority to function instead of the tariff structure, vertical differentiation in stead of horizontal differentiation. Monopolist of multiple products has advantage to sell more products, so when pricing one of products above than its marginal cost, it will create demand on other products artificially (Mazzeo, 2002). At present, China Mobile and China Unicom put out many different service products. However, those products have not enough difference in basic function. Instead, they made difference in tariff structure, which is what we called "tariff package". Therefore, the two enterprises actually do not execute competition of difference in the quality, but indirectly competition of price. The result of such competition is the same with the result of Bertrand model. In addition, for mobile communication service, there is no fundamental difference among products, so no foundation for complete horizontal differentiation. The two operators have emphasized on the difference level of their products, but that neglected consumers cognition degree on the product quality or vertical differentiation, so there are no benefits for getting larger market and profit (Day and Wensley, 1998). Based on that quality, standard depends on average effectiveness, namely, evaluation value of quality marginal effectiveness is different to evaluation value of average effectiveness. When marginal effectiveness' evaluation value is greater than average effectiveness,' the phenomenon of "oversupply" in quality will occur, whereas there is the other extreme when "undersupply" in quality (Jean, 1997). Due to the communication product involving a series services, there are some problems for a product such as "oversupply" in some services but "undersupply" in others. Recently, China Mobile have been complained to provide much SM service to consumers who really do not need.

9.2. To expand consumer's preference to the difference of quality

If the product differentiation strategy has not been utilized in the two operators' operation automatically, they have ignored the differentiation strategy of consumers' quality preference totally. From the model above, we can see that consumer's preference to the difference of quality has effect to the price of enterprise, market demand and profit, especially for China Unicom. In such situation when consumer's preference to the difference of quality is not obvious, China Unicom will face the result of no market demand. As a whole, the more obvious consumers' preference to the difference of quality, the more profits is. Therefore, enterprise needs to guide and expand consumer's preference to the difference of quality consciously (Kim, 2003).

From the aspects of development strategies, especially marketing strategies, these two enterprises have not realized it. Based on experience goods' product attribute, operators in other countries have realized that brand, price, and advertisement should be considered as a whole one (Caves and Greene, 1996). China Mobile's marketing is switched from technical features such as network coverage to the shape of enterprise's image. Moreover, China Unicom has not given prominence to its quality features, which helps display its standing value of consumer's preference on the quality level and add consumers' approbation on its product quality. To the opposite, both of them have stressed brand building. Although the processes of brand building is one important aspect in developing the consumer's preference to the difference of quality, the two enterprises have not stressed this aspect. Instead, they made their brand building from the angle of switching cost. They believe that in this competitive world, win the new consumers by brand and foster their loyalty is the key point for China's mobile communications market. Without propaganda and guidance, consumer did not know how to use and how to handle in some products and businesses. Therefore, the rates of using are low, and also lack the abilities of guidance and create new demand or product. In fact, according to the switching cost we considered above, the switching cost has only made some numerical changes in the growth of price, market share, and the amount of profits, whereas no fundamental change in conclusion. China Mobile benefits from the switching cost. From this point of view concerning brand building, China Mobile should concentrate on switching cost, whereas difference of consumers' quality preference for China Unicom.

10. Summary

Combined with the actual competition condition in China's mobile communication market, this article analyzes the Bertrand paradox issues in China's mobile communications market and points out reasons from six aspects in bringing the serious issues. After considering the quality difference in the establishment of the two oligarchies competition model. This article analyzes the calculation results from three aspects, price, market demand, and profit. Moreover, they are compared with the actual competition result of China's mobile communications market. The results showed that the model calculation is in line with actual data of China's mobile communications market, which demonstrates the model's explanatory power for practical competition case. According to the analysis results of model calculation and comparison, this article made an evaluation to operation strategies in China's mobile communications market and put forward two suggestions to adjust the strategy of products' quality differentiation and promote the development of the consumer's preference in the difference of quality.

Acknowledgments

Fund project of China education ministry new century excellent talents support plan: Oligarchy Monopoly Enterprise Competition Strategy (No. NCET–07–0124).

References

Anckar, B. and Incau, D., 2002. Value creation in mobile commerce: findings from a consumer survey. *Journal of Information Technology Theory & Application*, (4/1).

Bezzina, J. and Penard, T., 2000. Dynamic competition in the mobile market, subsidies and collusion. Working Paper.

Busse, M., 2000. Multimarket contact and price coordination in the cellular telephony industry. *Journal of Economics and Management Strategy*, 9(3).

Caves, R. and Greene, D., 1996. Brands' quality levels, prices, and advertising outlays: empirical evidence on signals and information costs. *International Journal of Industrial Organization*, 14(1).

Chen, Y.L., 2005. Analysis on game of 'price way' in China's mobile communication market. *Market Weekly Economics*, (4).

Day, G.S. and Wensley. R., 1998. Assessing advantage: a framework for diagnosing competitive superiority. *Journal of Marketing*, 52(Apr.).

Jean, T., 1997. *The Theory of Industrial Organization* (Chinese versions). Chinese Renmin University Press, Beijing.

Kim, Y., 2003. Estimation of consumer preferences on new telecommunications service: IMT–2000 service in Korea. *Korea Association for Telecommunications Policies*, (10).

Li, X.H. and Tang, X.D., 2006. Explanation on competition between China Mobile and China Unicom: double oligarchs price competition. *Economics Management*, (7).

Manuel, E., Sergio, R., and Jorge, P., 2006. Business development strategies for wireless broadband operators: the need for mobility integration towards profit returns. *International Telecommunications Society ITS 17th European Regional Conference* (August).

Mazzeo, M., 2002. Product choice and oligopoly market structure. *Rand Journal of Economics*, (33).

Ning, L.J., Sun, Q.M., and Zhang K., 2006. Analysis and suggestions on reasons of 'price way' in China's mobile communication market. *Comparative Economic & Social Systems*, (2).

Oz, S., 2002. A quick-and-easy method for estimating switching costs. *International Journal of Industrial Organization*, (20).

Penard, T., 2002. Competition and strategy on the mobile telephony market: a look at the GSM business model in France. *Communications & Strategies*, (45).

Shaked, A. and Sutton J., 1982. Relaxing price competition through product differentiation. *Review of Economic Studies*, (49).

Valletti, T. and Cave, M., 1998. Competition in UK mobile communications. *Telecommunication Policy*, 22(2).

Valletti, T., 1999. A model of competition in mobile communications. *Information Economics and Policy*, (11).

Wang, Y., 2006. *The Research of Customer Churn of China Mobile Company in S City*. Northwestern University, Xian.

Wen-Chueh, H., Pei-I, Y., and Tung-Lai H., 2004. A study on competitive advantage for mobile phone operators in Taiwan. *Taipei Technology University Academic Journal*, 37(1).

Wu, Y.T., Zhang, Q., and Li, Y., 2002. Game analysis of asymmetric competition in oligopoly market of telecommunications. *Quantitative & Technical Economics*, (2).

Zhang, L.N., 2006. *Price Regulation in Telecommunication Industry and Application Research in China*. Southeast University, Nanjing.

Building Chinese "World-Class Enterprises": The Advantages, Paths, and Strategy Choices

Hailin Lan

School of Business Administration,
South China University of Technology,
Wushan, Guangzhou 51064, China
bmhllan@scut.edu.cn

This paper principally discussed how to improve the international competitiveness of Chinese companies. Some typical strategic practices were analyzed by a case study of four Chinese companies. Using the concept "world-class enterprise" (WCE) and relevant international strategy theories, this paper proposed the necessity to develop WCE that results from country-specific advantages (CSAs) and firm-specific advantages (FSAs) in China. At last, it is concluded that several basic paths and alternative strategies for shaping Chinese WCE, which not only can help Chinese companies to formulate strategy to compete in world market but also can make theoretical contributions in the Chinese circumstance.

Keywords: International strategic management; World-class enterprises; Country-specific advantages.

1. Introduction

Recently a book named *"Dragons at Your Door"* attracted a wide attention aboard. In the book, Zeng and Williamson (2007) studied several global leading Chinese companies, such as CIMC, Galanz, and so on. While overseas media denounced the quality of Chinese products, these authors reminded Western companies that "Forget the idea that the rise of Chinese competitors simply means cheap, low-quality imitations flooding world markets. Chinese companies are starting to disrupt global competition by breaking the established rules of the game". This view is admirable in my opinion. Several Chinese companies rank at the top of industries or particular business because they have well-honed skills in paring down costs and squeezing the maximum benefit from limited resources. That is why they deserve to be called "world-class enterprises" (WCE). In the initial confrontation with multinational companies (MNCs), several Chinese companies competed against and entered traditional MNCs' territory. Although a few Chinese WCE exist, they do provide good examples for other Chinese companies to refer. Summarizing the successful practices and adopting some theoretical guidelines, business management scholars can provide some steps and strategic choices to develop a WCE. This will take effort, but it is worth doing now to improve the overall Chinese companies' international competitiveness.

2. Theoretical Background

2.1. *The concept of WCE*

WCE concept can be traced back to 1987, proposed in *Telecommunications* magazine. But till 1995, Professor William Newman, the former chairman of Academy of Management, firstly introduced this concept into China at a seminar held in Chengde. He said "China needs to develop its own WCE in competitive industries."

Clearly, Professor Newman was telling the truth based on three reasons. Firstly, at that time China had already possessed a state-running and lack-competitive "Global 500" company. Despite its large scale, this company hardly manifested itself in global competition. Secondly, as a fast-growing developing country, China had potential to breed world competitive companies by market competition instead of government planning. Thirdly, Chinese companies' ability is emerging at that time. Professor Newman noted that they should not aim for "World Fortune 500" judged by volumes and turnovers, but WCE in particular business because the second objective is more realistic and suitable.

With this in mind, I defined WCE as those ranking at the global leading positions of particular businesses. And it can be characterized by seven features as follows:

1. *Appropriate scale*: In initial stage, Chinese companies' intent to build huge business scale easily leads to a high degree of diversification and scatter their limited resources and ability. On the contrary, WCE just develops appropriate scale.
2. *High product quality and performance*: At first thought, Chinese companies mainly excel by low cost; however, logical this argument may be, it just skims the surface of the problem. Too much emphasis placed on cost advantage, for a long term, may obscure other facts to build international competence.
3. *Participating global competition*: Since a majority of MNCs entered China market and Chinese companies went abroad, a would-be WCE must be able to compete with global challengers or market incumbency.
4. *World standard operation*: A large number of Chinese companies benefited from government supports, incomplete market, and institutional deficiencies. But it is doubtful to approach WCE by these advantages. In the long run, WCE must highlight world standard operation.
5. *Cross-culture or cross-border management*: As economy globalization prevails, WCE in particular business or niche market also needs to compete and allocate resources transcending national borders. Therefore global view or cross-border management must be attached great importance.
6. *High flexibility*: Company's competence stems from its abilities to seek, satisfy, and maintain customers. If so, those would-be WCEs ought to have a keen eye for the change of customer need and maintain high flexibility and dynamics in terms of knowledge management, financial plan, organizational structure, and corporate culture.
7. *Making clear trade-off*: Provide that either opportunity or threat exists during the China's transition economy; those would-be WCEs must understand the importance of trade-off and make concentrated efforts. Because of this, they are expected to put the limited resources in right place and right time, so as to build and maintain core competence.

After 1998, Chinese companies increasingly felt compelled to focus on prime business areas and to build around core of shared competence. Affected by this thought, many of them began to write "to be WCE" in their strategy intent. For instance, Kelon aims to be WCE in making refrigeration appliance and CIMC's strategic intent reveal its ambition to be WCE in producing transport equipment.

2.2. Country-specific advantages

Why could Professor Newman foresee that Chinese WCE would emerge at the very beginning of transaction economy? The answer, in his view, is the country-specific advantages (CSAs) in China. Using case study method, we concluded several types of CSAs.

2.2.1. Cost advantage

It is commonly believed that the cost advantage is the main source of competence of Chinese companies. By cost advantage, firstly, native companies attracted foreign capitals, techniques, and human resources flowing into China, therefore formed manufacture sector at Chinese coastal areas; secondly, cheap labor moving from inner to coastal areas or plants moving from coastal to inner areas can secure more international industry transfer; thirdly, if Chinese companies buy foreign companies' unprofitable business in Western companies' portfolio capital and make it profitable again in China, there are only two options for Western companies: to exit market or go in China as well. Although currently economic globalization and international market, to some extent, undermine Chinese advantages in term of land and row material cost, the comparative advantage of human resource in China is expected to last long.

2.2.2. Large markets scale

As Western scholars depict, with a population of over 1.3 billion, China is a huge "elephant". If Chinese need some products, the huge demand would boost equivalent supply, therefore form many large manufacture center and stir other related industries rapidly. And in turn, other industries might be world leading by large supply. In this sense, China's large markets can facilitate Chinese companies to obtain either economy of scale or learning curve, which is indispensable to form world competitive cost advantage.

2.2.3. *Market structure advantage*

Since opening up, many MNCs, attracted by considerable market potential, entered and competed in the Chinese market. Meanwhile, a large group of SMEs, of different ownerships, ran their business flexibly and reinforced the competition level. So, in this highly intense, dynamic, and complex market, pulling ahead of these numerous rivals is no easy task, Chinese companies, naturally, not only got lot of experiences, but also established their own competencies in market interactions.

2.2.4. *Talent advantage*

The talent, mainly from three sources, is another advantage to develop WCEs in China. Firstly, Chinese higher education, especially of engineering, is relatively outstanding in the world; secondly, foreign-owned company, joint ventures, and cooperative enterprises help China train a large number of workers, engineers, and managers; thirdly, an increasing amount of foreign-born Chinese and overseas students return to China to work or invest. In sum, available human resources have bridged the gap and will continue to shorten the distance between Chinese and Western companies in terms of management, technology, and experience, ultimately enhancing Chinese companies' ability to innovate.

2.2.5. *Transition economy*

Many studies show that Chinese companies, during the process of economic change, normally suffer from the insufficient institutional deficiency and incomplete market economy. However, practical experiences reveal that centrally planned method, to some extent, is still working especially when government displayed its tremendous strength and speed to support an industry, or any companies. By this token, companies can also benefit from incomplete market, asymmetric information, and unequal opportunities at a certain time. So that having effective access to these kinds of available opportunities proves a source of specific advantages.

After nearly 30 years of reform and opening up, some critical Chinese CSAs have changed and needed reassessments. Rising costs underlines innovations and differentiations. If we combine cost advantage and innovation, therefore adopt cost innovation strategy, it might more likely to approach WCEs.

2.3. Firm-specific advantages (FSA)

Apart from CSAs necessary for being WCE, it is dispensable for going and competing oversea that company transfers CSAs into firm-specific advantages (FSAs). Chinese existing WCEs have proved that only by large-scale manufacturing, in a certain industry or product, Chinese companies can transform market scale advantages into the manufacturing cost advantage; only by controlling market, even monopoly, Chinese companies can maximize the profit by cost advantage; and only by continuous inputs to innovations Chinese companies can ultimately form integrative advantage in either cost leadership or differentiation. Therefore, based on FSAs, Chinese companies can find an effective way of achieving China's number one, then global number one, to develop into WCE.

To be WCE, a company must rely on the unique advantages to get largest share within a particular or niche market. This thought was proposed by Western scholars at Wharton West where a small seminar about Chinese enterprises was organized in 2002. Seminar participants hold a widely accepted view that before entering WTO, China mainly confronted difficulties in how to enhance the vitality of the market; therefore, the main driving force of economic development is the increasing number of companies and competitions among them. Although the economy in this period grew prosperously, there are several problems to all industries, such as the excessive number of companies, the low industry concentration, cut-throat peer competition, and decline of the industry average profit margins. Contrary to this situation, after entering WTO, China urgently need to address the issue of how to increase the international competence. Just as the United States in early 20th century developed some monopoly companies, such as DuPont, General Electric, and General Motors. Once we have such kind of monopoly companies that dominate in domestic market, it is likely to suppress the occupation of Chinese market by MNCs, only then Chinese companies are able to go out and grow into WCE, or else China will lose a historic opportunity to be "multinational corporation". For this reason, Western scholars suggested that Chinese companies should conduct M&A to integrate industries.

Actually, what amazed Western scholars and managers is not Chinese WCEs' cost advantage, but their learning and innovation capacity. Chinese companies, by cost advantage, have forced Western companies out of mass market and standardization produce, and back to the high-tech, customized, and specialist products markets, which still yield high profit. However, when Chinese companies, in steps, move to up-market in the same economical way, hardly Western companies can maintain their high profitability in the high-tech, customized, and specialist products markets. Ming Zeng has depicted this kind of threat: "Chinese companies are starting to disrupt global competition by breaking the established rules of the game. Their tool of choice is cost innovation: the strategy of using Chinese cost advantage in radically new ways to offer customers around the world dramatically more for less." And he also questions Western managers, "imagine a world where high technology, variety, and customization, along with specialist products, are available to customers at dramatically lower prices; a world where the value-for-money equation offered to global consumers has been transformed by Chinese multinationals. Could you survive this kind of dramatic change in the competitive climate?"

3. Case Study and Analysis

Chinese emerging companies normally face many restrictions and temptations as they grow: local governmental protectionism limited their market expansions; undeveloped capital market and business governance blocked integrations in dispersed industry; and opportunity-driven action always led to an unrelated diversification strategy. But Chinese managers should rethink that, compare with Western companies, Chinese companies lack resources, abilities, and experience, so they have to focus on one market, make clear trade-offs and improve their performance, that is a right way to turn weakness into strength for a long term.

Illustrated in cases of China International Marine Containers Group (CIMC), Guangdong Galanz Group (Galanz), Shenzhen Han's Laser Technology (Han's Laser), and Guangdong Donlim Group (Donlim) (Table 1). These Chinese WCEs normally have two strategic features: Firstly, rational corporate governance prevents institutional interference and the opportunism and, to a large degree, ensures them to center resources and

Table 1. Descriptions of four companies.

	CIMC	Galanz	Han's Laser	Donlim
Year founded	1980	1978	1996	1988
Headquarter location	Shenzhen	Shunde	Shenzhen	Shunde
Company ownership	List company (IPO in 1994)	Private company	List company (IPO in 2004)	Private company
Number of employees	50,000	30,000	5,000	20,000
Total assets (billion)	22.923	18	2	2.5
Turnover (billion)	30	18	1.6	4
Sector	Containers, trailers, tank equipments, and airport equipments	Microwave ovens, air conditioner, induction cookers, rice cookers, electric kettles, oven	Laser marker, laser cutter, laser welder, laser show system, sub-surface engraver	Electric kettle, coffee pot, toaster, Western-style small household appliances
Industry status	The world's largest container-manufacturing group penetrated every segment of the container market	Globally leading centers of microwave oven, air conditioners, and household appliances	Han's Laser is a global leader in the manufacture of professional laser equipment. Striving hard	Chinese largest exporter of small household appliance
Market	Dominate 70% global market share of standard container; Chinese first boarding bridge manufacturer	Dominate 70% global market share of microwave ovens in 2006; top position in terms of sales volume and market share of microwave ovens in China for 13 years consecutively	From 2005 till now, world largest laser marker manufacturer; world's third largest PCB drilling machine manufacturer	Dominate the global largest market share of electric kettle more than six years, Chinese largest exporter of electric kettle, coffee pot, and mixer

ability on specific products or industries for a long term. These companies concern competitive edge and "being stronger" more than increasing rate and "being larger", they underline correlation among products or industries instead of profitable possibility of a single product or industry. Secondly, adopting focus strategy and market diversification to build "FSA" and core competence, these companies integrate cost leadership with innovation, therefore enhance their performance.

The consequences that follow these Chinese competitors are nowhere better illustrated than in the case of CIMC. Far from being an overnight success, it was initially established in 1980 as one of the first Sino-foreign joint ventures in China. After its first container rolled off the line in 1982, CIMC had been globally number one in 1996, today CIMC is six times larger than its biggest rival, dominating the world of shipping containers with more than 55% of global market share and penetrating other segments. Far from being just a low-end, volume producer, CIMC has displayed a constructive growing path and strategy choice into WCE by steps.

3.1. Cost management

During 1980 to 1990, a combination of inexperienced management and a downturn in the market led the CIMC near disaster; in 1986, its production was shut down and most of its employees were laid off. But going through this period, CIMC formed strong cost management competence by 10,000 TEUs volume. Up to now, driven by the cost advantage and economical belief formed in difficult time, CIMC has captured one segment after another and reinforced its cost advantage.

3.2. Rational corporate governance

CIMC was restructured in 1990, China Merchant Group and COSCO, serving as two biggest shareholders of CIMC; they have 45% of the company shares each, while the rest 10% was shared by foreign and native employees. Now CIMC's state-owned shares have been gradually diluted to 17%, shares owned by natural persons increased. Such governance structure prevents CIMC from government's interference, as well as obtains government supports. Furthermore, it keeps CIMC growing at a high rate and away off unrelated diversifications.

3.3. Financing advantage

An aggressive expansion plan enables CIMC to pull away from its Chinese competitors. Taking advantage of new regulations that opened the way for initial public offerings (IPOs) in China, CIMC was public listed on the Shenzhen Stock Exchange in 1993. After that, CIMC has sufficient money to implement cost innovation strategy at every critical moment of its development.

3.4. Manufacture and distribution network

After 1993, CIMC used the money raised in stock market to buy up eight to nine Chinese competitors near ports. These acquisitions enabled CIMC to build up an unmatchable manufacture and distribution network, strengthening its logistics advantages at low cost.

3.5. Low procurement cost

As CIMC formed unchallenged manufacture and distribution network, it integrated acquired companies and new subsidiaries into a unified procurement of raw materials, kick-starting a virtuous cycle in which strong bargain power continued to reinforce economy of scale and economy of scope.

3.6. Global marketing

During M&A processes, CIMC unified marketing management, stream-lined the processes marketing, and therefore achieved economy of scope.

3.7. Acquisition skills

Acquiring and integrating one target companies after another, CIMC becomes proficient and skillful. So that it can transfer this knowledge to its product diversification and international development.

3.8. Cost innovation

Based on focus strategy, large business volume, and good liquidity, CIMC can capture the technical trend and invest in relevant R&D, so that CIMC learned advanced technology and knowledge borrowed from others. But CIMC's objective went far beyond imitating an established player. Instead its strategy was used in its lower cost design and engineering resources to improve on the technologies, it had acquired as well as to apply them to create a broader product range than its global competitors. As a result, CIMC began to drive hard to increase its market share in order to kick off a new cycle of cost reduction through scale economies and learning. Similarly, having secured its scale and cost advantages in the production of standard containers, CIMC's strategy was to set the new global standards for container transportation and barriers to entry to move up-market and carve out a large share of more sophisticated products.

4. Conclusion

Combining CSA and FSA, Chinese WCEs ventured into the global market and become world number one only after they built a strong position in the Chinese market. This strategy was discovered by Western scholars; they suggest Western companies fight the emerging "dragons" aggressively on their own turf in China through setting overseas subsidiary or joint venture so as to get CSA as well. In fact, there have been small numbers of foreign companies that were clearly aware of the problem and have been in China for more than 10 years. Some Western brands have occupied over 60% market share in China's carbonated drinks, tire, cars, and mobile phones industries, so that there are less chances to emerge Chinese WCEs in these industries. And if Western companies realize this situation, foray into the China market through acquisitions and mergers, seek large-scale manufacture, and share cost advantage, Chinese companies will leave themselves exposed to great threat in the long term. And if leading Western competitors to build large volume, cost advantage, and variety of products unchallenged in China, Chinese competitors are likely to be storing up trouble and stand little chance of being WCEs. Therefore, facing and defeating global incumbents, those would-be global competitive Chinese companies should adjust to Western companies' new strategic change and learn from existing Chinese WCEs, that means they must focus on particular business area, deploy cost innovation strategy, conduct M&A, and secure market share.

References

Hailin, L., 2000. Interpreting "world class enterprises". *CEO in 21th Century*, (2), 62–63 (in Chinese).

Hailin, L., 2001. Steps to "world class enterprises" — study on strategy management of Chinese company. *Enterprise Management Publishing House*, Beijing (in Chinese).

Hailin, L., 2007. Study on the evolution of the conception of business groups in China. *Chinese Journal of Management*, 4(3), 306–311 (in Chinese).

Hailin, L., 2007. *Study on Strategy Behavior of Chinese Company of Transition Economy*. South China University of Technology Press, Guangzhou (in Chinese).

Zeng, M. and Williamson, P., 2007. *Dragons at Your Door*. Harvard University Press, Boston.

Part 4

Achievements in Information Technology and Knowledge Management

Empirical Study of the Viscous Knowledge Transfer Effectiveness in Software Enterprises

Lingling Zhang[*,†,‖], Anqiang Huang[*,†], Yang Liu[*], Jun Li[†,§],
Li Wang[‡] and Yong Shi[†,¶]

*Management School of Chinese Academy of Sciences, Beijing 1001902
† Research Center on Fictitious Economy and Data Science,
Chinese Academy of Sciences, Beijing 100190
‡ Beijing Institute of Development Strategy, Beijing 100081, China
§ YingDa TaiHe Property Insurance Co., Ltd. Beijing 100005, China
¶ College of Information Science & Technology,
University of Nebraska at Omaha, Omaha, NE, 68182, USA
‖ zhangll@gucas.ac.cn

As knowledge has become the most important resource of an organization, the related knowledge becomes a vital approach to acquire core competitive power. In order to improve knowledge-transfer effectiveness, people have to identify significant influential factors of knowledge transfer and pay special attention to them. Based on existing research results at home and abroad, integrated with W-S-R systematic theory, this paper advances a model of influential factors of knowledge transfer, carries out empirical study of some China software enterprises by handing out questionnaires and gets some influential factors in the real world and some original results.

Keywords: Knowledge transfer; Empirical study; Influence factor; Software industry.

1. Introduction

Corresponding to the globalization of economy, enterprises are facing a furious competition and knowledge has become one of the most important strategic resources of an organization (Nonaka, 1994; Grant, 1996; Simonin, 1999). The ability of developing, maintaining and nurturing competitive advantage is mostly dependent on the ability of creating, transferring and utilizing its knowledge (Drucker, 1999; Hoopes and Postrel, 1999). However, knowledge transfer may encounter impedance, and knowledge cannot be relatively transferred (Attewell,1992; Zhang, Li, Zheng *et al.*, 2008; Zhang, Zheng *et al.*, 2008). Especially technological knowledge is often sticky to local circumstance (Anderson, 1999). Knowledge is difficult to be transferred from its owners to acceptors (Wang, 2005; Zhang, Li, Shi. *et al.*, 2009).

Software industry is a kind of high-tech industry, where knowledge sharing and transfer are important components. Software industry of China has its unique characters: (1) They depend heavily on some certain experts. (2) The workers in software industry have a high fluidity. According to the report about workers of China software industry, issued by Labor And Social Security Bureau, Shanghai and China Software Association on Oct. 24, 2005, in China more than one half of software companies have a job-quiting rate of 20%, while 79.3% of software companies have a job-quiting rate of 10%. As a result, knowledge transfer is a key to a software company's business development and business security.

This paper investigated in some software companies in china and explores a number of factors with influence of knowledge transfer effectiveness. The meaningful results of this paper provides practical potentials.

2. Literature Review

Researchers have studied a lot of influential factors of knowledge transfer. Based on empirical research of 10 productive enterprises, Shedian (1985) advanced 4 key influential factors of knowledge transfer effectiveness: (i) circumstance characters, such as market scale, policy and rules, etc.; (ii) experience and management ability of knowledge providers and acceptors. As included in Table 1; (iii) the difficulty of technology; (iv) technology transfer pattern. Davenport and Prusak (1998) concluded the impeditive factors and the corresponding solutions in Table 1.

Zander (1991) argued that knowledge's tacitness and articulability can heavily influence the degree of the difficulty. Szulanski (1996) further pointed out that tacitness and articulability have more influence than any other factor in some given knowledge-transfering process.

Table 1. Influential factors and solutions.

Hindering factors	Solutions
Lack of trust	Talk face to face, set the relationship of trust
Different culture, language and reference schema	Set up common sense through education, talk, journal, team, claim, etc.
Narrow definition of productive power and lack of meeting place	Provide for knowledge transfer, such as time and place
Lack of understanding ability	Provide learning time, employ workers who can accept new knowledge fast
The belief that knowledge is privilege of some certain groups	Apply super-class knowledge strategy, the nature of thought is more important than its' source.
Attributing both position and praise to workers	Evaluate the performance of workers and provide inducement of knowledge
Can't tolerate errors and the fact that people must cooperate with each other	Accept and encourage creative errors and cooperative patterns. One will not lose his job even he/she knows nothing about something

Kaiming Wang (2000) analyzed the influence factors of knowledge transfer from the aspect of cost and found the result that knowledge transfer cost is related to not only the contents and characters of knowledge, but also the experience of senders and acceptors and the calculation of knowledge and ability, the social environment and systems. Wang and Wu (2001) argued that the factors involved in the knowledge transfer process include the willingness and the protection awareness and the trust in the acceptor of the sender, the receptivity of the acceptor, the cultural distance between the sender and the acceptor, and the nature of the being-transferred knowledge. Chen (2002) provided the concepts that the ambiguity of the knowledge, including the particularity and complexity, is the main K-I factor.

Chang and Zou (2000) explored and advanced the idea that the characters and contents of knowledge could influence the speed of knowledge transfer, and they argued that influence factors of knowledge diffusion speed include knowledge character and contents, the ability of expression of knowledge senders, the ability of absorbency of acceptors, the differentiation and complementarity of knowledge structure, the expected profit and the cost of knowledge transfer. Kuang (2003) analyzed impeditive factors in the process of knowledge transfer and application which include knowledge tacitness, the baffle of absorption and understanding, the embeddedness, the difficulty of knowledge transfer, the tacit skills of knowledge application. Zhou (2003) believed that influence factors of knowledge transfer come from the sender, the acceptor, the knowledge itself, the approach of knowledge transfer and the enterprise environment, and so forth. Lin (2009) investigated the process of knowledge and thought that impeditive factors include the knowledge itself, the willingness and ability of the owner of knowledge, the intensity of motivation and the absorption capacity of the acceptor, and the differentiation of culture.

3. Model and Hypothesis

3.1. *Model*

Gu (1998) proposed W-S-R systematic theory, which argues that people must simultaneously think about three aspects — W, S, R — when people want to deal with problems. W stands for characters of subjects, S stands for arrangement, and R stands for the factors that have close relationship with persons (Gu and Tang, 2006). In the area of knowledge management, W stands for characters of knowledge itself, S stands for the enterprise's organization, arrangement and rules, etc., and R stands for the characters of knowledge provider and acceptor. Using W-S-R systematic theory, we categorize influential factors into W-factors, S-factors and R-factors. Details are shown in Fig. 1.

Based on the existing findings, this paper advances some new influencing factors, and designed a research model of the mechanism that depicts how the influencing factors work on knowledge transfer effectiveness.

3.2. *Dependent variables*

This paper uses knowledge transfer effectiveness as the dependent variable. There are two criteria of evaluating knowledge transfer effectiveness. One is the degree at which people can conveniently acquire the knowledge they need. The other is the degree at which people is satisfied with knowledge transfer in their enterprise. The score of knowledge transfer effectiveness is equal to the average of the two criteria above.

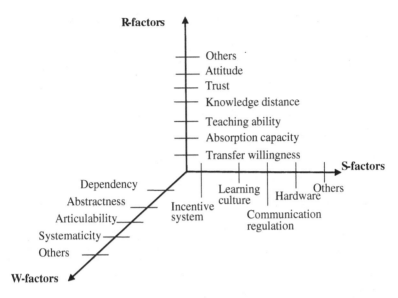

Fig. 1.   W-S-R factors.

3.3. *Independent variables*

According to W-S-R theory, we categorize the influencing factors of knowledge transfer effectiveness into W-factors, S-factors and R-factors as shown in Fig. 1.

3.3.1. *W-factors*

(1) Knowledge dependency refers to one of the characters of knowledge that knowledge clings to the particular people and environment. Once knowledge leaves the people and environment, it will lose its function. Knowledge dependency arises from knowledge embeddedness. Argote and Ingram (2000) argued that knowledge embeddedness comes from three aspects: members of organization, tools (including software and hardware) and task (reflecting organization's goal). Because of embeddedness, knowledge, especially tacit knowledge strongly clings to its environment and owner and is difficult to transfer from one person to another. The more strongly knowledge clings to its owner and environment, the more difficult it transfers, and thus the worse the

knowledge transfer effectiveness could be. Consequently Hypothesis 1 is developed as:

Hypothesis 1. Knowledge dependency is negatively related to knowledge transfer effectiveness.

(2) When knowledge is abstract, it will be very hard for people to express and learn it. Hakanson & Nobel (1998) found that knowledge observability and knowledge transfer vary with the same tendency. Considering the fact that when knowledge is abstract, it is also hard to be observed, this paper advances Hypothesis 2.

Hypothesis 2. Knowledge abstractness is negatively related to knowledge transfer effectiveness.

(3) Knowledge systematicity refers to the extent to which the transferred knowledge is integrated with other knowledge. A kind of knowledge with strong systematicity means to understand it needs to master more other kinds of knowledge. Consequently we have Hypothesis 3.

Hypothesis 3. Knowledge systematicity is negatively related to knowledge transfer effectiveness.

Knowledge articulability means that knowledge can be expressed by codes and scripts. The less effable knowledge is, the harder knowledge transfer could occur (Cummings J. L., Teng B. S., 2003). Encoded knowledge can be transferred more easily between organizations than what is difficult to be expressed (Kogut & Zander, 1992). Therefore we suggest:

Hypothesis 4. Knowledge articulability is positively related to knowledge transfer effectiveness.

3.3.2. R-factors

(1) Human is an indispensable factor of knowledge transfer, while human quality directly determines the effect of knowledge transfer and share. Cohen & Levinthal (1990) proposed the earliest conception of absorption capacity, and Zahra & George (2002) gave a further analysis that knowledge absorption capacity is a series of organizational lines and process in which company acquires, digests, transforms and utilizes knowledge to create dynamic organizational ability. Generally

speaking, most people accept the idea that absorption capacity promotes knowledge transfer. Therefore we hypothesize:

Hypothesis 5. Absorption capacity of acceptor is positively related to knowledge transfer effectiveness.

(2) Learning willingness has important influence on knowledge transfer (Shu, 2006). Assuming a person is reluctant to learn, knowledge transfer effectiveness can't be cheering even he has strong absorption capacity. As a result we hypothesize:

Hypothesis 6. The willingness is positively related to knowledge transfer effectiveness.

(3) Based on his research, Shu (2006) pointed out that both the owner's expressing ability and the willingness to teach affect knowledge transfer effectiveness heavily. According to this, we hypothesized:

Hypothesis 7. The expressing ability is positively related to knowledge transfer effectiveness.

Hypothesis 8. The willingness to teach is positively related to knowledge transfer effectiveness.

(4) A number of learners believe that trust between people plays a very important role in knowledge transfer because trust can facilitate knowledge transfer effectiveness. According to the research results by Kogut, Zander (1991), when people involved in KNOWLEDGE TRANSFER highly trust one another, they will protect less their knowledge, believe co-workers can bring them the prospecting profits, and is willing to teach their coworker really useful knowledge. With the same thoughts, acceptors tend to believe the ability and goodwill of the senders, trust the accuracy of knowledge and information offered by the senders, and consequently are inclined to absorb and use the transferred knowledge. Besides, Xu and Gao (2006) argued that through decreasing the transaction cost, trust substantially promotes knowledge transfer effectiveness. However, trust itself can not directly enhance knowledge transfer effectiveness, its substantial function is to increase the knowledge transfer willingness of both acceptors and senders, and then knowledge transfer willingness promotes knowledge transfer

effectiveness. Thus we assume:

Hypothesis 9. Trust is positively related to knowledge transfer effectiveness.

(5) Knowledge distance refers to the differentiation among knowledge transfer effectiveness bodies. Peng (2003) proposed that knowledge transfer effectiveness is a negative quadratic function of knowledge distance.

Hypothesis 10. The relationship between knowledge distance and knowledge transfer effectiveness follows a quadratic curve.

3.3.3. S-factors

Although many S-factors work on knowledge transfer effectiveness, this paper only cares about intra-organization factors as follows:

(1) One S-factor is hardware environment of an enterprise, such as intranet, case base, information management system, meeting room and so on. According to commonsense, it is reasonable to accept the idea that good hardware environment will arouse knowledge transfer effectiveness, and thus promote knowledge transfer effectiveness. Therefore we hypothesize:

Hypothesis 11. Hardware environment is positively related to knowledge transfer effectiveness.

(2) In case of expensive monitoring costs of tacit knowledge transfer, people must devise effective incentive system to encourage employees to share their tacit knowledge (Osterloh and Frey, 2000). Proper incentive system can enhance employee's knowledge transfer willingness, and make sharing knowledge into their conscious action. We hypothesize:

Hypothesis 12. Incentive system is positively related to knowledge transfer effectiveness.

(3) Organizational culture is the intrinsic quality of an organization, and the special mental brand which differentiates itself from others. Good organizational culture incessantly and imperceptibly educates and assimilates new employees so as to make them have the core quality of the organization. If an organization's culture permits "creative mistake", which is the mistake when employees try something

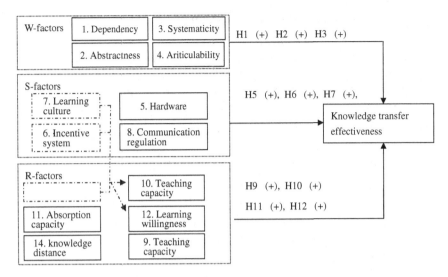

Fig. 2. Hypotheses of W-S-R.

new, arranges power and responsibility clearly, gives employees relatively enough time to think of new ideas, there will be a lot of knowledge transferred in the organization (Davenport and Prusak, 1998). Organizational culture can enhance knowledge transfer willingness and thus promote knowledge transfer effectiveness. So we hypothesize:

Hypothesis 13. Organizational learning culture is positively related to knowledge transfer willingness.

(4) When a new employee participates in an enterprise, he has a lot of new knowledge to learn, consequently the need for knowledge transfer is at its peak during this period. Under proper arrangement, new employees can learn fast the knowledge they need. Many enterprises have communication regulations, such as "communication meeting", which offer institutional guarantee of knowledge transfer. We hypothesize:

Hypothesis 14. Communicational regulation is positively related to knowledge transfer effectiveness. Based on 14 hypotheses above, we proposed the concept model of knowledge transfer as shown in Fig. 2.

4. Research Method and Data Collection

4.1. *Survey design and sample*

To test the hypotheses advanced in this study, we utilized a questionnaire survey method to seek response from six kinds of employees of the firms in our sample study. Through our review of the extant literature mainly reported in the Western academic journals, we identified key measurement items from several sources. We believe utilizing these previously validated measurements items would aid our study effectively.

We first compiled questionnaire in English, then translated it into Chinese. We consulted with business experts, who are three management professors at Management School of Graduate University of Chinese Academy of Sciences, to ensure the measurement items can reflect the fact Chinese firms face.

Our study population is composed of software firms in Beijing, Shanghai, Shenzhen, Tianjin and Haerbin. We undertook the main survey during winter 2008. We categorized firms into three kinds according to their scales, and split employees into six types. The details are shown in Table 2.

We provided our telephone number and email to informants to ensure that they can contact us in time whenever they have problems for filling the questionnaires. We handed out 100 questionnaires and 84 completed ones have been returned. After removing 6 of them with significant errors, we

Table 2. Statistics of employees and firms in the sample.

The scales of firms	Proportion (%)
<100	35
100~1000	35
>1000	30
Employee type	Proportion (%)
Management staff	22
Demand analyst	10
Program designer	13
Programmer	25
Tester	18
Else	11

had 77 valid questionnaires. We then contacted these informants to confirm their answers.

4.2. Reliability and validity analysis

Validity means that measurements in the questionnaire should actually weigh what we want to measure. In order to ensure the validity of this survey, we mainly applied the existing measurements published in several journals.

Reliability means that the results from the questionnaires should be steady, and the answers of questions under the same dimension should be in accord. People often use *Cronbach* α (Wang and Guo, 2001) to measure reliability, and believe that it is acceptable when *Cronbach* α is larger than 0.6.

We tested *Cronbach* α of W-factors, S-factors and R-factors, all of which were larger than 0.75, so we came to the conclusion that the reliability of this survey is acceptable.

4.3. Design of measurements

Based on many literatures, we chose some existing measurements and also advanced several measurements of our own. Parts of measurements are shown in Table 3.

5. Data analysis

5.1. Descriptive statistics

Through descriptive statistics, we found some interesting facts.

(1) The mean score of articulability is less than 3. Informants suggested that 30% of knowledge in software firms are difficult to express. The mean score of systematicity almost reaches 4, which implies that to understand knowledge in software firms requires much other knowledge. Consequently there is a lot of knowledge hard to be transferred in software firms.

(2) Learning culture, teaching willingness and learning willingness have high scores, while knowledge protection and self-respect problem got relatively low scores. This phenomenon shows most Chinese software

Table 3.   Measurement design and source.

Measurement	Meaning	Reference
Knowledge transfer effectiveness	1. At what degree people can acquire knowledge they want conveniently 2. At what degree people are satisfied with knowledge transfer in their firm	
Knowledge dependency	At what degree Knowledge is heavily dependent on particular environment, people and tools	Argote and Ingram, 2000
Knowledge abstractness	At what degree knowledge is vague and difficult to understand	
Knowledge systematicity	At what degree knowledge is integrated with other knowledge	Shu, 2006
Knowledge articulability	At what degree knowledge can be expressed by codes and scripts	Kogut and Zander, 1992; Cummings and Teng, 2003
Hardware environment	Enterprises should have some basic facilities for knowledge transfer, such as intranet, information management system, meeting room and so on.	Feng, Liu and Wang, 2006
Incentive system	At what degree employees are encouraged by incentive system	Osterloh and Frey, 2000
Learning culture	People will learn automatically when their live in a good learning atmosphere	Davenport and Prusak, 1998
Communication regulation	Enterprise have special rules to promote communication, for example a fixed-time meeting.	
Teaching ability	People can make themselves understood clearly	Shu, 2006
Teaching willingness	At what degree People is willing to teach others instead of protecting their knowledge	Shu, 2006
Absorption ability	People can learn and use new knowledge fast	Cohen and Levinthal, 1990
Learning willingness	How eagerly people want to learn	Shu, 2006
Trust	At what degree people trust their coworkers	Shu, 2006
Knowledge distance	The differentiation among Knowledge Transfer bodies	Peng, 2003

firms have good learning atmosphere, most employees neither refuse to consult others for self respect nor to secure their advantage over others through protecting their knowledge.

(3) Knowledge distance and systematicity have very high scores, which means employees in software firms have multi-discipline knowledge and their knowledge differs greatly.

(4) Teaching willingness have very high scores, compared to this, absorption capacity got low scores. One explanation is teaching willingness score was given by the informant himself (herself),[1] while absorption capacity scores were given by other informants.[2]

(5) The mean of "Firm's dependence on someone" is larger than 3. Statistically results suggested that 52% employees think the firm they are serving is heavily dependent on some expert.

5.2. One way ANOVA

(1) Influence of incentive method on knowledge transfer willingness.

Given the fact that employees on different positions get different incomes, happiness brought to them by money incentive is also different. In accordance with principle of diminishing marginal utility of wealth, employees with high incomes will weigh spiritual encourage more than material incentive. But to our surprise, the result of one way ANOVA suggested that there is no significant differentiation among employee on different positions and all employees prefer spiritual encourage. However considering that employees investigated may hide their real ideal of this issue, it seems to be more reasonable to keep the idea that people with low incomes prefer material incentive.

(2) Influence of firm scale on knowledge transfer effectiveness.

The scale of software firm is large, the same activities will correspondingly and frequently be repeated, and consequently the administrator has more motivation to pay more attention to knowledge transfer. It may be more reasonable to assume that the scale of firm is positively related

---

[1] Teaching ability question: "Are you able to articulate your thinking and make yourself understood?"
[2] Absorption capacity question: "Can others clearly give answers to your questions?"

to knowledge transfer effectiveness. The result of one way ANOVA indicates that the firm scale has no strong relationship with Knowledge transfer effectiveness, which means Chinese software firms, no matter how large the scales are, lie on a relatively low level of knowledge management.

5.3. Logistic regression analysis and conclusion

Our questionnaires were designed in the form of Likert Scale (Likert and Rensis, 1932), We use cumulative logistic regression model to testify our hypotheses advanced above.

We hypothesized that trust and incentive system and learning culture are positively related to teaching willingness and learning willingness above. In order to validate these hypotheses we calculated the correlation coefficients among 5 measurements. Details are shown in Table 4.

From the data in Table 4, we can conclude that trust, incentive system and learning culture are actually positively related to learning will, especially to teaching willingness. Hypothesis 9, Hypothesis 11 and Hypothesis 12 are validated.

In case of strong collinearity, we removed trust, incentive system and learning culture and used the remaining variables to set up model. Especially in order to testify Hypothesis 10, we added to model the variable "distance 2", which is equals to culture distance multiplied by culture distance. If the coefficient of "distance 2" is negative, then Hypothesis 10 is validated. After getting the result of model, we removed most variable who did not pass the test and used the remains to set up model, then we compared the results of the two models to check whether there is much difference between them or not.

Table 4. Correlation coefficients among 5 measurements.

	Teaching will	Learning will
Stimulus	0.78	0.26
Culture	0.65	0.35
Trust	0.68	0.39

Table 5. Results of hypotheses validation.

Hypothesis	Model I			Model II			Correlation analysis	Conclusion
	Coefficient	P-Value	Supported	Coefficient	P-Value	Supported	Supported	Supported
HP1(−): Dependency → KTE	0.11	0.75	No	—	—	No	—	No
HP2(−): Abstractness → KTE	0.28	0.33	No	—	—	No	—	No
HP3(−): Systematicity → KTE	−0.56	0.07	Yes	−0.48	0.1	Yes	—	Yes
HP4(+): Articulability → KTE	0.47	0.09	Yes	0.46	0.09	Yes	—	Yes
HP5(+): Absorption capacity → KTE	0.93	0.01	Yes	0.97	0	Yes	—	Yes
HP6(+): Learning willingness → KTE	0.68	0.12	No	0.64	0.13	No	—	No
HP7(+): Teaching ability → KTE	0.08	0.83	No	—	—	No	—	No
HP8(+): Teaching willingness → KTE	0.85	0.04	Yes	0.92	0.02	Yes	—	Yes
HP9(+): Trust → KTW	—	—	No	—	—	No	Yes	Yes
HP10: KTE is negatively related to the square of knowledge distance → KTE	−0.69	0.1	Yes	−0.57	0.16	No	—	Yes
HP11(+): Hardware → KTE	10.4	0.01	Yes	1.08	0	Yes	—	Yes
HP12(+): Incentive system → KTW	—	—	No	—	—	No	Yes	Yes
HP13(+): Learning culture → KTW	—	—	No	—	—	No	Yes	Yes
HP14(+): Communication regulation → KTE	0.98	0.01	Yes	0.9	0.01	Yes	—	Yes

Note: (1) The confidence level is 90%.
(2) "KTE" is short for "Knowledge transfer effectiveness".
(3) "KTW" is short for "knowledge transfer willingness".
(4)(−) represents a negative relationship, and (+) positive.

The results of model and model is as shown in Table 5, all the results have passed the related tests.

6. Conclusion

The final detailed results of hypotheses validation are shown in Table 5. According to the above analysis and Table 5, we came to the conclusions as follows.

(1) According to the result of analysis of variance, Chinese software firms contain a lot of sticky knowledge.

(2) Many Chinese software firms are highly dependent on one or two certain experts serving them.

(3) There is no notable difference of management levels among software companies in China. Compared with foreign companies, Chinese software companies, no matter how large they are, still at a relatively low level.

(4) Workers in software companies have more enthusiasm in studying, and won't quit opportunity to learn from others. They are willing to share the knowledge of their own. All of these make a solid basis of knowledge management.

(5) The result of the data suggests that employees' preference of the incentive methods (material methods or spirit method) has no significant difference, considering that people are inclined to hide their true ideas when it comes to the issue of money. However, we tend to accept the traditional idea that people on different positions attach different importance to material incentive.

(6) According to the result of the model, six variables, including articulability, systematicity, hardware, communication regulation, teaching willingness and absorption capacity, significantly promote knowledge transfer effectiveness. Knowledge distance significantly hinders knowledge transfer process and the coefficient of distance 2 is negative which means Hypothesis 10 is validated. Hardware, incentive system and learning culture are positively related to knowledge transfer effectiveness.

(7) Sorting the independent variables by the degree of influencing the dependent variable, we can get the descending result as follows:

hardware ≻ communication ≻ regulation ≻ absorption capacity ≻ teaching willingness ≻ systematicity ≻ articulability. Although the orders of knowledge distance in model and model are different, both of them are relatively high. Thus, knowledge distance has remarkable influence on knowledge transfer effectiveness.

(8) Model excluded three insignificant independent variables including abstractness, dependency and teaching ability. Comparing the results of model and Model, we conclude that abstractness, dependency and teaching ability have little influence on the dependent variable.

7. Summary

Through a survey, this paper has conducted an empirical study of the influencing factors of knowledge transfer effectiveness and made three significant contributions. First, we have studied the present knowledge management level of Chinese software firms and their existing problems, for the significance of applying knowledge management in Chinese software firms. Second, we have analyzed the characters of employees and their knowledge and cleared away people's misunderstandings. Third, we have found out the significant variables actually influencing knowledge transfer effectiveness and the order of these variables, which will permit people to distribute limited resources effectively and efficiently.

The future jobs can be two aspects: (1) knowledge transfer effectiveness should be evaluated by more measurements, such as: the improvement of economic criteria, the increase of firm's knowledge and so on. In this paper, with the data constraint, we only used two subjective measurements to evaluate knowledge transfer effectiveness, which may bring deviation from reality. Next step we will use comprehensive measurements, including subjective and objective criteria, to decrease the deviation. (2) The sampling data is not large enough. If we enrich our data sets, we may find more interesting results.

Acknowledgments

This work was partially supported by the President Fund of GUCAS (A) (Grant No.085102HN00). National Natural Science Foundation of China (Grant No. 70921061, 70501030, and 90718042), Beijing Natural Science Foundation (Grant No. 9073020).

References

Argote, L. and Ingram, P., 2000. Knowledge transfer: a basis for competitive advantage in firms. *Organizational Behavior and Human Decision Processes*, 82, 150–169.

Huang A.Q., Zhang L.L., Wang L. and Shi Y., 2007. The study on sticky knowledge transforming in enterprises based on W-S-R theory. *Chinese Journal of Management Science*, 15, 532–537 (in Chinese).

Baum, J.A.C. and Ingram, P., 1998. Survival-enhancing learning in the manhattan hotel industry. *Management Science*, 44, 996–1016.

Chang L. and Zou S.G., 2000. Knowledge management and formation of core competence of enterprises. *Science Research Management*, 21(2), 13–19.

Chen F.Q., 2002. Theory and descriptive research of enterprise knowledge. Alliance, Beijing Business Publisher: 43–45 (in Chinese).

Cohen, W.M. and Levinthal, D.A., 1990. Absorptive capacity: a new perspective on learning and innovation. *Administrative Science Quarterly*, 35, 128–152.

Cummings, J.L. and Teng, B.S., 2003. Transfering R&D knowledge: the key factors affecting knowledge transfer success. *Journal of Engineering and Technology Management*, 20, 39–68.

Davenport, T.H. and Prusak, L., 1998. Working Knowledge: How Organizations Manage What They Know. Harvard Business School Press, Boston.

Dong, X.Y., 2000. Knowledge transfer in enterprise informationization: the case of Lenovo. *Global Management Review*, 211, 28–35.

Feng, L.Y., Liu, Q., and Wang, X.Y., 2006. The formation and effective transfer of sticky knowledge. *Agriculture Network Information*, 3, 85–87.

Grant, R.M., 1996, "Toward a knowledge-based thory of the firm". Vol. 17, Special Issue: Knowledge and the Firm (Winter): 9–122.

Gu, J.F. and Gao, F., 1998. To See Wuli Shili Renli systems approach from the view of management science. *Systems Engineering Theory & Practice*, 8, 1–4 (in Chinese).

Hakanson, L. and Nobel, R., 1998. Technology characteristics and reverse technology transfer. Paper Presented at the Annual Meeting of the Academy of International Business. Vienna, Austria.

Kogut, B. and Zander, U., 1992. Knowledge in the firm, combinative capabilities and the replication of the technology. *Organization Science*, 3, 383–397.

Kuang, N.H., Hu, Q.Y., Yue, W.Y., and Du, R., 2003. A Framework of Orientation-Service-Inspiration for Knowledge-based Firms, Proc. of the 4th International Symposium on Knowledge and Systems Sciences (KSS'2003) and the 3rd International Workshop on Meta-Synthesis and Complex Systems (MCS'2003): 177–182.

Lane, P.J. and Lubatkin, M., 1998. Relative absorptive capacity and interorganizational learning. *Strategic Management Journal*, 19, 461–477.

Likert, Rensis, 1932. A Technique for the measurement of attitudes. Archives of Psychology 140, 1–55.

Lin, L., Zheng, X., and Ge, J.P., 2009. Study on the Knowledge Transfer Impacting Factors and Accelerating. Forum on Science and Techonolgy In China, 5, 39–43 (in Chinese).

Ma, Y.L., 2007. The empirical study on tacit knowledge transfer among management consultants. Xi'an University of Technology, Xi'an (in Chinese).

Muller, E. and Zenker, A., 2001. Business services as actors of knowledge transformation: the role of KIBS in regional and national innovation systems. *Research Policy*, 30, 1501–1516.

Nonaka, I., 1994. A dynamic theory of organizational knowledge creation. *Organ Sci* **5**, 14–37.

Osterloh, M. and Frey, B., 2000. Motivation, knowledge transfer, and organizational forms. *Organization Science*, 11, 538–550.

Peng, C., 2003. Knowledge transfer in regional innovation system: barrier and countermove. *Science and Technology Management Research*, 3, 166–169.

Shedian, E. H., 1985. Organizational culture and leadership. San Francisco: Jossey-Bass Senge.

Shu, L.B., 2006. Research on the process of knowledge transfer mechanisms and influencing factors in team. Zhejiang University, Zhejiang (in Chinese).

Simonin, B.L., 1999. Ambiguity and the process of knowledge transfer in strategic alliances. *Strategic Management Journal*, 20, 595–623.

Szulanski, G., 1996. Exploring internal stickiness: impediments to the transfer of best practice within the firm. *Strategic Management Journal*, 17, 27–43.

Wang, J.C. and Guo, Z.G., 2001. Logistic regression model-method and application. Beijing: Higher Education Press (in Chinese).

Wang, K.M. and Wan, J.K., 2000. Discussion on knowledge transfer and diffuse. *Foreign Economics and Management*, 10, 2–7

Wu, G.S. and Wang, Y., 2001. Sticky knowledge transfer in university-industry collaboration. *Science Research Management*, 6, 114–121 (in Chinese).

Xu, H.B. and Gao, X.Y., 2006. The mechanism that interpersonal trust facilitates knowledge transfer in organizational settings: an integrative framework. *Nankai Business Review*, 9(5), 98–106 (in Chinese).

Zander, U., 1991. Exploiting a technological edge: voluntary and involuntary dissemination of technology. Stockholm: Institute of International Business.

Zahra, S.A. and George, G., 2002. Absorptive capacity: a review reconceptualization an extension. *Academy of Management Review*, 27, 185–203.

Zhou, X.D. and Xiang, B.H., 2003. Internal transfer of enterprise knowledge: pattern, influence factors and mechanism analysis. *Nankai Management Review*: 7–10 (in Chinese).

Zhang, L.L., Li, J, Shi, Y., *et al.* 2009. Foundations of intelligent knowledge management. *Human System Management*, 28(4), 145–161.

Zhang, L.L, Li, J. Zheng, X.Y., *et al.* 2008. Study on a process-oriented knowledge management model. *International Journal of Knowledge and Systems Sciences*, 5(1), 37–44.

Zhang, L.L, Zheng, X.Y., *et al.* 2008. A Way to improving knowledge sharing: from the perspective of knowledge potential. *International Journal of Service Science and Management*, 10, 172–179.

Empirical Study on the Life Cycle of Web Information

Feicheng Ma and Yonghong Xia

School of Information Management,
Wuhan University, Luojia Hill, Wuchang 430072, China
fchma@whu.edu.cn

In this article, the life cycle of Web information is defined as the various phases and entire process of the Web information from the birth to out of utility value. The author selected representative Web sites such as Chinese academic resources, foreign academic resources, the forum, and news resources as the research objects. And this article uses citation analysis and hyperlink analysis to observe and record the phenomenon of the life cycle of Web information to reveal the basic laws and characteristics of the life cycle of general Web information.

1. Introduction

Web information generally refers to the kind of information unit, which is recorded in digital forms, expressed in multimedia format, attached to computer storage equipment, transmitted, identified and used through computer networks, and readily available during a certain period. Web information grows continuously and the new replaces the old constantly. The utility value of information loses gradually, which is called aging phenomenon in the information science community. Since Gosnell from the New York University explored the literature on aging phenomenon in 1943, many experts in this field have done extensive and in-depth researches, which have revealed the laws of information life evolution from a certain extent, and established a series of theoretical and mathematical models, and achieved some fruitful research results (Qiu, 2007).

Bar-Ilan and Peritz may be the first to attempt to study the dynamics of Web documents on a given topic over a period by using bibliometric methods for analysis. The results showed that substantial changes occurred to the "literature on the Web" on informetrics during this period. Three different trends were observed: documents disappear, others added to the Web and discovered by the search engines with time, and changes occurring to existing individual documents. These changes are mainly comprised of updates (Bar-Ilan and Peritz, 1999). Koehler considers two types of changes in Web pages and Web sites: content and structure. Finally, the study is concerned with understanding those constancy and permanence phenomena for different Web document classes. It is suggested that, from the perspective of information maintenance and retrieval, the WWW does not represent the revolutionary change. Web pages (or Web sites) demonstrate a significant variation in permanence and constancy. The Web page sizes contract and expand over time. In general, again like Web sites, Web pages on balance are increasing in size (Koehler, 1999). And in a four-year longitudinal study, Koehler revealed that (1) navigation pages have a better survival rate than content pages and (2) the longevity of a Web page is the complex function of domain type and page purpose. The findings suggest that we need to very closely examine the purpose, function, and use of Web pages and sites (Koehler, 2002).

Wang and Qiu point out that the main task of researches on the aging of Web information is to find out the indices of measure based on the research object and adopt various quantitative methods such as mathematical and statistical methods to make a quantitative description and statistical analysis of the aging of Web information to disclose its characteristics and inner law and further to establish corresponding mathematical model and put forward the theoretical interpretation system (Wang and Qiu, 2004). Based on analyzing the reasons and characteristics of obsolescence of Web information resources, Duan figured out that aging phenomenon should be considered in two aspects: the self-life cycle and the utilized degree. Static half-life, dynamic half-life, and lifetime are the indices to evaluate the self-life cycle; the macro-half-life and micro-half-life of Web information resources are the indices to evaluate the utilized degree (Duan, 2005).

In this article, we try to investigate the life cycle of Web information by empirical approaches. We select Chinese academic resources Web sites, foreign academic resources Web sites, the forum Web sites, news Web sites and top Web sites as the research objects, and use citation analysis and hyperlink analysis methods to observe and record the phenomenon of the life cycle of Web information to reveal the basic laws and characteristics of the life cycle of general Web information.

2. Method

2.1. The reasons of the aging of Web information

Web information aging means the attenuation of effective value and decrease of utilization ratio of intelligence in the Web information resources. Just as the aging of the traditional literature, aging is a widespread phenomenon (Duan, 2005).

The reasons of the aging of Web information are very complex and can be summarized as the following aspects:

1) Web information growth. As the total of Web information increases rapidly, the utilization ratio of each unit decreases, showing signs of aging. The former Soviet Union renowned intelligence scientist Mihailov notes, "At present, the growth, aging and discrete principles of the published articles, naturally, are regarded as the most fundamental principles that mark the development of scientific literature" (Qiu, 2007). The scientific literature not only grows, but also ages. Growing in the process of aging, growth is the main trend. The growth rate of Web information is extremely astonishing. According to the statistics of China Internet Web information Centre, by 31 December 2007, the number of Web sites in China has reached 1.5 million, with the annual growth rate of 78.4%; the total number of Web pages has reached 8.47 billion, with the annual growth rate of 89.4%, as Fig. 1 (The 21st China Internet Development Report, 2008) shows.

2) Web information update. Web information update refers to the changes in the content of knowledge and intelligence contained in the Web information, while the features, such as the vector form, the way of data organization and the URL are constant. The emergence of new Web information can accelerate the aging rate of the old. A research found that 97% of the sites would be changed within six months, and the proportion would rise up to 99% if the observation time has been one year. As to Web pages, the proportions were 98.3% and 99.1% (Zhao et al., 2005).

Hundred Million

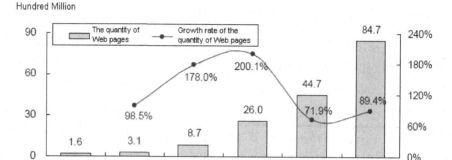

Fig. 1.   The growth of Web information in China.

3) Web information disappearance. Web information disappearance means the Web information is removed from the system, and can be accessed and used no longer, which means the end of the life cycle of Web information. A study showed that 68% of the Web pages would be removed from the Internet one year later; 12.2% of the Web sites and 20.5% of the Web pages could not be accessed any longer six months later, and the proportion would rise up to 17.7% and 31.8% after one year (Duan, 2005).

4) Web information pragmatic attenuation. Pragmatics refer to the utility value of Web information to the recipients. As to recipients, only the information demanded is worth transmitting. Even if the Web information is demanded, there is still a "saturation law or border effect" problem, that's to say, with the realization of the recipients' demands, although the objective value of Web information has not changed, the utility value to the recipients reduces, because of the similar information they have received (Yan, 1996). In addition, the value of Web information is restricted by time. Scientific theories, technical creation and economic information have periods of validity. If beyond the time frame, their values will disappear immediately.

There are also some other factors that affect the aging of Web information. The type, property, and development stages of Web information are the internal reasons; the advancement of science and technology, changes of users' demands, and social environment are the external reasons.

2.2. *Characteristics of the aging of Web information*

Compared to the traditional literature information, the aging of Web information shows some new characteristics, mainly include:

1) Rapidity. The rapidity of access and dissemination of Web information leads to the result that it will be exploited soon after publication, then replaced by new information quickly, aged because of lose of utility value. Generally speaking, the aging of Web information is much faster than traditional literature information.

2) Carrier independency. The external form and content of traditional literature are inseparable. Even if the information on carrier completely loses its utility value, the carrier usually will be saved, and the information will not disappear. Amendments and updates of the original information and the generation of new information will inevitably be accompanied by the formation of new carriers. Therefore, the quantity of traditional literature information is always increasing. But the external form and content of Web information can be mutual independent. Web information will usually disappear completely after losing its utility value, and new information is likely to overwrite the old, which does not necessarily mean the growth of the total quantity of information.

3) Dynamics. Information in the Web environment is a third category of information between two states: permanent existence and immediate disappearance after generation. Update and disappearance are the normal states of its existence and motion (Duan, 2005). The existence, update, and disappearance of Web information are a dynamic equilibrium system in the Web environment.

4) Complexity. Traditional literature is carrier dependent, which facilitates the relevant institutions' unified management, and control. But many characters of the Web information lead to complexity of the phenomenon of aging. So, it will be difficult to measure its quantity accurately and trace its historical states systematically.

The characteristics of the aging of Web information are closely linked and complemented by one another, and determined by the nature of Web information. The rapidity of the aging of Web information leads to its dynamics, and the dynamics and carrier independency result in its complexity.

2.3. The definition of the life cycle of Web information

Life cycle is originally a biological term, which means the various phases and entire process experienced by an organism from birth to death (CNKI academic definition, 2008). After extension and expansion, life cycle is widely applied in many fields, such as physics, engineering management, enterprise management and informetrics, and becomes an important research method, which divides the entire process from birth to death of the research object into several successive, even repeated stages.

Just as the aging phenomenon, Web information also shows obvious characteristics of life cycle. From the perspective of users' experiences, the author defines life cycle of the general Web information as the various phases and entire process of the Web information from the birth to out of utility value.

2.4. Citation analysis and hyperlink analysis

Citation analysis is a methodology that has many proponents that view it as a vital research area within the field (McDonal, 2007). An important application of citation analysis is the evaluation of performance, which is based on the assumption that citations indicate a positive sign of the value of the cited documents for subsequent research (Luukkonen, 1997). Though critics of citation analysis (Peritz, 1992; MacRoberts and MacRoberts, 1986, 1989) have long challenged the assumption that citations can be used as valid indicators of quality, utility or even impact, a compelling body of research findings have been achieved to support the core contention (Baldi, 1998; Braam, 1991). In some sense, the frequency a paper is cited can be used as a rough-and-ready indicator of its merit-granting, of course, variations in the citation's importance and the inevitable amount of error and noise. Consequently, citations can be viewed as legitimate objects of research (Peritz, 1992). As the famous academician of Chinese Academy of Science Zou notes, "We can't say that the higher the citation frequency, the greater the utility value, but generally speaking, the citation frequency is proportional to the utility value" (Zou, 2004).

Some studies have applied citation analysis and other bibliometric principles and techniques (often with modifications) to the analysis of characteristics and link structures of the Web (Zhao and Strotmann, 2007).

As Larson notes, "The notion of citation is fundamental both to the scholarly enterprise and to hypertext networks where it provides the primary mechanism for connection and traversal of the information space" (Larson, 1996). The principles of citation indexing find their echo in the dynamically reticulated structure of the Web, hence the proliferation of neologisms, such as cybermetrics, netometrics, webometrics and influmetrics, probably have the opportunities for measurement and evaluation in new environment (Kim, 2000). If citations can be tracked, counted and weighted, then why are not the links connected to Web sites (Cronin, 2001)?

2.5. Data sample and manipulation

Based on the previous discussion, we propose a hypothesis for the present empirical study: the more Web information is used, the more the topicality, and the higher the utility value; the less Web information is used, the less the topicality, and the lower the utility value. The forms of usage are various, such as citation, reading, comment, and link.

This article will collect data by the software NetGet and the search engine AlltheWeb through experimental observation, citation analysis, hyperlink analysis methods, and use Excel and SPSS for data processing and statistics to study the life cycle of Web information empirically.

We select China Journal Net, Wiley InterScience Platform, Strong China Forum of People's Daily Online, Netease News Center and Alex top 50 Web sites as the research objects, observe, record and analyze the situation of life cycle of the Web information in different types.

1. Citation of electronic documents in Chinese journals

Select published articles in 1994 from the main four kinds of Chinese journals of information science as concrete objects, and use the advanced retrieval functions of the China Journal Net to count the quantity of articles cited each year from 1994 to 2006, as Table 1 indicates (the data were acquired on 3 May 2007).

We take the data of each kind of journal for normalization. Let the year as abscissa, the average value of total times cited in each year as ordinate, and we can get the broken line as Fig. 2 shows.

Suppose that we can measure the utility value of literature information by its times cited, then Fig. 3 reflects the laws of changes in utility value

Table 1. Citation of articles in 1994 from the main four kinds of Chinese journals of information science.

Cited journals	Year												
	1994	1995	1996	1997	1998	1999	2000	2001	2002	2003	2004	2005	2006
Journal of the China society for scientific and technical information	3	46	56	26	26	19	16	9	8	7	13	8	6
Information science	8	25	24	20	22	11	14	15	11	8	5	14	12
Journal of information	6	37	33	15	17	9	11	4	9	9	3	8	7
Journal of information theory and practice	2	40	38	25	22	13	13	5	10	11	13	4	3

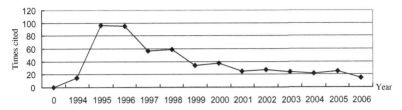

Fig. 2. Citation of articles in 1994 from the main four kinds of Chinese journals of information science.

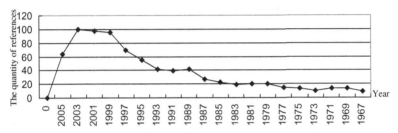

Fig. 3. The quantity of references cited each year from 1967 to 2006 by articles published in 2006 on Wiley InterScience platform.

of literature information with the time passing by. Just as Alvarez and Escalona point out that the topicality would be reflected in the citations that appear in the later papers. If a paper is being cited less over time, this points to a declining research interest in the work which is consequently losing topicality — it is becoming old or obsolescent. With "topicality," the behavior of the citations to papers published previously in the journals of an area of knowledge over a period has a common characteristic: at the beginning of the period, the number of citations rises, to be followed by a decline (Alvarez and Escalona, 2000).

2. Citation of electronic documents in foreign journals

Select the total references cited by articles published in 2006 on Wiley InterScience platform as specific subjects, and use the advanced retrieval functions of the platform to obtain the quantity of references cited in each year from 1967 to 2006, as Table 2 indicates (the data was acquired on 15 November 2007).

Table 2. The quantity of references cited in each year from 1967 to 2006 by articles published in 2006 on Wiley InterScience platform.

Year	2005–2006	2003–2004	2001–2002	1999–2000	1997–1998	1995–1996	1993–1994	1991–1992	1989–1990	1987–1988
The total number of references	1,317	2,063	2,017	1,957	1,423	1,144	853	796	841	554
Year	1985–1986	1983–1984	1981–1982	1979–1980	1977–1978	1975–1976	1973–1974	1971–1972	1969–1970	1967–1968
The total number of references	454	383	417	414	314	288	216	279	279	176

We take the data of each year for normalization. Let the year as abscissa, the total quantity of references cited each year as ordinate, and we can get the broken line as Fig. 3 shows.

As Table 2 and Fig. 3 show, the quantity of references cited by articles published in 2006 on Wiley InterScience platform diminishes as time moves forward. Suppose that we can measure the utility value of literature information in a certain year by the quantity of references cited, and Fig. 3 reflects the laws of changes in utility value of literature information with the time passing by.

3. The posts read

We randomly select 100 posts from the Strong China Forum of People's Daily Online published between 10 and 11 February 2008, and make a follow-observation. Use automatic recording function of the Web site and the software NetGet to obtain the read frequency of each post in every half an hour after publication (the total observation times are 20), and select the observational data of 20 posts most frequently read, as shown in Table 3.

We take the data of each column in Table 3 for normalization. Obtain the average of the data of each observation time. Let the observation times as abscissa, the average of the data of each observation time as ordinate, and we can get the broken line as Fig. 4 shows.

Suppose that we can measure the utility value of posts in forums by reading frequency, and Fig. 4 reflects the laws of changes in utility value of posts with the time passing by.

4. The news commented

We randomly select 100 pieces of news from the Netease News Center published between February 10 and 11 in 2008, and make a follow-observation. Use automatic recording function of the Web site and the software NetGet to obtain the commented frequency of each piece of news in every two hours after publication (the total observation times are 15), and select the observational data of 20 pieces of news most frequently commented, as shown in Table 4.

We take the data of each column in Table 4 for normalization. Obtain the average of the data of each observation time. Let the observation times as

Table 3. The posts read in the Strong China Forum of People's Daily Online.

Observation times	Posts ID																			
	1	2	3	4	5	6	7	8	9	10	11	12	13	14	15	16	17	18	19	20
1	15	26	6	28	64	30	31	46	11	14	5	17	25	32	15	21	12	10	23	6
2	33	49	7	15	63	42	50	57	15	11	5	25	55	50	7	16	23	14	38	15
3	78	61	6	1	48	50	47	50	16	7	2	41	38	22	11	11	13	15	44	6
4	54	145	0	1	25	66	35	13	30	5	3	35	29	2	2	3	2	27	20	2
5	29	1,586	0	0	13	74	27	2	16	4	0	23	11	3	0	0	0	16	4	0
6	41	1,174	0	0	11	32	21	7	18	2	0	2	4	1	0	0	0	24	8	2
7	28	262	2	3	21	35	16	0	13	0	0	4	13	2	0	0	0	15	12	0
8	17	375	0	0	11	13	11	2	9	0	0	6	9	2	1	0	0	13	7	0
9	6	228	0	0	4	9	10	0	7	0	0	13	10	1	0	0	0	3	6	3
10	10	154	0	0	8	8	3	0	3	0	0	19	0	0	0	0	0	4	2	1
11	19	29	0	0	11	0	1	0	1	0	0	9	4	0	0	0	0	4	39	1
12	6	19	0	0	5	2	0	0	0	0	0	5	3	0	0	0	0	8	0	0
13	5	14	0	0	3	0	0	0	0	0	0	3	0	0	0	0	0	8	2	0
14	2	11	0	0	1	5	4	0	6	0	0	1	0	0	0	0	0	2	1	1
15	3	0	0	0	0	9	3	0	4	0	0	0	0	0	0	0	0	2	0	0
16	1	8	0	0	0	15	7	0	7	0	0	0	0	0	0	0	0	5	0	0
17	0	8	0	0	0	10	5	0	3	0	0	0	1	0	0	0	0	0	0	0
18	1	0	0	0	1	14	23	0	2	0	0	1	3	0	0	0	0	0	0	0
19	0	18	0	0	2	22	16	0	13	0	0	1	0	0	0	0	0	0	0	0
20	0	33	0	0	3	11	8	0	0	0	0	1	0	0	0	0	0	0	0	0

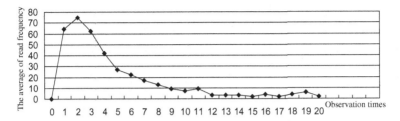

Fig. 4. The posts read in the Strong China Forum of People's Daily Online.

abscissa, the average of the data of each observation time as ordinate, and we can get the broken line as Fig. 5 shows.

Suppose that we can measure the utility value of news by commented frequency, and Figure 5 reflects the laws of changes in utility value of news with the time passing by.

5. Update of the links of top Web sites

We randomly select 10 Web sites from the top 50 Web sites measured by Alexa, that is Google, Windows Live, Microsoft Corporation, Wikipedia, EBay, Sina News Centre, Index, The Internet Movie Database, Seznam, and Megaupload. Use hyperlink analysis function of the Web site AlltheWeb to obtain the quantity of updated links based on time distribution (take every three days as a segment from 24 January 2008 to 23 November 2007, and the total observation times are 20), as Table 5 (the data were acquired on 25 January 2008) shows.

We take the data of each column in Table 5 for normalization. Obtain the average of the data of each observation time. Let the observation times as abscissa, the average of the data of each observation time as ordinate, and we can get the broken line as Fig. 6 shows.

Suppose that we can measure the utility value of information in top Web sites by the quantity of updated links, and Fig. 6 reflects the laws of changes in utility value of information in top Web sites with the time passing by.

3. Results

Record the broken lines from Fig. 2 to Fig. 6 as L1, L2, L3, L4, L5, integrate them in one figure, as shown in Fig. 7:

Table 4. The news commented in Netease News Center.

Observation times	News ID																			
	1	2	3	4	5	6	7	8	9	10	11	12	13	14	15	16	17	18	19	20
1	1	25	4	34	150	4	7	4	2	7	9	0	3	3	67	6	15	8	2	21
2	4	15	3	126	72	6	11	1	7	15	11	2	3	1	69	7	4	5	13	17
3	3	21	5	136	51	7	9	3	9	6	3	4	2	2	46	2	16	6	4	19
4	3	21	0	103	37	3	3	3	12	6	3	2	0	2	48	3	12	8	2	9
5	2	17	3	104	18	4	3	3	8	1	3	1	1	4	47	2	12	3	1	8
6	2	12	2	76	24	7	3	0	3	0	4	0	1	0	42	0	9	4	1	5
7	1	4	0	15	8	1	0	0	0	1	0	0	2	0	8	1	1	2	3	1
8	0	2	1	27	8	1	0	0	0	3	0	4	0	0	11	0	0	2	2	0
9	0	0	0	19	1	0	0	0	1	0	0	0	2	0	4	0	0	0	0	0
10	0	5	1	9	1	1	0	1	2	0	0	0	0	1	9	0	2	1	0	0
11	1	1	1	18	2	0	0	1	1	0	0	0	1	0	21	2	3	2	0	2
12	1	2	0	32	8	1	0	0	0	0	0	0	2	0	2	1	1	0	0	0
13	1	1	0	6	1	1	0	0	1	0	0	0	0	0	0	0	0	1	1	0
14	2	1	0	4	5	1	0	0	0	0	0	0	0	1	4	1	1	0	2	1
15	1	1	0	3	4	0	0	0	0	0	0	0	0	0	6	0	0	0	0	0

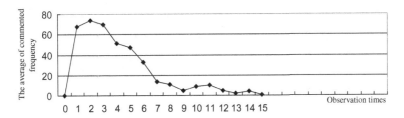

Fig. 5. The news commented in Netease News Center.

From Fig. 7, it is not difficult to find that although the five broken lines are not identical, the changes trends are similar. When Web information is released, its utility value will rise into the maximum very soon, and then attenuate gradually over a longer period, approaching zero.

On each broken line in Fig. 7, as the change trend on one side of the point with maximum ordinate is different from the other, we regard these points as boundaries, and L1, L2, L3, L4, L5 each can be divided into two broken lines, recorded respectively as L1a, L1b, L2a, L2b, L3a, L3b, L4a, L4b, L5a, L5b. Make regression analysis and curve estimates of the divided broken lines in Fig. 7, and the regression equations are shown in Table 6.

In Table 6, we can see that the fitting curves of L1a, L2a, L3a, L4a, L5a are quadratic curves, which can be recorded in the mass as

$$Yna = a0 + a1X1 - a2X1^2 \quad (n = 1, 2, 3, 4, 5)$$

The fitting curves of L1b, L2b, L3b, L4b, L5b are negative exponential curves, which can be recorded in the mass as:

$$Yn = Ke^{-ax2} \quad (n = 1, 2, 3, 4, 5)$$

The analytical data from SPSS shows that the goodness-of-fit of these curves is good, and the equations are highly and significantly effective.

If we take the average value of every three adjacent points' abscissa and ordinate respectively on L1 and L4 in Fig. 7 (the abscissa ranges respectively are [1, 12], [1, 15]), there will be corresponding new points, and these points constitute new broken lines recorded as M1 and M4 as shown in Fig. 8. Similarly, if we take the average value of every five adjacent points' abscissa and ordinate respectively on L2, L3 and L5 in Fig. 7 (the abscissa ranges are

Table 5.　Update of the links of top Web sites.

Observation times	Website ID									
	1	2	3	4	5	6	7	8	9	10
1	1,240	7,560	26,200	11,300	20,600,000	196,000	2,230	98,900	1,580	1,900
2	1,590	1,010	14,100	7,000	10,700,000	100,000	3,430	17,700	1,130	275
3	42,300	42,600	324,000	94,700	9,350,000	611,000	205,000	364,000	63,900	39,400
4	70,500	690,00	632,000	175,000	13,800,000	997,000	353,000	738,000	182,000	452,000
5	59,600	52,500	512,000	165,000	8,810,000	915,000	262,000	746,000	175,000	405,000
6	26,000	25,600	238,000	92,900	10,600,000	573,000	117,000	609,000	87,200	96,000
7	12,100	11,300	105,000	51,200	6,250,000	272,000	44,800	480,000	40,000	50,100
8	6,360	20,100	72,000	35,300	10,400,000	180,000	23,100	327,000	21,900	33,900
9	8,780	10,700	27,600	21,400	7,090,000	111,000	14,800	241,000	12,200	24,600
10	9,970	7,210	23,000	18,200	685,000	150,000	13,600	171,000	8,630	27,200
11	6,610	5,150	17,600	18,100	2,060,000	155,000	9,020	99,100	12,500	18,900
12	6,460	8,640	19,700	33,500	1,590,000	121,000	9,040	80,200	20,400	81,800
13	5,650	12,300	32,000	46,600	1,970,000	153,000	11,300	76,900	42,200	26,7000
14	4,060	9,080	26,000	34,800	869,000	76,600	61,300	61,000	35,100	237,000
15	1,330	5,080	21,400	18,800	2,640,000	133,000	31,100	161,000	19,400	76,500
16	990	2,620	26,800	9,740	2,120,000	57,200	13,700	124,000	8,600	51,900
17	1,110	2,560	12,700	7,770	659,000	105,000	12,800	44,800	6,470	51,200
18	1,080	2,710	11,500	7,790	774,000	72,000	11,400	112,000	5,250	55,000
19	2,120	2,120	19,100	6,220	346,000	67,400	11,100	109,000	4,700	54,700
20	848	1,550	14,400	4,740	196,000	86,000	8,700	89,900	4,460	44,800

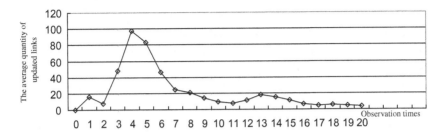

Fig. 6. Update of the links of top Web sites.

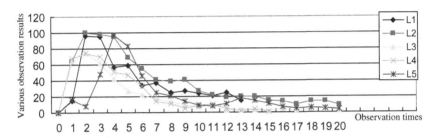

Fig. 7. Observational results of life cycle of Web information in five categories.

[1, 20]), there will be corresponding new points, and these points constitute new broken lines recorded as M2, M3, and M5 as shown in Fig. 8.

Make regression analysis and curve estimates of the broken lines in Fig. 8, and the regression equations are shown in Table 7.

In Table 7, we can see that the fitting curves of M1, M2, M3, M4, and M5 are negative exponential curves, which can be recorded in the mass as:

$$Yn = Ke^{-ax} \quad (n = 1, 2, 3, 4, 5)$$

The analytical data from SPSS shows that the goodness-of-fit of these curves is good, and the equations are highly and significantly effective.

We find that the negative exponential curves are appropriate to the negative exponential function proposed by Brookes in 1970. From a diachronic study, Mr. Brookes put forward that the attenuation process of the cited frequency of scientific periodical literature with the passage of time is

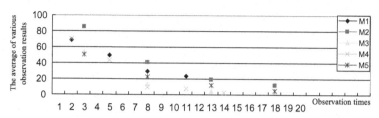

Fig. 8. The average of observational results of life cycle of Web information in five categories.

Table 6. Regression equations of the broken lines in Fig. 7.

Broken lines	Rsq	F	Sig.	Regression equations
L1a	1.000	0.000	0.000	$Y1a = 1.03E - 014 - 18.481X1 + 33.125X1^2$ $(0 \leq X1 \leq 2)$
L1b	0.895	84.979	0.000	$Y1b = 227.994 \times e^{-0.981 \times 2}$ $(2 \leq X2 \leq 13)$
L2a	1.000	0.000	0.000	$Y2a = 1.66E - 014 + 77.678X1 - 13.839X1^2$ $(0 \leq X1 \leq 2)$
L2b	0.952	334.010	0.000	$Y2b = 125.917 \times e^{-0.136 \times 2}$ $(2 \leq X2 \leq 20)$
L3a	1.000	0.000	0.000	$Y3a = -3.0E - 014 + 90.500X1 - 26.500X1^2$ $(0 \leq X1 \leq 2)$
L3b	0.818	76.435	0.000	$Y3b = 66.731 \times e^{-0.189 \times 2}$ $(2 \leq X2 \leq 20)$
L4a	1.000	0.000	0.000	$Y4a = -1.0E - 014 + 99.000X1 - 31.000X1^2$ $(0 \leq X1 \leq 2)$
L4b	0.914	128.331	0.000	$Y4b = 163.718 \times e^{-0.308 \times 2}$ $(2 \leq X2 \leq 15)$
L5a	0.955	21.185	0.045	$Y5a = 4.886 - 9.971X1 - 8.143X1^2$ $(0 \leq X1 \leq 4)$
L5b	0.803	61.301	0.000	$Y5b = 104.905 \times e^{-0.168 \times 2}$ $(4 \leq X2 \leq 20)$

approximately appropriate to the simple negative exponential function. The function can be represented as $C(t) = Ke^{-at}$, in which $C(t)$ represents the cited frequency of literature published t years ago; K represents a constant, varies with different subjects; a represents the aging rate of literature; t represents time (Brookes, 1970).

Table 7. Regression equations of the broken lines in Fig. 8.

Broken lines	Rsq	F	Sig.	Regression equations
M1	0.982	109.098	0.009	$Y1 = 88.769 \times e^{-0.125\times}$
M2	0.988	171.163	0.006	$Y2 = 119.460 \times e^{-0.132\times}$
M3	0.906	19.338	0.048	$Y3 = 72.214 \times e^{-0.187\times}$
M4	0.947	54.076	0.005	$Y4 = 149.743 \times e^{-0.302\times}$
M5	0.996	525.201	0.002	$Y5 = 77.667 \times e^{-0.146\times}$

4. Discussion and Conclusion

Based on the results of empirical analysis in Fig. 7 and Table 6, we can draw the Web information life cycle curve qualitatively, as shown in Fig. 9:

In Fig. 9, the horizontal axis represents time, and the vertical axis represents utility value. The curve qualitatively describes the approximate change trend in utility value of Web information from production to extinction. This article divides the process into three stages: growing period (as indicated in fragment AB), mature period (as indicated in fragment BC) and recession period (as indicated in fragment CD). Point A represents the production of Web information, and point D represents the extinction of Web information.

From Fig. 9, we can see that Web information quickly accesses into growing period soon after its production, the access amount rapidly rises, and the change trend presents the law of quadratic curve. Subsequently, Web information accesses into the mature period, and its access amount reaches the maximum. Its value will be fully utilized in this stage. Then

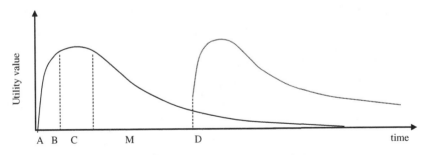

Fig. 9. Web information life cycle curve.

Web information accesses into the recession period, when access amount will gradually reduce and approach zero, and the change trend presents the law of power curve. Generally speaking, the length of A–B will be far smaller than the length of C–D, that is to say, the growing period is far shorter than the recession period.

Point M represents the case that Web information in recession period or even has died out is reactivated. It will begin a new life cycle, similarly, in accordance with the three stages of development, including growth, maturity, and decline. The cause of activation may be the update of Web information, changes in the external environment, and so on. For example, the content of a Web site is outdated and its access amount is very small due to the lack of management in a long time. Not until an institution takes over the Web site and strengthen its management and maintenance, does the access amount rise rapidly. Another example, a photo of more than 30 years' old is not necessarily of great value from the news point of view. But after the "9/11" incident, it became one of the most popular internet photos, because one person in the photo is considered as the appearance of Bin Laden when he was a child (Liang, 2004). For more instance, national confidential documents lose their utility value of confidentiality when they reach a certain age. But after the declassification and announcement, the documents' utility value rises rapidly, because there are many organizations and individuals interested in them, which will be collected and used.

In this article, we reveal the basic laws and characteristics of the general Web information's life cycle from the perspective of users' experiences and through empirical research methods, and divide the stages of Web information's life cycle roughly. However, Web information in reality is very complex. The overall ecological environment of Web information is constantly changing, and the differences among all types of Web information are very obvious. Further understanding of the characteristics of life cycle of Web information in different types, and applying the life cycle theory to effective management and reasonable utilization of Web information are significant subjects for further study.

References

Alvarez, P. and Escalona, I., 2000. What is wrong with obsolescence. *Journal of the American Society for Information Science and Technology*, 51(9), 812–815.

Baldi, S., 1998. Normative versus social constructivist processes in the allocation of citations: a network analytic model. *American Sociological Review*, 63, 829–846.

Bar-Ilan, J. and Peritz, B.C., 1999. The life span of a specific topic on the web — the case of "informetrics": a quantitative analysis. *Scientometrics*, 46(3), 371–382.

Braam, R.R., 1991. *Mapping of Science: Foci of Intellectual Interest in Scientific Literature* (DSWO Press, University of Leiden).

Brookes, B.C. 1970. The growth, utility, and obsolescence of scientific periodical literature. *Journal of Documentation*, 26(4), 283–294.

CNKI academic definition. Retrieved 27 January 2008, from http://define.cnki.net/define_result.aspx?searchword=%E7%94%9F%E5%91%BD%E5%91%A8%E6%9C%9F.

Cronin, B., 2001. Bibliometrics and beyond: some thoughts on web-based citation analysis. *Journal of Information Science*, 27(1), 1–7.

Duan, Y.F., 2005. Study on obsolescence of web information resources. *Knowledge of Library and Information Science*, (4), 28–31.

Kim, H.J., 2000. Motivations for hyperlinking in scholarly electronic articles: a qualitative study, *Journal of the American Society for Information Science*, 51(10), 887–899.

Koehler, W., 1999. An analysis of web page and web site constancy and permanence. *Journal of the American Society for Information Science*, 50(2), 162–180.

Koehler, W., 2002. Web page change and persistence — a four-year longitudinal study. *Journal of the American Society for Information Science and Technology*, 53(2), 162–171.

Larson, R.R., 1996. Bibliometrics of the World Wide Web: an exploratory analysis of the intellectual structure of cyberspace. In: S. Hardin (ed.), *Global Complexity: Information, Chaos and Control. Proceedings of the 59th ASIS Annual Meeting* (Information Today Inc., Medford, NJ, and ASIS).

Liang, Z.J., 2004. Phases to achieve information lifecycle management. *Science Technology for China's Mass Media*, (7).

Luukkonen, T., 1997. Why has Latour's theory of citations been ignored by the bibliometric community? Discussion of sociological interpretations of citation analysis. *Scientometrics*, 38(1), 27–37.

MacRoberts, M.H. and MacRoberts, B.R., 1986. Quantitative measures of communication in science: a study of the formal level. *Social Studies of Science*, 16(1), 151–172.

MacRoberts, M.H. and MacRoberts, B.F., 1989. Problems of citation analysis: a critical review. *Journal of the American Society for Information Science and Technology*, 40(5), 342–349.

McDonal, J.D., 2007. Understanding journal usage: a statistical analysis of citation and use. *Journal of the American Society for Information Science and Technology*, 58(1), 39–50.

Peritz, B.C., 1992. On the objectives of citation analysis: problems of theory and method. *Journal of the American Society for Information Science and Technology*, 43(6), 448–451.

Qiu, J.P., 2007. *Informetrics* (Wuhan University Press, Wuhan).

The 21st China Internet Development Report. Retrieved 27 January 2008, from http://www.cnnic.cn/uploadfiles/pdf/2008/1/17/104156.pdf.

Wang, H.X. and Qiu, J.P., 2004. Some issues concerning the research on the aging of web information. *Information Studies: Theory & Application*, (4), 433–435.

Yan, Y.M., 1996. *Modern Information Science Theory* (Wuhan University Press, Wuhan).

Zhao, R.Y., Duan, Y.F., and Qiu, J.P., 2005. Study on webometrics (Part 1) — status quo and trends of hyperlink analysis studies. *Journal of the China Society for Scientific and Technical Information*, (2), 181–192.

Zhao, D.Z. and Strotmann, A., 2007. Can citation analysis of web publications better detect research fronts. *Journal of the American Society for Information Science and Technology*, 58(9), 1285–1302.

Zou, C.L., 2004. Some views on the Sci-Tech Academic Journal. Retrieved 19 April 2008, from http://scitech.people.com.cn/GB/25509/55787/74836/74845/5085220.html.

Customer Analysis for Lube Oil Marketing Strategies: A Data Mining Approach

Quan Chen[*,†], Ling-Ling Zhang[*,†,‖], Jun Li[†,‡], Li Wang[§] and Yong Shi[†,¶]

[*] Management School, Graduate University of the Chinese
Academy of Sciences, Beijing 100190, China
[†] Research Center on Fictitious Economy and Data Science,
Chinese Academy of Sciences, Beijing 100190, China
[‡] YingDa TaiHe Property Insurance Co., Ltd. Beijing 100005, China
[§] Beijing Institute of Development Strategy, Beijing 100081, China
[¶] College of Information Science & Technology,
University of Nebraska at Omaha, Omaha,
NE 68182, USA
[‖] zll933@163.com

With the development of information technology, Knowledge Discovery in Database (KDD) or Data Mining (DM) has been widely used in our daily life. However, as for the marketing of lube oil, especially customer analysis of lube oil, the application of KDD is very limited at present. Therefore, this paper presents a customer analysis model for lube oil marketing. It first introduces customer segmentation model according to customer value, and establishes corresponding Evaluation Index System. Then the paper uses K-means clustering and Decision Tree for customer analysis. Based on the established customer analysis model, this paper analyzes the customer data of Great Wall lube oil in the Fujian area, classifies the customers into four categories, and explores the behavioral characteristics and marketing strategies of each category.

Keywords: Data Mining; Customer analysis; Cluster analysis; Decision tree; Lube oil marketing.

1. Concept of Data Mining

1.1. *Current research in data mining*

The word "KDD" first appeared in the first International Conference on KDD, which was held in Detroit, 1989. There were only a few dozen people who took part at that time, but these grew to 577 persons and 17 companies in 1997. At present, it is generally accepted that: knowledge discovery is to find novel, effective, and potentially available, and ultimately understandable patterns can be processed from large data sets (Fayyad *et al.*, 1996; Fayyad and Stolorz, 1997). In1999, the third KDD Conference was held in Beijing. With discussion and research, the conference demonstrated the rapid development trend of KDD. IEEE Journal of Knowledge and Data Engineering published a special issue on KDD technology in 1993. At present, the international research community also regards KDD as data mining. Specifically, given all types of real databases, data mining uses statistics, inductive learning, approximate reasoning, artificial neural networks, genetic algorithms, conceptual advance algorithm, associated algorithms, classification algorithms, rough theory, modern mathematical analysis and its integrated approach to explore useful information as knowledge.

Compared with international activities, domestic research on knowledge discovery started later, there is no overall strength. The National Natural Science Foundation of China (NSFC) first supported the research projects in the field in 1993. At present, many domestic scientific research units and institutions of higher learning compete to carry out techniques of data mining and applied research. In the applications, through access to literature, the main can be summarized as follows: (1) Knowledge Discovery in government decision making, scientific research, business decision making in various fields such as applied research; (2) the application of Knowledge Discovery in CRM, e-commerce, and such new areas; (3) knowledge discovery systems and software building; (4) the cross-penetration between knowledge and other subject, including relation with other disciplines (Chris *et al.*, 2002; Chen *et al.*, 2006).

Although the research on data mining techniques is not long, up to now is still a very new research topics, the speed of theoretical research and software development are very alarming. Data mining quickly has many successful applications for its potential to create huge economic benefit for the enterprises.

1.2. The application of knowledge discovery in customer analysis

Knowledge discovery or data mining technology are originally application oriented. At present, it can be found to play an active role in many critical areas. Especially in the fields such as banking, telecommunications, insurance, transportation, retail, and other business areas. Among all these applications, the practice of data mining in marketing is undoubtedly the most successful one. Its application in marketing can be summed up as follows: (1) customer analysis, (2) deviation analysis (fraud detection), (3) trend analysis (estimating product performance and marketing, as well as for prediction of future sales (Michael *et al.*, 2001). Among them, applications of data mining on customer analysis have significant effect on the development of marketing strategy, which is also the focus of this paper.

The main applications of data mining in the customer analysis are the customer segmentation based on cluster analysis, customer buying behavior analysis based on association rules, customer value analysis based on decision tree, customer loyalty analysis and customer churn analysis, customer satisfaction analysis based on fuzzy AHP analysis; marketing program development based on neural network, etc.

2. Customer Analysis Model

2.1. The overall of customer analysis model

In this paper, we utilize a two-step analysis model to practice customer analysis. First step is the selection of appropriate customer segmentation model, and the application of K-means clustering method on customer segmentation. Based on the different customer clusters, the second step applies decision tree to describe customer behavior of each cluster, thus provides both theorical and practical basis for enterprises to develop marketing strategy better. Customer analysis model is shown in Fig. 1.

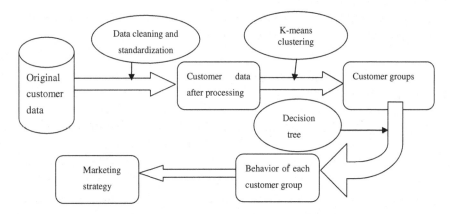

Fig. 1.   Customer analysis model.

2.2. Customer segmentation model

2.2.1. Meaning of customer segmentation

Customer segmentation is the division customer set according to customer attributes. Customer segmentation is one of the core concepts in customer relationship management, and the critical tool and link on implementing a customer relationship management. 80/20 rule indicates that 80% of the profits of enterprise come from 20% of its customers. For enterprises, a relatively small part of customers may create a great quantity and profits. Thus, enterprises should develop differentiated marketing strategy and make rational allocation of their resources (Marcus and Claudio, 1998; Chris *et al.*, 2002).

2.2.2. Selection of customer segmentation methods

Traditional methods of customer segmentation, in general, can be summed up as: (1) customer segmentation based on demographics; (2) customer segmentation based on customer behavior, such as Recency, Frequency, and Monetary (RFM) analysis, and customer value Matrix analysis; (3) customer segmentation based on the life cycle variables; and (4) customer segmentation based on customer value (Suzanne, 1992; Arthur, 1996).

The current marketing practices of brand lube oil in China are mainly based on indicators like purchase quantity and profits to conduct customer

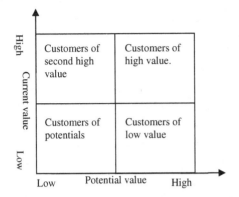

Fig. 2. Two dimensional customer value matrx.

segmentation. Generally, customers are divided into key customers, general customers, and retail customers. Obviously, such a rough customer classification can only reflect one aspect of customer value. It is difficult to accurately guide the brand lube oil to make decision in terms of input resources on customers and strategy maintenance, as well as to meet needs of customer relationship management.

This paper holds that maintenance of customer needs a great deal of effort and cost. In addition, the contribution of different customers is disparity. Therefore, the value of customers for brand lube oil should be regarded as the basis for customer segmentation. In this way, this paper draws on the value of customer life cycle segmentation model, brought up by Chen Mingliang (Chen, 2001). This model takes into account customer's current value and potential value comprehensively, and is simple for application (Fig. 2).

2.3. Customer segmentation index system

2.3.1. Index system

The above-mentioned two-dimensional model (Fig. 2) has four quadrants, considering the customer's current value and potential value of the existing oil industry, customer classification, customer value based on more scientific breakdown. In this paper, the introduction of customer value and evaluation system framework, two-dimensional model of customer value in the oil industry based on the characteristics of the evaluation of

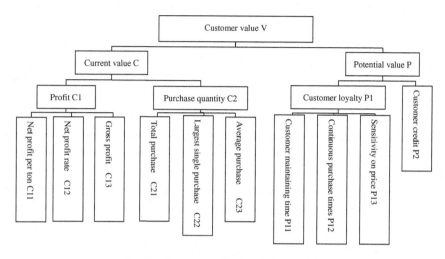

Fig. 3. Customer evaluation index system.

the establishment of specific indicators. The specific terms are as shown in Fig. 3.

2.3.2. Determination of weights of evaluation indexes

The establishment of customer value evaluation index system provides a basis for concrete measurement of customer's current value and potential value. This paper conducts Analytic Hierarchy Process (Saaty, 1980) to evaluate the weights of indicators. Due to space constraints, there is nonspecific description of the calculation here. The weights of each level are shown in Table 1, and the formula for customer's current value (C) and potential value P is as follows:

$$C = (C11^*0.4 + C12^*0.4 + C13^*0.2)^*0.667 + (C21^*0.54 + C22^*0.297 + C23^*0.163)^*0.333$$

$$P = (P11^*0.625 + P12^*0.239 + P13^*0.136)^*0.667 + P2^*0.333$$

Based on formula of customer's current value and potential value, the value of these two indicators can be calculated according to the specific customer data. The next step, by selecting appropriate clustering method, we can divide customers into groups based on their current and potential value.

Table 1. Weights of index system.

First level	CR	Second level	CR	Third level	CR
Customer value V	Current value C 0.667	CR = 0.00	Profit C1 0.667	CR = 0.00	Net profit per ton C11 0.400	CR = 0.00
					Net profit rate C12 0.400	
					Gross profit C13 0.200	
			Purchase quantity C2 0.333			
					Total purchase C21 0.540	CR = 0.08
					Largest single purchase C22 0.297	
					Average purchase C23 0.163	
	Potential value P 0.333		Customer loyalty P1 0.667	CR = 0.00	Customer maintaining time P11 0.625	CR = 0.02
					Continuous purchase times P12 0.239	
					Sensitivity on price P13 0.136	
			Customer credit P2 0.333			

3. An Empirical Study Based on the Great Wall Lube Oil Marketing in Fujian Province

3.1. *Data preparation and cleaning*

In this paper, the original 350 customer transactions are selected randomly from the Fujian Great Wall Lubricating Oil customer database. After selection of corresponding fields according to the customer evaluation index and data cleaning, there are 318 effective transactions for analysis. Due to space limitations, only 10 customer transactions are listed in Table 2.

3.2. Data discretization

Since the various dimensions of indexes, as well as the problem of comparison of qualitative data and quantitative data, data discretization should be conducted. This paper uses artificial methods to partition intervals based on consulting experts of lubricating oil marketing. Evaluation index value is discreted into five intervals, given 1 to 5 of 5 score respectively. Data discretization standards and the five customer transactions after discretization, are shown in Tables 3 and 4.

According to formula of customer's current value and potential value, as well as discrete customer data, we can calculate the 1st customer's two dimensions value:

$$C = 2^*0.4 + 2^*0.4 + 3^*0.2)^*0.667 + (4^*0.54 + 3^*0.297$$
$$+ 2^*0.163)^*0.333 = 2.59$$
$$P = (3^*0.625 + 5^*0.239 + 3^*0.136)^*0.667 + 5^*0.333 = 3.98$$

The top 10 customers' two dimensions value are shown in Table 5.

3.3. Customer segmentation based on cluster analysis

The types of cluster analysis methods are mainly divided as hierarchical methods, density-based methods, network-based methods, and model-based methods (Zait and Messatfa, 2004). In this case, K-means cluserting is utilized. The algorithm has good scalability and efficiency (AIsabti *et al.*, 2002). Meanwhile, Spss Clementine 11.0 is chosen to practice K-means based on the calculated value of the customer's current value and potential value. Corresponding to the two-dimensional model of customer value segmentation, we set the numbers of clusters to 4 ($k = 4$). After clustering analysis, the results are shown in Fig. 4 and Table 6.

Table 2. Original customer data.

No	Net profit per ton	Net profit rate	Gross profit	Total purchase	Largest single purchase	Average purchase	Customer maintaining time	Continuous purchase times	Sensitivity on price	Customer credit
1	110	1.47	22435	65597	19010	5124	5	21	General	Excellent
2	454	7.81	75214	110000	110000	110000	12	2	Low	Good
3	656	9.21	13768	14672	6120	2096	3	7	Low	Fair
4	262	5.18	37564	81056	28900	6768	4	17	High	Fair
5	70	1.23	8105	52067	34570	13017	2	4	General	Fair
6	160	2.45	24646	77086	25296	3854	3	20	Low	Good
7	435	7.14	33712	63600	37200	9086	3	7	Low	Excellent
8	44	0.67	3560	21540	6960	5385	2	4	General	Fair
9	261	5.90	47876	191000	94650	63667	2	5	General	Fair
10	280	4.44	3865	8780	8780	8780	2	3	High	Fair

Table 3. Discretization standards.

Index Net profit per					
ton (Yuan)	>1000	500–1000	200–500	100–200	<100
Net profit rate	>8%	5%–8%	3%–5%	1%–3%	<1%
Gross profit					
(Yuan)	>50000	20000–50000	10000–20000	5000–10000	<5000
Total purchase					
(ton)	>100	50–100	30–50	15–30	<15
Largest single					
purchase (ton)	>80	30–80	15–30	8–15	<8
Average					
purchase (ton)	>50	20–50	8–20	3–8	<3
Customer					
maintaining					
time (year)	>10	5–10	3–5	2–3	<2
Continuous					
purchase					
times	>20	10–20	5–10	2–5	<2
Sensitivity on					
price	Very low	Low	General	High	Very high
Customer credit	Excellent	Good	Fair	Poor	Very poor
Discretized					
value	5	4	3	2	1

3.4. Further analysis of customer value based on decision tree

After K-means clustering analysis, this paper then analyzes features of customers in the same group through decision tree, and the results of the analysis are presented as rules. The paper uses the C5.0 model in Clementine, C5.0 is a commercial version of C4.5. Through setting pruning severity (cutting purity) to 100, we get a decision tree with three levels, with an accuracy of 97.8% (Figs. 5 and 6), the decision tree structure is shown in Fig. 7.

3.5. Corresponding marketing strategies

From the above-mentioned analysis process, we can see the best development of relations between enterprise and its customers, maintain customers of high value, and change other three types of customers into customers of

Table 4. Customer data after data discretization.

No	Net profit per ton	Net profit rate	Gross profit	Total purchase	Largest single purchase	Average purchase	Customer maintaining time	Continuous purchase times	Sensitivity on price	Customer credit
1	2	2	3	4	3	2	3	5	3	5
2	4	4	5	5	5	5	5	2	4	4
3	5	5	3	2	2	1	3	3	4	4
4	3	4	4	4	3	2	3	3	2	3
5	1	2	2	4	4	3	2	5	3	3
6	2	2	3	4	3	2	3	3	4	4
7	4	4	4	2	4	3	3	3	4	5
8	1	1	1	2	2	3	2	3	3	3
9	3	4	4	5	5	5	2	3	3	3
10	3	3	1	1	2	3	2	2	2	3

Table 5. Two dimensions value.

No	1	2	3	4	5	6	7	8	9	10
Current value C	2.59	4.47	3.68	3.53	2.34	2.59	3.95	1.39	4.07	2.27
Potential value P	3.98	4.07	3.42	2.91	2.55	3.74	3.76	2.55	2.55	2.36

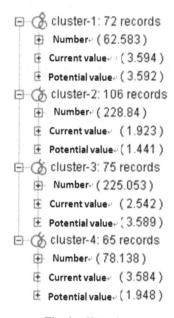

Fig. 4. Clustering.

high value. The following section will discuss how to conduct correspond-ing strategy for each type of customers.

3.5.1. *Customers of high value*

This kind of customers has both high present value as well as high potential value. According to the results of cluster analysis, this kind of customers takes up one-fifth of the total amount of customers, which basically reflects the 80/20 market law. In the decision tree analysis, these customers show two main characteristics: first is that they have a relatively long period of business with the company; and second is that their purchases are usually

Table 6. Segmentation result.

Customer type	Customers of high value Group 1		Customers of low value Group 2		Customers of potentials Group 3		Customers of second high value Group 4	
	Mean value	Evaluation	Mean value	Evaluation	Mean value	Evaluation	Mean value	Evaluation
Current value	3.594	High	1.923	Low	2.542	Low	3.584	High
Potential value	3.592	High	1.441	Low	3.589	High	1.948	Low
Number of sample	72		106		75		65	
Proportion	22.6%		33.4%		23.6%		20.4%	

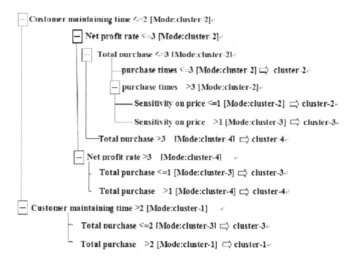

Fig. 5. Decision tree.

⊟···Results for output field $KM1-K-Means
  ⊟···Comparing $C-$KM1-K-Means with $KM1-K-Means

Correct	311	97.8%
Wrong	7	2.2%
Total	318	

Fig. 6. Accuracy of decision tree.

big. Therefore, the brand lube oil company should allocate its resources to maintain and promote the relationships with this kind of customers. On one hand, the company can offer them some priorities with oil supplies and also some favored prices. On the other hand, the company may support them with comprehensive necessary services, such as pre-sale market information supports and order services, in-sale reception services and freights, and after-sale door-to-door services and technical guidance.

3.5.2. *Customers of second high value*

This type of customers has high present value, but low potential value. The decision tree analysis indicates that although these customers will maintain short relationships with a certain brand, they have quite large purchase amounts and can provide high profits. Accordingly, the brand lube oil

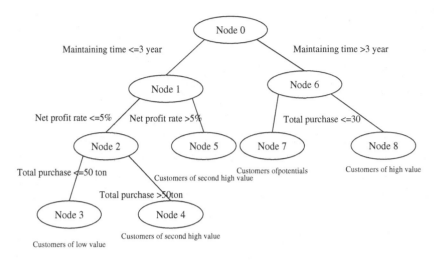

Fig. 7. Result of decision tree.

company should take measures to stop their swaying between different suppliers, so as to improve their potential value. The company can provide free-of-charge consulting services and achieve positive communication with them. Senior leaders may pay regular visits to the customers with large purchase amounts or high profit to find out their needs in time. The company can utilize proper services to maintain the customers' satisfaction and loyalty with the brand, trying to improve their potential value.

3.5.3. Customers of potentials

This kind of customers has low present value, however pretty high potential value. The results of decision tree analysis show that although these customers have relatively long relationships with a certain brand, their present purchase amounts still remain to increase. In terms of marketing strategies, the brand should increase the width and depth of sales, encouraging the customers to repeat their purchasing. Since they have long relationships with the brand, the company can provide them cash-on-delivery services, that is, the customers can pay after delivering of the goods. In addition, promotions can be made in certain times, in order to open their purchase potential. By such developing, they can turn high-value customers to the brand.

3.5.4. *Customers of low value*

This type of customers has both low present value and potential value. Decision tree analysis indicates that neither do they maintain long relationships with the brand, nor do they have large purchase amounts or provide high profits. This type of customers are of the largest number; however, they provide limited profit for the brand, sometimes even results in negative profits. The company may not input any resources for most of these customers. It can even encourage those inferior customers turn to other competitors.

4. Conclusions

This paper has first reviewed the application of knowledge data mining in marketing, especially in customer analysis. The application of data mining in lube oil marketing is new. Based on characteristics of lube oil marketing, the paper has proposed two-steps customer analysis model by using data mining for the customer value segmentation. As a case study, customer data of Great Wall lube oil in Fujian area has been analyzed and its customers have been classified into four categories. The behavior characteristics and marketing strategies of each category have also been identified. The findings of this paper have indicated that if lube oil enterprises in China can utilize scientific methods to explore customers' value, and develop targeted marketing strategies as well as providing differentiated services according to different types of customers, they will win the increasing market competition.

Acknowledgments

This work was partially supported by the President Fund of GUCAS (Grant No. 085102HN00), National Natural Science Foundation of China (Grant No. 70621001, 70531040, 70840010, 70501030, and 90718042), Beijing Natural Science Foundation (Grant No. 9073020), 973 Project of Chinese Ministry of Science and Technology (Grant No.2004CB720103), and BHP Billiton Corporation, Australia.

References

AIsabti, K., Ranka, S., and Singh, V., 2002. An efficient K-means clustering algorithm. hi/SSwIS, club Pl.cdu/ranka/.

Arthur, M.H., 1996. Making your database payoff using recency frequency and monetary analysis [DB/OL]. http://www.dbmarketing.com/articles/Art104a.htm.

Chen, M., Li, Zh, 2001. Study on value segmentation and retention strategies of customer. *Group Technology & Production Modernization*, 18(4), 9–11.

Chen, Y., Zhang, G., Hu, D., and Wang, S., 2006. In: *International Federation for Information Processing (IFIP)*, Vol. 207, *Knowledge Enterprise: Intelligent Strategies in Product Design, Manufacturing, and Management*, Wang, K., Kovacs, G., Wozny, M., and Fang, M. (Boston: Springer), pp. 288–293.

Chris, R., Jyun-Cheng, W., and Yen, D.C., 2002. Data mining techniques for customer relationship management. *Technology in Society*, 24, 483–502.

Fayyad, U.M., 1996. The KDD process for extracting useful knowledge from volumes of data. *Communications of the SCM*, 39(11), 27–34.

Fayyad, U.M., Piatesky, G., and Smyth, P., 1996. *Advances in Knowledge Discovery and Data mining.* Cambridge, MA: AAA|MIT Press.

Marcus, C., 1998. A practical yet meaningful approach to customer segmentation. *Journal of Consumer Marketing*, 15(5), 494–504.

Michael, J.S., Chandrasekar, S., Gek, W.T., and Welge, M.E., 2001. Knowledge management and data mining for marketing. *Decision Support Systems*, 31(1), 127–137.

Saaty, T.L., 1980. *The Analytic Hierarchy Process: Planning, Priority Setting, Resource Allocation*, McGraw-Hill, New York.

Suzanne, D., 1992. What can customer segmentation accomplish? *Banker Magazine*, 175(2), 72–81.

Usama, F. and Paul, S., 1997. Data mining and KDD: promise and challenge. *Future Generation Computer Systems*, 13, 99–115.

Zait, M. and Messatfa, H., 2004. A comparative study of clustering methods. *Future Generation Computer Systems*, 13, 149–159.

Design and Implementation of Intelligent Mobile Information System for Campus Safety Management

Li-Shan Chen

No. 92, Ciwun Rd., Cishan Township,
Kaohsiung County, Taiwan 84251
sun56@ms8.hinet.net

If information technology can be utilized for campus safety, it would be helpful for school staff to monitor all situations in schools. This study is based on campus safety management and is aimed at establishing an intelligent mobile information system in colleges; this will facilitate the installation of video recorders in the rush areas (at the entrance and exit of the campus) and inconspicuous places on campuses. This study adopts the Windows Media Player along the RTP/RTSP protocol in order to embed the mobile information system into the users' machines (personal digital assistants or smart phones). In this study, we randomly select 40 school staff and 100 students to test the intelligent system. Further, the results were compared with those from a conventional school safety system. Forty-two percent of users were satisfied with the conventional safety system and 96% of the users were satisfied with the intelligent mobile system when using personal digital assistants. The software integrity satisfaction was 99.99%; usability satisfaction, 96%; correctness, 95%; and reliability, 95%.

Keywords: Campus safety; Intelligent system; Mobile; RTP/RTSP.

1. Introduction

Recently, the mobile telecommunication industry has experienced significant advances and it will continue to evolve in the near future (Barco *et al.*, 2008). The success of wireless and mobile communications in the

21st century has resulted in a large variety of wireless technologies such as second-, third-, and fourth-generation cellular, satellite, Wi-Fi, Bluetooth, and WiMAX (IEEE 802.16) services. IEEE 802.16 is designed to support high capacities, high data rates, and multimedia services. The aim of IEEE 802.16 is to fill the gap between the high data rates of wireless local area networks (WLANs) and the high mobility of cellular wide area networks (WANs) (Kim *et al.*, 2008). Technological developments in content-based analysis of digital video information are undergoing much progress, with ideas for fully automatic systems now being proposed and demonstrated (Hyowon *et al.*, 2006). In the near future, several radio access technologies will coexist in Beyond 3G mobile networks (B3G) and they will be eventually transformed into one seamless global communication infrastructure. Self-managing systems (i.e., those that self-configure, self-protect, self-heal, and self-optimize) are the solution to tackle the high complexity inherent to these networks (Barco *et al.*, 2008). Digital representations are widely used for audiovisual content, enabling the creation of large online repositories of video and allowing access such as video on demand (Justin and Timothy, 2006). Digital artifacts created via transformational technologies often embody implicit knowledge that must be correctly interpreted to successfully act upon the artifacts (Leonardi and Bailey, 2008). With continued advances in communication network technology and sensing technology, there is astounding growth in the amount of data produced and made available through cyberspace (Keke and Ling, 2006). An additional major benefit is whether a partial prototype implementation can be automatically generated from a given software architecture design or not (Yujian *et al.*, 2007). For campus safety in schools nowadays, digital monitors and IP-Cams are connected to form an imaging system. Thus, an image information system network is established. Such networks help school staff monitor the situations at schools. The staff can select images that they want to observe. Simultaneously, they also can notice the general images of the campus, corner areas, entrance of the school, and areas around the information system. In this study, we randomly selected 40 school staff and 100 students to test the intelligent system and software. Further, the obtained results were compared with those from a conventional school safety system.

2. Related Study

2.1. *For mobile communication*

Wireless communication research is evolving toward integration, inter-working, and convergence of wireless systems, which will yield several concepts of simultaneous use (Ferreira *et al.*, 2006). Malek and Frank (2006) have focused on determining a near-optimal collision-free path because of its importance in robot motion planning, intelligent transportation systems, and any autonomous mobile navigation system. Yang and colleagues (2006) have presented a perspective on the future vision of mobile communications and services, which is referred to mobile ubiquitous service environments. Dixit identified the key barriers to achieving true network convergence. The influence of the provision of security is evaluated in the protocols and applications/scenarios where sensors can be used (Gao and Zhang, 2008), and more than 80,000 scalar multiplications per second are performed to enhance security in wireless mobile applications (Masi and Vitria, 2008). A distributed channel assignment protocol based on a cross-layer approach has been proposed, and it has been shown that the proposed protocol can substantially increase throughput and reduce delay in wireless ad hoc networks (Chakraborty and Pal, 2008). Pavlou documented a historic evolution, highlighted important design choices, and explained the reasons behind the various frameworks and technologies.

Sánchez and colleagues presented a model to design and implement mobile applications to support the displacement and dynamic decision making of users with visual disabilities, and the problem of scheduling packets for downlink transmissions in the time slots of a frame is addressed in such a way that the quality-of-service requirements are fulfilled (Ku *et al.*, 2008). A spanning tree is based on the auto configuration of mobile ad hoc networks and a novel approach for efficient distributed address auto configuration (Su *et al.*, 2008). Fingerprint technicians' occupationally defined values and norms have played an important role in structuring their existing work practices, as well as the tension produced by organizationally mandated efforts to restructure the logic of their expertise-based hierarchies (Flesca *et al.*, 2008). Pavlou and colleagues build upon the principal–agent perspective to propose a set of four uncertainty mitigating factors — trust, Web site information, product diagnostics, and social presence.

An interface between the applications and the underlying transport network has been defined that offers the dynamic and efficient management of network resources based on a policy-based resource control engine (Rothenberg and Ross, 2008).

Gao and Zhang (2008) have proposed an effective technique to determine the number and distribution of equilibria and a new supervised linear feature extraction technique for multiclass classification problems particularly suited to the nearest-neighbor classifier technique (Masip and Vitria, 2008). Two connectionist schemes, namely, (1) detection of bad/derogatory groups of features online and (2) the elimination of the effect of these bad features while performing function approximations or classification tasks (Chakraborty and Pal, 2008).

Payne (2008) examines the Web service paradigm from an open multi agent system perspective and contrasts the formally grounded knowledge-centric view of agents with a pragmatic declarative bottom-up approach adopted by Web services. The architecture modeling system can identify different elements and styles in a variety of buildings (Liu *et al.*, 2008); location-based spatial queries having certain unique characteristics can be revealed, which traditional spatial query-processing systems employed in centralized databases do not address (Ku *et al.*, 2008). Medium access control protocols have quality-of-service support topology independent link activation transmission scheduling — for mobile code-division multiple-access ad hoc networks (Su *et al.*, 2008).

Flesca and colleagues (2008) investigated the minimization problem for a wide fragment of XPath (namely *XP*), where the use of the most common operators (child, descendant, wildcard, and branching) is allowed with some syntactic restrictions; a novel approach is developed for static index pruning that considers the locality of occurrences of words in the text (Moura *et al.*, 2008), and more nuanced understanding of consumer channel choices is developed (Vivek and Elena, 2008). The context-aware query processing system enhances the semantic content of Web queries using two complementary knowledge sources: lexicons and ontology (Storey *et al.*, 2008).

2.2. For monitoring system

Tan and colleagues (2008) investigated the performance of those 3G networks in terms of their data throughput, latency, video and voice calls handling capacities, and their ability to provide service guarantees to different traffic classes under saturated and lightly loaded network conditions.

A software architecture design has many benefits including aiding comprehension, supporting early analysis, and providing guidance for subsequent development activities (Justin and Timothy, 2006).

The monitoring system is digitized and the information transfer is systematized. The definition of a photograph in this information system and the convenience in its management are apparently different from those of a conventional system; a video frame can be viewed via a network. The previous studies have focused on mechanical monitors and the control of the bottoms; they did not add intelligent functions on the bottoms. The mobile information system has facilitated convenience in campus safety management. Nowadays, intelligent systems are extensively being applied for monitoring at homes and companies for safety management and burglary prevention; however, intelligent systems have not yet been widely applied for campus safety management.

3. Research Method

The mobile information system is developed in the environment of: Microsoft Windows Server 2008, Internet Information Services 7.0 (IIS 7.0), Microsoft Structured Query Language (MS SQL) Server 2005, and Visual Studio 2008 (VS 2008). The human-computer-interface software is developed in the environment of Microsoft Windows Embedded CE 6.0 release 2, MS SQL server 2005, and edited using VS 2008. The programming languages are Extensible Markup Language (XML) and C#.

3.1. Several parts are stated as below in this study

This study is conducted on the basis of a distributed system. Thus, the display layer, image retrieved layer, agent layer, and information could be

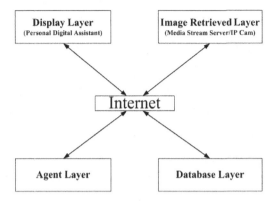

Fig. 1. Main frame of the general concept of this study.

placed at any point on the Internet (Fig. 1). The advantage of using a frame in this study is its high availability; any layer, when shutting down, can be restarted in another location. It is unlimited and the server should be placed in local schools.

The practical frame diagram for a single school is shown in Fig. 2.

The wireless IP-Cam is linked through a wireless access point (802.11g); the wired IP-Cam is connected to switch via an RJ-45 connector. The switch is linked to a media-streaming server on the Intranet of the campus for saving and retrieving images. The media-streaming server builds a broadcasting point through which images are collected from the inner network and broadcast on the outer network for the users to monitor.

The images that the users want to monitor are automatically retrieved through agents and downloaded to the users' mobile tools after they login to their accounts. Moreover, the users can monitor in-time images of any classroom or any corner of the campus through the agents.

3.2. Establishment of the database

This study adopts the relational database management system to establish the database. The Boyce-Cod Normal Form (BCNF) is used for database normalization. During the process of standardization, a larger amount of time is required to integrate the joins when checking the segment of relational joins. Therefore, a balanced point should be obtained between the flexibility and efficiency of the database. As a result of the high-speed

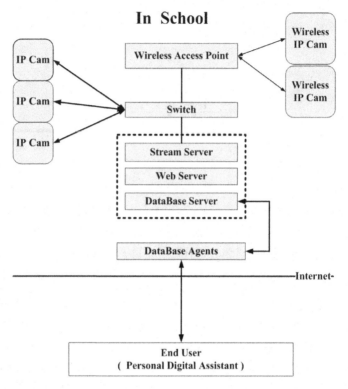

Fig. 2. Practical frame diagram for a single school.

reaction in time, and for obtaining a balanced point between flexibility and efficiency, a compromise task is required for obtaining the BCNF. Microsoft SQL Server 2005 is adopted for the platform in the database management system.

The study adopts the "three-layer frame", which is the basic frame of the N-Tier architecture. The three-layer frame is shown in Fig. 3.

Each layer has its own responsibility, and they are stated as follows:

1. *Database layer*: It stores the data. The basic information of the users and children are stored in this layer.
2. *Agent layer*: When the users expect certain information, the agent retrieves it and replies to the users. The agent layer can be considered to be a middle layer between the Internet and database server. When the users send a request for monitoring the images of their children in the

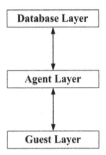

Fig. 3. Three-layer frame.

class, the agents will begin to find the data demanded by the users (for example, the location of the student in the class). Since the expected information is expressed in a worded pattern, it must be uploaded to the streaming server and converted to string flow images. Then, the stream images are transferred to the users' machines.

3. *Guest layer*: It means the end user. Users send a request through the Internet to the agent layer, and the agent layer is responsible for storing or retrieving the information from the database.

3.3. *Steam images*

Stream images play an important role in this study because they are the means by which the users receive image information of situations that they expect to monitor. As shown in Fig. 4, the Microsoft Media Server (MMS) protocol is employed between the Web server and the media-streaming server (Microsoft, 2007).

The process of linking is described by an example of a WMV file of 300 Kbps in the linking of 500 Kbps. In this example, users request a 300 Kbps WMV file from the server with a speed of 500 Kbps; then, the server will send the information for approximately the first 10 s in order to store in the buffer area. In this process, the linking speed is 500 Kbps; however, the remaining stream information utilizes the speed of 300 Kbps to transmit to the users, as shown in Fig. 5.

The problems with IP-Cams can be solved by establishing a streaming media server. Hence, the problems related to simultaneous transfer of information and limited bandwidth can be solved; further, in order to

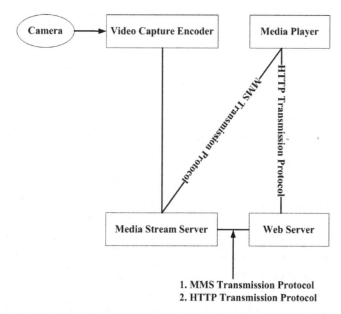

1. MMS Transmission Protocol
2. HTTP Transmission Protocol

Fig. 4. MMS protocol used between the Web server and media-streaming server.

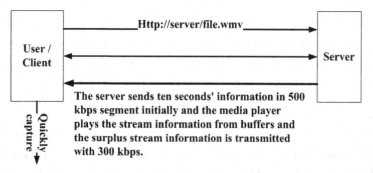

Fig. 5. The linking speed is 500 Kbps; however, the remaining stream information utilizes the speed of 300 Kbps to transmit to the users.

achieve the monitoring demanded by the users, the retrieved images can be transmitted in a planned and systematic manner.

When the users login to the system, they will search the images from the database and the agents will capture the images to transfer them to the users from the streaming server, as shown in Fig. 6.

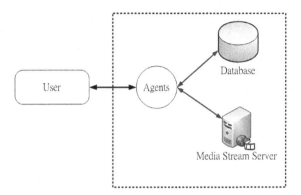

Fig. 6. Users login to the system.

```
"select * from Parent join Student " +
        "on Parent.uid = Student.uid join Class_of_Student " +
        "on Class_of_Student.std_number = Student.std_number join Course " +
        "on Course.class = Class_of_Student.class " +
        "where Parent.uid = '" + name + "' and " +
        "datepart(weekday,getdate()-1) = week " +
        "and datepart(hour,getdate()) between datepart(hour,beg) and datepart(hour,en) " +
        "and
convert(int,REPLACE(SUBSTRING(CONVERT(char(16),getdate(),120),12,16),':','')) " +
        "between
convert(int,REPLACE(SUBSTRING(CONVERT(char(16),beg,120),12,16),':','')) " +
        "and    convert(int,REPLACE(SUBSTRING(CONVERT(char(16),en,120),12,16),':','')) 
";
```

Fig. 7. Portion of database server codes.

A portion of the database server codes programmed with the Virtual C# language is shown in Fig. 7.

3.4. Comparison of new system and old system

From 15–19 March 2008, the former 50 persons who entered the campus in the morning were tested the new system and old system. They also tested the software satisfaction. In this study, there were 40 school staff and 100 students taking part in testing the new system, old system, and software. They compared image transmitting velocity, clear, personal service, and convenient usage between new system and old system.

Fig. 8. Login frame.

Fig. 9. Selection frame.

4. Result and Discussion

4.1. *Result*

The mobile information system for PDAs has been developed successfully, as shown in Figs. 8–10.

This study provides a solution (including hardware solutions) to promote campus safety management. The system developed will be more advantages for school staff and students.

Fig. 10. Campus frame.

4.2. Discussion

In this study, we randomly selected 40 school staff and 100 students for testing the intelligent system and software. These users satisfied with the conventional safety system when using their PDAs (student: 44/100; staff: 15/40) and the users satisfied with the intelligent mobile information system when using their PDAs (student: 95/100; staff: 39/40), are shown in Fig. 11.

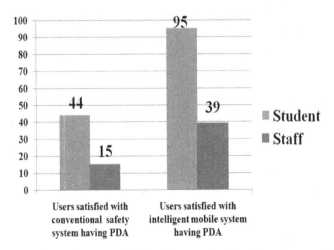

Fig. 11. Comparison of users satisfied with conventional safety system and intelligent mobile system having PDA.

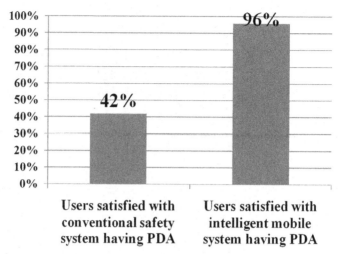

Fig. 12. Comparison of users satisfied with conventional safety system and intelligent mobile system having PDA.

In Fig. 12, the vertical axis represents the total satisfaction percentage. The satisfaction percentage for the conventional safety system is 42% and that for the intelligent mobile system is 96%.

The software integrity satisfaction percentage can be as high as 99.99% (student: 100/100; staff: 40/40). The software usability satisfaction percentage is 96% (student: 96/100; staff: 38/40), The software accuracy is 95% (student: 96/100; staff: 37/40). The software reliability is 95% (student: 95/100; staff: 38/40), as shown in Figs. 13 and 14.

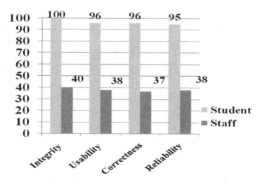

Fig. 13. Numbers of software integrity, usability, correctness, and reliability satisfaction.

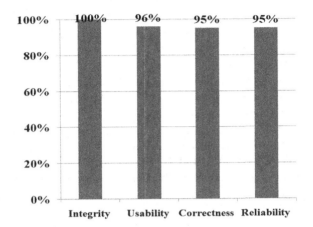

Fig. 14. Percentage of software integrity, usability, correctness, and reliability.

5. Conclusion

In this study, we have adopted a new generation technology to alter a conventional safety system. The size of the software is 20 kilobits; therefore, the software is not a liability for the users' mobile tools. Users need not use the browser; they can directly communicate with the intelligent mobile system via mobile tools. School staff can monitor classroom situations through the system and direct visits are not required.

References

Barco, R., Lázaro, P., Díez, L., and Wille, V., 2008. Continuous versus discrete model in autodiagnosis systems for wireless networks. *IEEE Transactions on Mobile Computing*, 7(6), 673–681.

Bashirullah, A.K. and Jayaro, X., 2006. Consortium: a solution to academic library services in Venezuela. *Library Collections, Acquisitions and Technical Services*, 30(1–2), 102–107.

Chakraborty, D. and Pal, N.R., 2008. Selecting useful groups of features in a connectionist framework. *IEEE Transactions on Neural Networks*, 19(3), 381–396.

Ferreira, L., Serrador, A., and Correia, L.M., 2006. Concepts of simultaneous use in mobile and wireless communications. *Wireless Personal Communications*, 37(3–4), 317–328.

Flesca, S., Furfaro, F., and Mascian, E., 2008. On the minimization of XPath queries. *Journal of the ACM (JACM)*, 55(1), Article No. 2.

Gao, B. and Zhang, W., 2008. Equilibria and their bifurcations in a recurrent neural network involving iterates of a transcendental function. *IEEE Transactions on Neural Networks*, 19(5), 782–794.

Hyowon, L., Alan, F.S., Noel, E.O'., and Barry, S., 2006. User evaluation of Físchlár-news: an automatic broadcast news delivery system. *ACM Transactions on Information Systems (TOIS)*, 24(2), 145–189.

Justin, Z. and Timothy, C.H., 2008.

Justin, Z. and Timothy, C.H., 2006. Detection of video sequences using compact signatures. *ACM Transactions on Information Systems (TOIS)*, 24(1), 1–50.

Keke, C. and Ling, L., 2006. iVIBRATE: interactive visualization-based framework for clustering large datasets. *ACM Transactions on Information Systems (TOIS)*, 24(2), 245–294.

Kim, K.J., Kim, B., Um, J.W., Son, J.J., and Choi, B.D., 2008. Delay analysis of extended rtPS for VoIP service in IEEE 802.16e by matrix analytic method. *Annals of Operations Research*, 162(1), 85–107.

Ku, W.S., Zimmermann, R., and Wang, H., 2008. Location-based spatial query processing with data sharing in wireless broadcast environments. *IEEE Transactions on Mobile Computing*, 7(6), 778–791.

Leonardi, P.M. and Bailey, D.E., 2008. Transformational technologies and the creation of new work practices: making implicit knowledge explicit in task-based offshoring. *MIS Quarterly*, 32(2), 411–436.

Liu, Y., Xu, C., Zhang, Q., and Pan, Y., 2008. The smart architect: scalable ontology-based modeling of ancient Chinese architectures. *IEEE Intelligent Systems*, 23(1), 49–56.

Malek, M.R. and Frank, A.U., 2006. A mobile computing approach for navigation purposes web and wireless geographical information systems. *Lecture Notes in Computer Science*, 4295, 123–134.

Masip, D. and Vitria, J., 2008. Shared feature extraction for nearest neighbor face recognition. *IEEE Transactions on Neural Networks*, 19(4), 586–595.

Microsoft, 2007. http://www.microsoft.com.

Moura, E.S., Santos, C.F., Araujo, B.D.S., Silva, A.S., Calado, P., and Nascimento, M.A., 2008. Locality-based pruning methods for web search. *ACM Transactions on Information Systems*, 26(2), Article No. 9.

Payne, T.R., 2008. Web services from an agent perspective. *IEEE Intelligent Systems*, 23(2), 12–14.

Rothenberg, C.E. and Roos, A., 2008. A review of policy-based resource and admission control functions in evolving access and next generation networks. *Journal of Network and Systems Management*, 16(1), 14–45.

Storey, V.C., Jones, A.B., Sugumaran, V., and Purao, S., 2008. A methodology for context-aware query processing on the World Wide Web. *Information Systems Research*, 19(1), 3–25.

Su, Y.S., Su, S.L., and Li, J.S., 2008. Topology-independent link activation scheduling schemes for mobile CDMA ad hoc networks. *IEEE Transactions on Mobile Computing*, 7(5), 599–616.

Tan, W.L., Lam, F., and Lau, W.C., 2008. An empirical study on 3G network capacity and performance. *IEEE Transactions on Mobile Computing*, 7(6), 737–750.

Vivek, C. and Elena, K., 2008. The relative advantage of electronic channels: a multidimensional view. *MIS Quarterly*, 32(1), 179–200.

Yang, J.I., Ping, Z., Zheng, H., Xu, W., Yinong, L., and Xiaosheng, T., 2006. Towards mobile online exchange relationships: a principal–agent perspective. *MIS Quarterly*, 31(1), 105–136.

Yujian, F. Zhijiang, D., and Xudong, H., 2007. A translator of software architecture design from SAM to Java. *International Journal of Software Engineering and Knowledge Engineering*, 17(6), 709–755.

Part 5

Management Challenges from Chinese Society

Effectiveness of Transformational Leadership and Transactional Leadership in Higher Education in China*

Kan Shi[†], Wenjing Chen[‡], Changjang Xu[§] and Wayne Daniel Jones[¶]

[†] School of Management, Graduate University,
Chinese Academy of Sciences, Beijing 100190, China
shik@gucas.ac.cn

[‡] School of Economics and Management,
Beijing University of Posts and Telecommunications,
Institute of Psychology, Chinese Academy of Sciences,
Beijing 100101, China

[§] School of Educational Science and Technology,
Zhejiang Normal University, Jinhua 321004,
Institute of Psychology, Chinese Academy of Sciences,
Beijing 100101, China

[¶] College of Business Administration,
Roosevelt University, Chicago, IL, USA

A great deal of attention had been paid to transformational leadership and transactional leadership in the existing research; however, there is little empirical research that explores the effectiveness of transformational leadership and transactional leadership in the context of higher education in China. A questionnaire was used to determine the effectiveness of transformational leadership and transactional leadership in this context. The following are the main findings.

First, there was a statistically significant relationship between transformational leadership and leadership effectiveness (e.g., job satisfaction, organizational commitment, and job performance). At the same time, there was a statistically significant relationship between transactional leadership and leadership effectiveness.

Correspondence: Kan Shi School of Management, Graduate University, Chinese Academy of Sciences, Beijing 100190, China. e-mail: shik@gucas.ac.cn
*This article is supported by Chinese Natural Scientific Committee, No. 70471060, 70573108.

Second, the comparison of the two type of leadership showed that transformational leadership could explain extra variance for predicting the job satisfaction and organizational commitment after the variable of transactional leadership was controlled. Additionally, transactional leadership explained extra variance for predicting the job performance after the variable of transformational leadership was controlled.

Keywords: Transformational leadership; Transactional leadership; Leadership effectiveness; Higher education.

1. Introduction

With the development of Chinese economy, people are becoming more interested in educational and mental development needs. Youths of 18–20 years are thirsting for higher education after they finish their high school studies (Maoyuan, 2002). Based on the overall population of China, the department of education made the decision to increase the number of college students since 2000. Along with this initiative, there are several related policies that followed, such as the merging and assimilation of smaller universities into other institutions to achieve the greater economies of scale, as well as the socialization of student-logistical-management system. The more the students who attend college, the greater the challenges that the leaders of higher education face. (Daguang, 2002). It has become of great importance to find the best means of dealing with the new challenges associated with being an efficient and effective leader of the colleges and universities.

Transactional and transformational leadership have become the focus of scholars in recent years (Bass, 1985; Judge and Piccolo, 2004). Many studies have been conducted within the field of education to determine the effectiveness of transformational leadership (Roueche *et al.*, 1989; Segiovanni, 1990; Seagren *et al.*, 1993; Lucas, 1994; Jantzi, 1996; Leftwich, 2001) There are multiple studies that show positive correlations between leaders' effectiveness and the components of transformational leadership, although effectiveness has also been found to be positively related to the contingent reward component of transactional leadership (Lowe *et al.*, 1996; see also DeGroot *et al.*, 2000; Eagly and Johannesen-Schmidt, 2003; Lim and Ployhart, 2004; Bono and Anderson, 2005; Wang *et al.*, 2005; Keller, 2006). Most of the studies in the area of education are focused on transformational leadership and tend to neglect the effectiveness of transactional leadership. There is little research on the effectiveness of transactional leadership in China. Moreover, there are even fewer empirical studies that examine both transformational and transactional leadership at the same time.

Is transformational or transactional leadership more appropriate in higher education in China? What effect would transformational and transactional leadership have in this context? This study is designed to address these issues.

2. Method

2.1. Samples

Samples were selected in the five universities in the Zhejiang and Liaoning Provinces of China. The average age for all the participants was approximately 35 years old. The participants had worked for the universities for about 10 years, and they reported being in their current positions for about 7 years.

The job categories sampled were nearly evenly divided between faculty (59.7%) and staff (45.8%). More than 99% of the participants had obtained a college degree, and approximately one-fourth of the participants had advanced degrees (Master's or Ph.D.).

Data were collected by questionnaires that were distributed in a packet. Each packet contained a letter from the researchers assuring complete confidentiality to the participants and the complete questionnaires (Table 1).

2.2. Measures

2.2.1. Transformational leadership behaviors

Podsakoff and colleagues (1990) Transformational Leadership Behavior Inventory (TLI) was used to assess the leadership behaviors measured in the study. The six dimensions were: (a) articulating a vision (five items; sample item: "Inspires others with his/her plans for the future"), (b) providing an appropriate model (three items; sample item: "Leads by 'doing', rather than simply by 'telling'"), (c) fostering the acceptance of group goals (four items; sample item: "Get the group to work together for the same goal"), (d) having high performance expectations (three items;

Table 1. Summary of sample characteristics.

Variable	Character	N	%
Gender			
	Male	188	38.4
	Female	290	59.3
	Missing	11	2.2
	Total	489	100.0
Level of education			
	Beneath college	6	1.2
	Junior college	21	4.3
	Bachelor or equivalent	285	58.3
	Master or equivalent	153	31.3
	Ph.D. or equivalent	13	2.7
	Missing	11	2.2
	Total	489	100.0
Position			
	Faculty	292	59.7
	Staff	165	35.8
	Others	4	0.8
	Missing	18	3.6
	Total	489	100.0

sample items: "Show us that he/she expects a lot from us"), (e) providing individualized support (four items; sample item: "Show respect for my personal feeling"), and (f) providing intellectual stimulation (four items, sample item: "Challenge me to think about old problems in new ways").

2.2.2. Transactional leadership behaviors

A five-item contingent reward behavior scale (Podsakoff *et al.*, 1984) was used to measure transactional leadership behaviors. An illustrative sample item from the scale was "Always gives me positive feedback when I perform well." Contingent punishment was assessed with three items from Podsakoff and colleagues (1984) contingent punishment scale. The sample item was "Lets me know about it when I perform poorly."

2.2.3. Job satisfaction

The three-item Satisfaction scale was used to measure the job satisfaction (Cammann *et al.*, 1983). An example item was, "All in all, I am satisfied with my job."

2.2.4. *Organizational commitment*

The eight-item Meyer and Allen (1997) measure was used to assess the affective commitment to the organization. An example item was, "I would be very happy to spend the rest of my career with this organization."

2.2.5. *Job performance*

The four-item scale selected from Gould (1979) and Pazy (1988) was used to measure the job performance. An example item was, "Compared to my colleague, my performance is petty good".

Five-point-Likert scales ranging from "(1) Strongly Disagree" to "(5) Strongly Agree" were used to assess all of the components in the present study.

2.3. Data analysis

Hierarchical regression analyses (Cohen *et al.*, 2003) were conducted to test the hypothesis that transformational leadership adds to transactional leadership in association with leadership effectiveness. Transactional leadership was initially entered into the regression equation. Then, transformational leadership was added separately to each equation. This was done to determine whether transformational leadership added significant, unique variance to account for the effectiveness measures. The two-step hierarchical regressions were performed on each of the three effectiveness measures. As a point comparison, the regressions were repeated, entering transformational leadership followed by transactional leadership into regression equations.

3. Results

3.1. Factor analysis and assessment of reliability

The means, standard deviations, reliabilities, and correlations for all variables used in the present study are reported in Table 2. As indicated in this table, the Cronbach alpha internal consistency reliability estimates were all above Nunnally's (1978) recommended level of 0.70, except for high performance expectation and contingent punishment, which had alphas of 0.63 and 0.61, respectively.

Table 2. Means, standard deviations, reliabilities, and correlations.

Variable	Mean	SD	1	2	3	4	5	6	7	8	9	10	11
1. Articulation a vision	3.55	0.71	**0.84**										
2. Providing an appropriate model	3.63	0.88	0.67**	**0.87**									
3. Fostering group goals	3.69	0.72	0.77**	0.75**	**0.83**								
4. High performance expectation	3.81	0.61	0.65**	0.56**	0.65**	**0.63**							
5. Individualized support	3.40	0.82	0.55**	0.73**	0.65**	0.38**	**0.84**						
6. Intellectual stimulation	3.41	0.72	0.74**	0.61**	0.70**	0.58**	0.52**	**0.79**					
7. Contingent reward	3.56	0.67	0.68**	0.67**	0.69**	0.56**	0.63**	0.63**	**0.81**				
8. Contingent punishment	3.62	0.67	0.40**	0.38**	0.41**	0.37**	0.37**	0.43**	0.46**	**0.61**			
9. Job satisfaction	3.70	0.68	0.27**	0.30**	0.32**	0.24**	0.26**	0.18*	0.26**	0.14*	**0.65**		
10. Organizational commitment	3.41	0.64	0.39**	0.42**	0.40**	0.33**	0.41**	0.33**	0.38**	0.22**	0.55**	**0.78**	
11. Job performance	3.31	0.56	0.24**	0.20**	0.24**	0.22**	0.24**	0.21**	0.29**	0.15**	0.23**	0.27**	**0.78**

Note: $N = 489$. * $p < 0.05$; ** $p < 0.01$.

3.2. The effectiveness of transformational leadership and transactional leadership

Hierarchical regression analyses were conducted to find the effectiveness of transformational leadership and transactional leadership. As can be seen in the upper portion of Table 3, for each effectiveness measure, transactional leadership accounted for significant variance. More importantly, transformational leadership added unique variance in the effectiveness measures of job satisfaction and organizational commitment. Except for the job performance measure, transformational leadership added no significant variance beyond that contributed by transactional leadership.

As an alternative model, the hierarchical regression analyses were repeated by first entering transactional leadership followed by transformational leadership. It was found that there was a statistically significant relationship between transformational leadership and leadership effectiveness, such as job satisfaction, organizational commitment, and job performance. The result shown in the lower portion of Table 3 indicates how the measures of job satisfaction, organizational commitment, and transactional leadership added no significant variance beyond that contributed by transformational leadership. But for the job performance, transactional leadership added significant variance beyond that contributed by transformational leadership.

4. Discussion

In this study, we compared the effectiveness of transformational leadership and transactional leadership. The conclusion of Bass (1985) was that "transformational leadership had extra effectiveness of influence to the follows than transactional leadership." In this study, we found that transactional leadership explained extra variance for predicting the job performance after the variable of transformational leadership was controlled. As mentioned before that transformational leadership emphasizes on emotion while transactional leadership emphasizes on rationality and instrumentalism. For the measurement of leadership effectiveness, the variables of job satisfaction and organizational commitment belonged to the emotional aspect of leadership effectiveness. Thus, the relationship between transformational leadership and job satisfaction and organizational commitment might be

Table 3. Hierarchical regression of transformational and transactional leadership.

		Job satisfaction	Organizational commitment	Job performance
First ordering				
1. Transactional leadership				
Contingent reward	(Beta)	0.250***	0.346***	0.290***
Contingent punishment	(Beta)	0.059	0.061	0.051
	(R^2)	0.074	0.134***	0.094***
2. Transactional leadership				
Contingent reward	(Beta)	0.007	0.029	0.177*
Contingent punishment	(Beta)	0.020	0.003	0.031
3. Transformational leadership				
Articulation a vision	(Beta)	0.046	0.154*	0.095
Providing an appropriate model	(Beta)	0.167*	0.098	−0.065
Fostering group goals	(Beta)	0.176*	−0.003	−0.046
Individualized support	(Beta)	0.094	0.090	0.113
Intellectual stimulation	(Beta)	0.060	0.218**	0.118
High performance expectation	(Beta)	−0.119	−0.004	−0.016
	(Total R^2)	0.141***	0.220***	0.111***
	(ΔR^2)	0.066***	0.085***	0.016
Second ordering				
1. Transformational leadership				
Articulation a vision	(Beta)	0.048	0.159*	0.170
Providing an appropriate model	(Beta)	0.163*	0.102	−0.061
Fostering group goals	(Beta)	0.178*	0.001	−0.019
Individualized support	(Beta)	0.097	0.093	0.132
Intellectual stimulation	(Beta)	0.065	0.226**	0.179*
High performance expectation	(Beta)	−0.114	0.001	−0.022
	(R^2)	0.140***	0.219***	0.077***
2. Transformational leadership				
Articulation a vision	(Beta)	0.046	0.154*	0.095
Providing an appropriate model	(Beta)	0.161*	0.098	−0.065
Fostering group goals	(Beta)	0.176*	−0.003	−0.046
Individualized support	(Beta)	0.094	0.090	0.113
Intellectual stimulation	(Beta)	0.060	0.218**	0.135
High performance expectation	(Beta)	−0.119	−0.004	−0.016
3. Transactional leadership				
Contingent reward	(Beta)	0.007	0.029	0.175*
Contingent punishment	(Beta)	0.020	0.003	0.031
	(Total R^2)	0.141***	0.220***	0.111***
	(ΔR^2)	0.001	0.001	0.024*

Notes: $N = 489$.
* $P < 0.05$.
** $P < 0.01$.
*** $P < 0.001$.

more direct. Then why did transformational leadership not explain extra variance of prediction for job performance beyond transactional leadership as the conclusion draw by researchers of Western countries? We must look into the Chinese culture itself to find out the reason.

As we all knew that China was the country with large power distance. The followers must rely on his or her superior to get all kinds of resources in his or her organization, including the job resources, necessary equipment and persons, and reward such as promotion and raising the payment. And the followers relied on the oral or spiritual support of his or her superior to meet his or her needs as well. Walder (1983) especially emphasized that the followers needed to rely on the superior to make a living after he did some researches on the state-owned corporations of mainland China. Why did this happen in China? Because the superior was in charge of all sorts of resources, and the distribution of these resources was different according to different people. The influence of individual power was much larger than system or rules. Westwood (1992) brought forward the concept of "headship" after he researched the corporations owned by the foreign citizen of Chinese origin in southeast Asian. It was quite different from the Western leadership which emphasized on system or rules. In these organizations, the leader controlled all resources and the distribution of these resources, because of the position of the "head of the organization" he or she owned.

Furthermore, the followers of Chinese culture faced the higher uncertainty than followers of other cultures, because the leader of Chinese culture was plenipotentiary while the followers had little power to doubt the relationship between the distribution of resource and the job performance. Moreover, the most important information to accomplish the job or task was held and transmitted by the leader such as how to set down the goal, how to appraise the performance, and how to assign the job. Based on the social fact in China that the influence of "person-governed" society was much stronger than the nomocracy of the Western countries, and the social fact that the leader in Chinese culture controlled the resources and the system of reward and punishment, the behaviors of transactional leaders such as to be fair-and-square to distribute the resources and tasks, to set the job target fairly, to give appropriate reward or punishment to the followers according to their actual performance was much more important than the behaviors of transformational leaders such as to articulate a vision to the followers, to provide an appropriate model, and to provide individual support to the fellows.

In the specific Chinese culture, there is larger power distance than that in the Western countries (Zheng and Fan, 2000). People tend to respect the power itself as the strength. And some researches found that the educational organizations are the loosely coupled system (Weick, 1976), which carried out the dual system (Owens, 2001). Ramsden (1998) found the leaders in the higher education system were always in the process between "tense up and balance." The most important competency for the leaders in the higher education system was adaptability. In the higher education situation, the combination of the transformational leadership and the transactional leadership might be the most effective way to run the leadership of higher education.

References

Avolio, B.J., 1999. *Full leadership development: building the vital forces in organizations.* Thousand Oaks, CA: Sage.

Avolio, B.J. and Bass, B.M., 2002. *Manual for the Multifactor Leadership Questionnaire (Form 5X).* Redwood City, CA: Mindgarden.

Avolio, B.J., Bass, B.M., and Jung, D., 1999. Re-examining the components of transformational and transactional leadership using the multifactor leadership questionnaire. *Journal of Occupational and Organizational Psychology,* 7, 441–462.

Barling, J., Weber, J., and Kelloway, E.K., 1996. Effects of transformational leadership training on attitudinal and financial outcomes: a field experiment. *Journal of Applied Psychology,* 81, 827–832.

Bass, B.M., 1985. *Leadership and Performance Beyond Expectations.* New York: Free Press.

Bass, B.M., 1998. *Transformational Leadership: Individual, Military and Educational Impact.* Mahwah, NJ: Erlbaum.

Bass B.M. and Avolio B.J., 1993. Transformational leadership: a response to critics. In Chemers, M. and Ayman R. (eds.). *Leadership Theory and Research: Perspectives and Directions.* San Diego: Academic Press, pp. 49–80.

Beng-Chong, L. and Ployhart, R.E., 2004. Transformational leadership: relations to the five-factor model and team performance in typical and maximum contexts. *Journal of Applied Psychology,* 89(4), 610.

Burns, J.M., 1978. *Leadership.* New York: Harper & Row.

Bycio, P., Hackett, R.D., and Allen, J.S., 1995. Further assessments of Bass's (1985) conceptualization of transactional and transformational leadership. *Journal of Applied Psychology,* 80, 468–478.

Cammann, C., Fichman, M., Jenkins, D., and Klesh, J., 1983. Assessing the attitudes and perceptions of organizational member. In Seashore, E.L., Mirvis, P., and Cammann, C. (eds.). *Assessing Organizational Change: A Guide to Methods, Measure and Practices*. New York: John Wiley, pp. 71–138.

Daguang, W., 2002. The characters of the enlargement policy and the responsibility of the government in China. *Education Research*, (3–4), 24–27.

Dvir, T., Eden, D., Avolio, B.J., and Shamir, B., 2002. Impact of transformational leadership on follower development and performance: a field experiment. *Academy of Management Journal*, 45, 735–744.

Hui, W., Law, K.S., Hackett, R.D., Wang, D., and Chen, Z.X., 2005. Leader-member exchange as a mediator of the relationship between transformational leadership and followers' performance and organizational citizenship behavior. *Academy of Management Journal*, 48(3), 420.

Jantzi, D.L.K., 1996. Toward an explanation of variation in teachers' perceptions of transformational school leadership. *Educational Administration Quarterly*, 32, 512–538.

Joyce, E. and Anderson, B.M.H., 2005. The advice and influence networks of transformational leaders. *Journal of Applied Psychology*, 90(6), 1306.

Judge, T.A. and Piccolo, R.F., 2004. Transformational and transactional leadership: a meta-analytic test of their relative validity. *Journal of Applied Psychology*, 89(5), 755–768.

Keller, R.T., 1992. Transformational leadership and the performance of research and development project groups. *Journal of Management*, 18, 489–501.

Keller, R.T., 2006. Transformational leadership, initiating structure, and substitutes for leadership: a longitudinal study of research and development project team performance. *Journal of Applied Psychology*, 91(1), 202.

Leftwich, P.R., 2001. Transformational leadership at the department chair level in North Carolina community colleges. *North Carolina State University*, Ed.D.

Leithwood, K., 1992. The move toward transformational leadership. *Educational Leadership*, 49(5), 8–12.

Lowe, K.B., Kroeck, K.G., and Sivasubramaniam, N., 1996. Effectiveness correlates of transformational and transactional leadership: a metaanalytic review. *Leadership Quarterly*, 7, 385–425.

Lucas, A.F., 1994. *Strengthening Departmental Leadership: A Team-Building Guide for Chairs in Colleges and Universities*. San Francisco: Jossey-Bass Publishers.

MacKenzie, S.B., Podsakoff, P.M., and Rich, G.A., 2000. Transformational and transactional leadership and salesperson performance. *Journal of the Academy of Marketing Science*, 29(2), 115–134.

Maoyuan, P., 2002. The strategy for the development of higher education in China in the 21st century. *China Higher Education Research*, (1–8), 33–37.

Owens, R., 2001. Organizational behavior in education: instructional leadership and school reform, 7th edn. Allyn & Bacon.

Podsakoff, P.M., Todor, W.D., Grover, R.A., and Huber, V.L., 1984. Situational moderators of leader reward behavior and punishment behaviors: fact or fiction? *Organizational Behavior and Human Performance*, 34, 21–63.

Podsakoff P.M., Mackenzie, S.B., Moorman, R.H., and Fetter, R., 1990. Transformational leader behaviors and their effects on followers' trust in leader, satisfaction, and organizational citizenship behaviors. *Leadership Quarterly*, 1(2), 107–142.

Ramsden, P., 1998. Learning to lead in higher education. New York: Routledge.

Roueche, J.E, Baker, G.A., and Rose, R.R., 1989. *Shared Vision: Transformational Leadership in American Community Colleges*. Washington, DC: American Association of Community and Junior Colleges.

Segiovanni, 1990. *Value-added Leadership: How to Get Extraordinary Performance in School*. New York: Harcourt Brace Jovanovich.

Shamir, B., Zakay, E., Breinin, E., and Popper, M., 1998. Correlates of charismatic leader behavior in military units: Subordinates' attitudes, unit characteristics, and superiors' appraisals of leader performance. *Academy of Management Journal*, 41, 384–409.

Sosik, J.J., 1997. Effect of transformational leadership and anonymity on idea generation in computer-mediated groups. *Group & Organization Management*, 22(4), 460–487.

Sosik, J.J., Avolio, B.J., and Kahai, S.S., 1997. The impact of leadership style and anonymity on group potency and effectiveness in a GDSS environment. *Journal of Applied Psychology*, 82, 89–103.

Waldman, D.A., Bass, B.M., and Einstein, W.O., 1987. Leadership and outcomes of performance appraisal process. *Journal of Occupational Psychology*, 60, 177–186.

Waldman, D.A., Bass, B.M., and Yammarino, F.J., 1990. Adding to contingent-reward behavior: the augmenting effect of charismatic leadership. *Group and Organizational Studies*, 15, 381–394.

Weick, K.E., 1976. Educational organizations as loosely coupled systems. *Administrative Science Quarterly*, 21, 1–19.

Yukl, G., 1999. An evaluation of conceptual weaknesses in transformational and charismatic leadership theories. *Leadership Quarterly*, 10, 285–305.

Impact of the Speed of Innovation Arrival on Innovation Adoption Timing: The Case of Two Generations of Future Innovations*

Jia He[†] and Yong Zeng[‡,*]

[†] *Department of Finance, The Chinese University of Hong Kong, Shatin, NT, Hong Kong*

[‡] *School of Management and Economics, The University of Electronic Science and Technology of China, Chengdu, Sichuan 610054, China*
zengy@uestc.edu.cn

Based on previous studies of Grenadier and Weiss (1997) and He and Zeng (2001), this article realizes the concept of treating the adoption of technology innovations as a sequence of real options more completely by introducing the second generation of future innovations. The solutions to the values of the real options and the triggers to adopt the current innovation, to leapfrog or upgrade to the future innovation are discussed in detail. By assuming the first as well as the current innovation emerges over the sales recording period, the relevant probability model regarding adoption timing is given analytically. Our numerical illustrations show that while there is a significant turning point in the impact of the speed of technology progress when only one generation of future innovation is expected and it emerges over the recording period, the impact becomes much less nonmonotonic or even monotonic when a further generation of improvements is expected. This confirms the intuitive and our previous empirical results.

Keywords: Real options; Technology innovation; Adoption timing.

* The work described in this article was supported by a grant from the Research Grants Council of Hong Kong Special Administrative Region (Project No. #CUHK4041/99H) and a grant from National Natural Science Foundation of China (Grant No. 70272001).
*Contact author.

1. Introduction

Technology innovation has made great contributions to the growth of the world economy and becomes even more important in the competitive strategy of a firm in new economy. Since the technology progress is an unceasing and uncertain process, the adoption behaviors and diffusion patterns of technology innovations are strongly influenced by expectations concerning the timing and significance of future improvements as well as the uncertainty of the technology progress. Actually, uncertainty of technology progress creates flexibility that can be represented by a sequence of real options, and thus value for a firm to make strategic investment decisions in adopting the innovations. While facing the current innovation provides a firm with the option to adopt now or delay the adoption till the arrival of the future innovation, by purchasing the current technology a firm has an opportunity of learning by doing and holds an option to upgrade in the future at low cost. Therefore, a current innovation should be viewed as a link in a chain of future investment options rather than considered in isolation. The real option concept created by Myers (1977) and the real option approach to capital budgeting pioneered by Brennan and Schwartz (1985) has received considerable attention in the literature, and it provides an effective approach for evaluation of adoption decisions under uncertain technological environments.[1]

Although the influence of future improvements of technology innovations on current investment decision has been dealt with in a few papers such as Balcer and Lippman (1984), Nair (1995), and Rajagopalan *et al.* (1998), formal theoretic analysis in this line of analysis has only aroused interest in recent years. In a notable recent theoretic piece, Grenadier and Weiss (1997) treat explicitly the investment in technology innovations as a stream of embedded options. By defining four adoption strategies and using an option-pricing approach, Grenadier and Weiss derived analytically the conditions and likelihood as when one of these four strategies will be the optimal migration strategy under uncertainty of technology innovations. They further examine the impact of various characteristics of technology

---

[1] Please see Pindyck (1991), Dixit and Pindyck (1994), Trigeorgis (1995, 1996), Amram and Kulatilaka (1999), Alleman and Noam (1999), and Copeland and Antikarov (2001) among many others.

environments on a firm's strategy of technology migration. In another recent paper, Farzin and colleagues (1998) investigate the optimal technology adoption timing through the real option approach and by characterizing the arrival of innovations as a Poisson jump process.[2] However, in their analysis only the critical technology state (the trigger) to adopt the innovation has been dealt with. As pointed out by Ingersoll and Ross (1992) in their discussion about the effect of the level of interest-rate uncertainty on the optimal timing of investment in a project, the trigger may not suffice to describe the waiting time. Furthermore, the triggers cannot be observed in conducting the empirical studies since only adoption timing is recorded in the data. Thus, a model directly characterizing the adoption timing is desirable.

Empirical results on this subject are also rather limited. The initial empirical support was provided based on case studies. Kaplan (1986) illustrates how the opportunity of learning by doing and the option to migrate influence the investments of firms in technology innovations. In Rosenthal (1984), the effects of the speed of technology progress and the significance of the future improvements are illustrated by the adoption of computer-integrated manufacturing techniques (CIM). In a formal empirical study, Weiss (1994) investigates the effects of technology environments on the adoption of "surface-mount technology" (SMT) in the printed-circuit assembly equipment market. Based on a survey of 85 firms with automated assembly lines for manufacturing printed circuit boards, Weiss estimates a multinomial logic model to test the relationship between the decision states and the factors such as the speed, significance and certainty of improvements, the adoption and search cost.

Based on previous studies, He and Zeng (2001) investigate the diffusion process of medical technology innovations and specifically studies adoption timing both empirically and theoretically. By using a data set characterized by a large sample size of hospitals (4,767, including for-profit and not-for-profit, large and small hospitals), and multiple product lines of medical equipment (7, including CT, MRI, PET, SPECT, Ultra-sonic, Angioplasty, and Lithotripter), we study the adoption behavior and diffusion patterns

---

[2] Huisman and Kort (1999, 2000) further extend their model to analyze the strategic technology adoption in a duopoly framework.

of innovations under different technological environments and internal conditions of hospitals. We extend previous theoretical results by providing probability models of adoption timing under different assumptions about the state of technology progress and data recording.

Our empirical study shows adoption behavior and diffusion patterns of innovations differ drastically according to technological environments and internal conditions of hospitals. While rapid technology progress, great adoption cost, significant future improvement, or small bed size encourage the delay of adoption and imply the typical S-shaped diffusion, we may not see the points of inflection indicating market maturity and saturation in the opposite cases. The characteristics of diffusion patterns are more evident in the adoption of for-profit hospitals. The empirical findings are well explained by our models through numerical illustrations. By combining various characteristics of technology environments, our models provide more insights into the adoption behaviour and thus better explanations for the recorded diffusion patterns of different medical equipment. However, only one generation of future innovation is considered in our previous models. As a result, when assuming the "future" innovation emerges over the recording period and the recorded sales are the total sales of the "current" and the "future" innovation, the impact of the speed of innovation on adoption timing is not monotonic. This is not consistent with the empirical results. An intuitive explanation for the inconsistency stems from the unceasing property of technology progress which produces further improvements even after the second generation of innovation has emerged in the market. Thus, expecting the third (and even the fourth) generation in the future, a firm may delay the adoption decision to its arrival, especially in the markets with rapid innovations. In this case, the speed of innovation may only exhibit monotonic impact.

The primary objective of this article is to verify formally the intuitive explanation by introducing the second generation of future innovations. By assuming the first as well as the current innovation emerges over the sales recording period, the relevant probability model regarding adoption timing is given analytically. Our numerical illustrations show that while there is a significant turning point in the impact of the speed of technology progress when only one generation of future innovation is expected and it emerges over the recording period, the impact becomes much less nonmonotonic or even monotonic when a further generation of improvements is expected. This confirms the intuitive and our previous empirical results.

The remainder of this article is organized as follows. In Sec. 2, we present a summary of the theoretic framework. In Sec. 3, we first derive the values of the real options through contingent claims analysis, then we discuss the solutions to the values of the real options and the triggers to adopt the current innovation, to leapfrog or upgrade to the future innovation in detail. Section 4 provides the theoretical model of adoption timing and presents a series of numerical illustrations of our model. Section 5 concludes.

2. The Framework

A firm is confronted with a current innovation (CI) and also expects two generations of improvements in the current version (1FI and 2FI). The state of technology progress is assumed to follow a Geometric Brownian motion

$$dX_t = \alpha X_t dt + \sigma X_t dW_t. \tag{1}$$

The initial state is X_0. The trigger X_{h1} and X_{h2} indicate the arrival of 1FI and 2FI respectively, where $X_{h2} > X_{h1} > X_0$. The value of CI to the firm is P_0, and its adoption cost is C_e. We assume that $P_0 > C_e$. The value of 1FI P_{T1} and the value of 2FI P_{T2} are uncertain, which are represented as $P_{T1} = P_0 + \varepsilon_1$, $\varepsilon_1 \sim N(\mu_1, v_1^2)$ and $P_{T2} = P_{T1} + \varepsilon_2$, $\varepsilon_2 \sim N(\mu_2, v_2^2)$. ε_1, ε_2, and dW_t are independent. The firm's optimal technological migration strategy is

Prior to adopting CI (and before 1FI arrives), the firm holds an option to purchase CI. The firm's optimal exercise strategy is to adopt CI the first moment that $X(t)$ falls below the trigger X_{l1}, prior to the arrival of 1FI.

If the firm invests in CI prior to the arrival of 1FI, it will receive an option to upgrade. After 1FI emerges and before the arrival of 2FI, the firm will upgrade to 1FI the first moment $X(t)$ falls below the trigger X_{l2} if $P_{T1} - P_0 - C_{u0}^{(1)} \geq 0$, where $C_{u0}^{(1)}$ denotes the upgrade cost of exchanging CI for 1FI. Otherwise, it will postpone the decision of upgrading to the arrival of 2FI.

If the firm does not invest in CI prior to the arrival of 1FI, then after 1FI emerges and before the arrival of 2FI, it will leapfrog to 1FI the first

moment $X(t)$ falls below the trigger X_{l3} if $P_{T1} - C_{l1} \geq P_0 - C_{d0}^{(1)}$, or purchase CI at a discounted price $C_{d0}^{(1)}$; where $C_{d0}^{(1)}$ denotes the cost of adopting CI after the arrival of 1FI and before the arrival of 2FI, and C_{l1} denotes the cost of adopting 1FI. Otherwise, it will further postpone the decision of adoption to the arrival of 2FI.

At the arrival of 2FI, if the firm has invested neither in CI nor in 1FI, it will leapfrog to 2FI at a cost C_{l2}, leapfrog to 1FI at a discounted price C_{d1} or purchase CI at a further discounted price $C_{d0}^{(2)}$, depending on which is the largest of $P_{T2} - C_{l2}, P_{T1} - C_{d1}$ or $P_0 - C_{d0}^{(2)}$. If the firm has already adopted CI but not 1FI, it will upgrade directly to 2FI, upgrade to 1FI or give up upgrading depending on which is the largest of $P_{T2} - P_0 - C_{u0}^{(2)}, P_{T1} - P_0 - C_{u0}^{(1)}$ or 0; where $C_{u0}^{(2)}$ denotes the upgrade cost of exchanging CI for 2FI. If the firm has already invested in 1FI, it will upgrade to 2FI if $P_{T2} - P_{T1} - C_{u1} \geq 0$; where C_{u1} denotes the upgrade cost of exchanging 1FI for 2FI.

We further assume the following reasonable relationships among the adoption and upgrading costs:

$C_{d0}^{(1)} \leq C_e$ and $C_{d1} \leq C_{l1}$ *to mean discount;*

$C_{u0}^{(1)} < C_{l1}, C_{u1} < C_{l2}$ and $C_{u1} < C_{u0}^{(2)}$ *to incorporate the*
ability of learning by doing;

$C_{l1} < C_e + C_{u0}^{(1)}, C_{l1} \leq C_{d0}^{(1)} + C_{u0}^{(1)}, C_{l2} < C_{l1} + C_{u1},$

$C_{l2} \leq C_{d1} + C_{u1}, C_{l2} \leq C_{d0}^{(1)} + C_{u0}^{(2)},$

and $C_{u0}^{(2)} \leq C_{u0}^{(1)} + C_{u1}$ to prevent some forms of adoption arbitrage.
The triggers and adoption timing are illustrated by Fig. 1.

3. The Values of the Options and the Solutions

Let $G(X)$, $F_1(X)$ and $F_2(X)$ denote the value of the option to purchase CI, the value of the option to upgrade to 1FI from CI and the value of the option to exchange 1FI for 2FI respectively.

Assume dW_t can be spanned by asset or portfolio V_t, which follows

$$dV_t = \mu V_t dt + \sigma V_t dW_t.$$

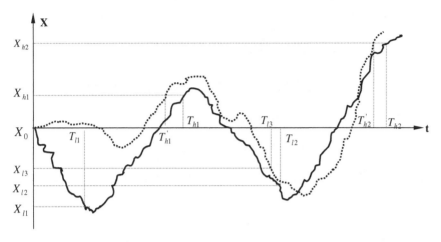

Fig. 1.

First, suppose the firm has already adopted 1FI. Consider the following portfolio: Hold the option to upgrade from 1FI to 2FI and go short $n = F_2(X)X/V$ units of the spanning asset. The value of this portfolio is $P = F_2(X) - nV$. By Ito's lemma, we have

$$dP = \left[\frac{1}{2}\sigma^2 X^2 F_2''(X) - \delta X F_2'(X)\right] dt,$$

where $\delta = \mu - \alpha$, which is the difference between the equilibrium rate of return μ and the "capital gain" α. Because dP is nonstochastic, this portfolio is risk-free and its rate of return should be risk-free interest rate r, i.e., $dP = rPdt$. Therefore,[3]

$$\frac{1}{2}\sigma^2 X^2 F_2''(Z) + (r - \delta)X F_2'(X) - r F_2(X) = 0.$$

Similarly, we can derive the differential equations that $F_1(X)$ and $G(X)$ satisfy.

---

[3]By dynamic programming, we can get $\frac{1}{2}\sigma^2 X^2 F_2''(X) + (\rho - \delta)X F_2'(X) - \rho F_2(X) = 0$, where ρ is the discount rate. Using risk neutral argument, we can get $\frac{1}{2}\sigma^2 X^2 F_2'' + \alpha X F_2' - r F = 0$. Therefore, the three approaches are equivalent if we assume risk neutrality, i.e., $\rho = \mu = r$.

Thus, we have

$$G(X) = A_{g1}X^{-\beta_1} + A_{g2}X^{\beta_2}, \tag{2}$$

$$F_1(X) = A_{f11}X^{-\beta_1} + A_{f12}X^{\beta_2}, \tag{3}$$

$$F_2(X) = A_{f21}X^{-\beta_1} + A_{f22}X^{\beta_2}, \tag{4}$$

where

$$\beta_1 = \frac{[(r-\delta) - \sigma^2/2] + \sqrt{[(r-\delta) - \sigma^2/2]^2 + 2r\sigma^2}}{\sigma^2} > 0,$$

$$\beta_2 = \frac{-[(r-\delta) - \sigma^2/2] + \sqrt{[(r-\delta) - \sigma^2/2]^2 + 2r\sigma^2}}{\sigma^2} > 1.$$

The boundary conditions which $G(X)$, $F_1(X)$, and $F_2(X)$ must satisfy can be derived according to the above optimal technological migration strategy.

First, assume the firm has invested in 1FI prior to the arrival of 2FI. $F_2(X)$ should satisfy

$$F_2(X_{h2}) = E[\max(P_{T2} - P_{T1} - C_{u1}, 0)] = K_4. \tag{5}$$

Because X_t has an absorbing barrier at zero, the option would never be exercised if X_t ever falls to zero. Thus

$$F_2(0) = 0. \tag{6}$$

From Eqs. (5) and (6), we have

$$A_{f21} = 0,$$

$$A_{f22} = K_4(X_{h2})^{-\beta_2}.$$

Second, assume the firm has invested in CI but not 1FI prior to the arrival of 2FI. $F_1(X)$ should satisfy

$$F_1(X_{h2}) = E[\max(P_{T2} - P_0 - C_{u0}^{(2)}, P_{T1} - P_0 - C_{u0}^{(1)}, 0)] = K_3 \tag{7}$$

According to our assumptions, we have $K_3 > K_4$ if $\mu_1 \geq C_{u0}^{(1)}$. Furthermore, if CI is adopted prior to the arrival of 1FI, $F_1(X)$ should also satisfy

$$F_1(X_{l2}) = \Pr(P_{T1} - P_0 - C_{u0}^{(1)} \geq 0)[E(P_{T1} - P_0 - C_{u0}^{(1)}|P_{T1} - P_0$$
$$- C_{u0}^{(1)} \geq 0) + F_2(X_{l2})] + \Pr(P_{T1} - P_0 - C_{u0}^{(1)} < 0)F_1(X_{l2})$$

which can be rearranged as

$$F_1(X_{l2}) = \frac{K_{12}}{1 - \phi_2} + F_2(X_{l2}) \tag{8}$$

with related smooth-pasting condition

$$F_1'(X_{l2}) = F_2'(X_{l2}), \tag{9}$$

where $K_{12} = E[\max(P_{T1} - P_0 - C_{u0}^{(1)}, 0)]$,

$$\phi_2 = \Pr(P_{T1} - P_0 - C_{u0}^{(1)} < 0).$$

Third, assume the firm has invested neither in CI nor 1FI prior to the arrival of 2FI. $G(X)$ should satisfy

$$G(X_{h2}) = E[\max(P_{T2} - C_{l2}, P_{T1} - C_{d1}, P_0 - C_{d0}^{(2)})] = K_2. \tag{10}$$

According to our assumptions, we have $K_2 > K_3$. If the firm does not adopted CI before the arrival of 1FI, at the trigger X_{l3} $G(X)$ satisfies

$$G(X_{l3}) = \Pr(P_{T1} - C_{l1} \geq P_0 - C_{d0}^{(1)})[E(P_{T1} - C_{l1}|P_{T1} - C_{l1} \geq P_0$$
$$- C_{d0}^{(1)}) + F_2(X_{l3})] + \Pr(P_{T1} - C_{l1} < P_0 - C_{d0}^{(1)})$$
$$[(P_0 - C_{d0}^{(1)}) + F_1(X_{l3})]$$

which can be rearranged as

$$G(X_{l3}) = K_{13} + \phi_3 F_1(X_{l3}) + (1 - \phi_3)F_2(X_{l3}) \tag{11}$$

with related smooth-pasting condition

$$G'(X_{l3}) = \phi_3 F_1'(X_{l3}) + (1 - \phi_3)F_2'(X_{l3}) \tag{12}$$

where $K_{13} = E[\max(P_{T1} - C_{l1}, P_0 - C_{d0}^{(1)})]$,

$$\phi_3 = \Pr(P_{T1} - C_{l1} < P_0 - C_{d0}^{(1)}).$$

In addition, before the arrival of 1FI, at the trigger X_{l1} $G(X)$ should also satisfy the value matching and smooth-pasting conditions

$$G(X_{l1}) = K_{11} + F_1(X_{l1}) \tag{13}$$

$$G'(X_{l1}) = F_1'(X_{l1}) \tag{14}$$

where $K_{11} = P_0 - C_e$.

As there are 10 equations with nine unknown parameters (A_{g1}, A_{g2}, A_{f11}, A_{f12}, A_{f21}, A_{f22}, X_{l1}, X_{l2}, and X_{l3}), in general the system has no ordinary solution unless there exist redundant equations. We deal with this problem later. Before doing that, let us investigate the subsystems of the equations.

Firstly, consider the subsystem comprising Eqs. (5)–(10) and (13)–(14). The solution to the subsystem can be decomposed into two basic equations:

$$c_1(X_{h2})^{-\beta_1}(\varpi_1)^{-\beta_1/\beta_2} + \varpi_1(X_{h2})^{\beta_2} = K_2 - K_3, \tag{15}$$

$$c_2(X_{h2})^{-\beta_1}(\varpi_2)^{-\beta_1/\beta_2} + \varpi_2(X_{h2})^{\beta_2} = (1 - \phi_2)(K_3 - K_4), \tag{16}$$

where

$$c_1 = \frac{\beta_2}{\beta_1}\left[\frac{\beta_1}{\beta_1 + \beta_2}K_{11}\right]^{(\beta_1+\beta_2)/\beta_2},$$

$$c_2 = \frac{\beta_2}{\beta_1}\left[\frac{\beta_1}{\beta_1 + \beta_2}K_{12}\right]^{(\beta_1+\beta_2)/\beta_2},$$

$$X_{l1} = \left[\frac{\beta_1}{\beta_1 + \beta_2}\frac{K_{11}}{\varpi_1}\right]^{1/\beta_2},$$

$$X_{l2} = \left[\frac{\beta_1}{\beta_1 + \beta_2}\frac{K_{12}}{\varpi_2}\right]^{1/\beta_2}.$$

Accordingly, we have

$$A_{g1}^{(1)} = (K_2 - K_3)(X_{h2})^{\beta_1} - \left(\frac{\varpi_2}{1 - \phi_2} + \varpi_1\right)(X_{h2})^{\beta_1+\beta_2},$$

$$A_{g2}^{(1)} = \frac{\varpi_2}{1 - \phi_2} + \varpi_1 + K_4(X_{h2})^{-\beta_2},$$

$$A^{(1)}_{f11} = (K_3 - K_4)(X_{h2})^{\beta_1} - \left(\frac{\varpi_2}{1 - \phi_2}\right)(X_{h2})^{\beta_1 + \beta_2},$$

$$A^{(1)}_{f12} = \frac{\varpi_2}{1 - \phi_2} + K_4(X_{h2})^{-\beta_2}.$$

Secondly, consider the subsystem comprising Eqs. (5)–(12). The solution to the subsystem can be decomposed into Eq. (15) and the following basic Eq. (17):

$$c_3(X_{h2})^{-\beta_1}(\varpi_3)^{-\beta_1/\beta_2} + \varpi_3(X_{h2})^{\beta_2}$$
$$= (K_2 - K_3) + (1 - \phi_3)(K_3 - K_4) \tag{17}$$

where

$$c_3 = \frac{\beta_2}{\beta_1}\left[\frac{\beta_1}{\beta_1 + \beta_2}K_{13}\right]^{(\beta_1 + \beta_2)/\beta_2},$$

$$X_{l3} = \left[\frac{\beta_1}{\beta_1 + \beta_2}\frac{K_{13}}{\varpi_3}\right]^{1/\beta_2}.$$

Accordingly, we have

$$A^{(2)}_{g1} = (K_2 - K_3)(X_{h2})^{\beta_1} - \left(\frac{\varpi_3 - \varpi_1}{1 - \phi_3} + \varpi_1\right)(X_{h2})^{\beta_1 + \beta_2},$$

$$A^{(2)}_{g2} = \frac{\varpi_3 - \varpi_1}{1 - \phi_3} + \varpi_1 + K_4(X_{h2})^{-\beta_2},$$

$$A^{(2)}_{f11} = (K_3 - K_4)(X_{h2})^{\beta_1} - \left(\frac{\varpi_3 - \varpi_1}{1 - \phi_3}\right)(X_{h2})^{\beta_1 + \beta_2},$$

$$A^{(2)}_{f12} = \frac{\varpi_3 - \varpi_1}{1 - \phi_3} + K_4(X_{h2})^{-\beta_2}.$$

Thus, we can see the only difference between the solutions to the two subsystems is between $\frac{\varpi_2}{1 - \phi_3}$ and $\frac{\varpi_3 - \varpi_1}{1 - \phi_3}$. Before we examine further the coincidence of the solutions, we have a discussion about the characteristics of the solution to the basic equations.

Define

$$f(\varpi) = c(X_h)^{-\beta_1}\varpi^{-\beta_1/\beta_2} + \varpi(X_h)^{\beta_2} + (\Gamma_1 - \Gamma_2)$$

and $X_l = \left[\frac{\beta_1}{\beta_1+\beta_2}\frac{\Gamma_0}{\varpi}\right]^{1/\beta_2}$, where $c = \frac{\beta_2}{\beta_1}\left[\frac{\beta_1}{\beta_1+\beta_2}\Gamma_0\right]^{(\beta_1+\beta_2)/\beta_2}$, $\Gamma_0 > 0$ and $\Gamma_2 > \Gamma_1 > 0$. Therefore,

$$f'(\varpi) = c(-\beta_1/\beta_2)(X_h)^{-\beta_1}\varpi^{-\beta_1/\beta_2-1} + (X_h)^{\beta_2}$$

with an unique zero point at

$$\varpi^{(0)} = (X_h)^{-\beta_2}\left(\frac{\beta_1}{\beta_2}c\right)^{\frac{\beta_2}{\beta_1+\beta_2}} = \left(\frac{\beta_1}{\beta_1+\beta_2}\Gamma_0\right)(X_h)^{-\beta_2}.$$

Because $f''(\varpi) = c\left(\frac{\beta_1}{\beta_2}\right)\left(\frac{\beta_1+\beta_2}{\beta_2}\right)(X_h)^{-\beta_1}\varpi^{-\beta_1/\beta_2-2} > 0$ for $\varpi > 0$, ϖ_0 is the minimum point of $f(\varpi)$. In addition,

$$f(\varpi^{(0)}) = \Gamma_0 - (\Gamma_2 - \Gamma_1)$$

and

$$f(\varpi^{(1)}) = c(\Gamma_2 - \Gamma_1)^{-\beta_1/\beta_2} > 0,$$

$$f(\varpi^{(2)}) = [c/(\Gamma_2 - \Gamma_1)]^{\beta_2/\beta_1} > 0,$$

where $\varpi^{(1)} = (\Gamma_2 - \Gamma_1)(X_h)^{-\beta_2}$ and $\varpi^{(2)} = [c/\Gamma_2 - \Gamma_1]^{\beta_2/\beta_1}(X_h)^{-\beta_2}$. Thus, there exist solutions to equation $f(\varpi) = 0$ for $\Gamma_0 \leq (\Gamma_2 - \Gamma_1)$ and no solution for $\Gamma_0 > (\Gamma_2 - \Gamma_1)$. Furthermore, for $\Gamma_0 = (\Gamma_2 - \Gamma_1)$, there exists a unique solution at ϖ_0. For $\Gamma_0 < (\Gamma_2 - \Gamma_1)$,

$$f'(\varpi^{(1)}) = \left[1 - \left(\frac{\beta_1}{\beta_1+\beta_2}\cdot\frac{\Gamma_0}{\Gamma_2-\Gamma_1}\right)^{\frac{\beta_1+\beta_2}{\beta_2}}\right]\cdot(X_{h2})^{\beta_2} > 0,$$

$$f'(\varpi^{(2)}) = \left[1 - \left(\frac{\beta_1+\beta_2}{\beta_2}\cdot\frac{\Gamma_2-\Gamma_1}{\Gamma_0}\right)^{\frac{\beta_1+\beta_2}{\beta_1}}\right]\cdot(X_{h2})^{\beta_2} < 0.$$

Therefore, there are two solutions, which are within $(\varpi^{(0)}, \varpi^{(1)})$ and $(\varpi^{(2)}, \varpi^{(0)})$ respectively. Denote them by $\hat{\varpi}_1$ and $\hat{\varpi}_2$ respectively. Because $X_l(\varpi^{(0)}) = X_h$, $\hat{\varpi}_1 > \varpi^{(0)}$ and $\hat{\varpi}_2 < \varpi^{(0)}$, $X_l(\hat{\varpi}_1) < X_h$ and $X_l(\hat{\varpi}_2) > X_h$. Thus, there is only one meaningful solution to Eqs. (15), (16), or (17) if any of them have two solutions.

For $K_{12} > (1 - \phi_2)(K_3 - K_4)$, there exists no solutions to Eq. (16). This implies that once the firm adopts CI, it will never upgrade to 1FI prior to the arrival of 2FI. Similarly, $K_{13} \geq (K_2 - K_3) + (1 - \phi_2)(K_3 - K_4)$ implies once the firm does not adopt CI prior to the arrival of 1FI, it will not adopt CI or leapfrog to 1FI prior to the arrival of 2FI. $K_{11} \geq (K_2 - K_3)$ implies that the firm should not adopt CI prior to the arrival of 1FI.

For $K_{12} > (1 - \phi_2)(K_3 - K_4)$, the triggers X_{l1} and X_{l3} as well as the option values can be uniquely determined by the subsystem comprising Eqs. (5)–(12) for $K_{11} < (K_2 - K_3)$ and $K_{13} < (K_2 - K_3) + (1 - \phi_2)(K_3 - K_4)$. Even if $K_{13} > (K_2 - K_3) + (1 - \phi_2)(K_3 - K_4)$ or $K_{11} > (K_2 - K_3)$ in addition to $K_{12} > (1 - \phi_2)(K_3 - K_4)$, Eq. (15) or (17) can be derived from subsystem comprising Eqs. (7), (10), (13), and (14), or subsystem comprising Eqs. (7), (10), (11), and (12). Thus, the trigger X_{l1} or X_{l3} can be uniquely determined although the option values are undermined. That is enough for the analysis of adoption timing. Similarly, For $K_{13} > (K_2 - K_3) + (1 - \phi_2)(K_3 - K_4)$, the triggers X_{l1} and X_{l3} as well as the option values can be uniquely determined by the subsystem comprising equations subsystem comprising Eqs. (5)–(10) and (13)–(14) for $K_{11} < (K_2 - K_3)$ and $K_{12} < (1 - \phi_2)(K_3 - K_4)$. However, for $K_{11} < (K_2 - K_3)$, $K_{12} < (1 - \phi_2)(K_3 - K_4)$ and $K_{13} < (K_2 - K_3) + (1 - \phi_3)(K_3 - K_4)$, the equations are potentially inconsistent. Now we have an examination on the extent of coincidence of the solutions. The basic conclusion is that for reasonable adoption and upgrading costs, the extent of inconsistency is minors. The arguments for this conclusion are as follows.

Firstly, for the basic equation $f(\varpi) = 0$ and $\Gamma_0 < (\Gamma_2 - \Gamma_1)$, the solution $\hat{\varpi}_1$, which corresponds to a X_l less than X_h, can be approximated at high accuracy by $\varpi^{(1)}$, which can be obtained by neglecting the nonlinear item in the basic equation. Thus we can see the only difference between the solutions to the two subsystems, i.e., that between $\frac{\varpi_2}{1-\phi_2}$ and $\frac{\varpi_3 - \varpi_1}{1-\phi_3}$, may be neglected. Denote $q_w = \frac{\varpi_3 - \varpi_1}{1-\phi_3} / \frac{\varpi_2}{1-\phi_2}$ for further discussion.

Secondly, with the solution to the subsystem comprising Eqs. (5)–(12), $F_1(X)$ and its derivative with respect to X, $F_{1X}(X)$, can be represented as

$$F_1^{(1)}(X) = \left\{ \left[(K_3 - K_4)(X_{h2})^{-\beta_2} - \frac{\varpi_3 - \varpi_1}{1 - \phi_3} \right] \left(\frac{X_{h2}}{X} \right)^{\beta_1 + \beta_2} \right.$$

$$\left. + \frac{\varpi_3 - \varpi_1}{1 - \phi_3} \right\} X^{\beta_2} + F_2(X),$$

$$F_{1X}^{(1)}(X) = \left\{ \left(-\frac{\beta_1}{\beta_2}\right) \left[(K_3 - K_4)(X_{h2})^{-\beta_2} - \frac{\varpi_3 - \varpi_1}{1 - \phi_3} \right] \left(\frac{X_{h2}}{X}\right)^{\beta_1 + \beta_2} \right.$$

$$\left. + \frac{\varpi_3 - \varpi_1}{1 - \phi_3} \right\} (\beta_2 X^{\beta_2 - 1}) + F_{2X}(X).$$

Similarly, with the solution to the subsystem comprising Eqs. (5)–(10) and (13)–(14), $F_1(X)$ and $F_{1X}(X)$ can be represented as

$$F_1^{(2)}(X) = \left\{ \left[(K_3 - K_4)(X_{h2})^{-\beta_2} - \frac{\varpi_2}{1 - \phi_2} \right] \left(\frac{X_{h2}}{X}\right)^{\beta_1 + \beta_2} \right.$$

$$\left. + \frac{\varpi_2}{1 - \phi_2} \right\} X^{\beta_2} + F_2(X),$$

$$F_{1X}^{(2)}(X) = \left\{ \left(-\frac{\beta_1}{\beta_2}\right) \left[(K_3 - K_4)(X_{h2})^{-\beta_2} - \frac{\varpi_2}{1 - \phi_2} \right] \left(\frac{X_{h2}}{X}\right)^{\beta_1 + \beta_2} \right.$$

$$\left. + \frac{\varpi_2}{1 - \phi_2} \right\} (\beta_2 X^{\beta_2 - 1}) + F_{2X}(X).$$

Define

$$qf = \left[F_1^{(1)}(X_{l2}) - F_1^{(2)}(X_{l2}) \right] / F_1^{(2)}(X_{l2}),$$

$$qdf = \left[F_{1X}^{(1)}(X_{l2}) - F_{1X}^{(2)}(X_{l2}) \right] / F_{1X}^{(2)}(X_{l2}).$$

We can illustrate that $qf \ll 1$ and $qdf \ll 1$ for reasonable adoption and upgrading costs. This implies Eqs. (13) and (14) will be satisfied at high accuracy if we approximate ϖ_2 with $\frac{1 - \phi_2}{1 - \phi_3}(\varpi_3 - \varpi_1)$, where ϖ_1 and ϖ_3 are solutions to the basic Eqs. (15) and (17).

Similarly, define

$$qg = \left\{ \left[G^{(1)}(X_{l3}) - F_1^{(1)}(X_{l3}) \right] \right.$$

$$\left. - \left[G^{(2)}(X_{l3}) - F_1^{(2)}(X_{l3}) \right] \right\} / \left[G^{(1)}(X_{l3}) - F_1^{(1)}(X_{l3}) \right],$$

$$qdg = \left\{ \left[G_X^{(1)}(X_{l3}) - F_{1X}^{(1)}(X_{l3}) \right] \right.$$

$$\left. - \left[G_X^{(2)}(X_{l3}) - F_{1X}^{(2)}(X_{l3}) \right] \right\} / \left[G_X^{(1)}(X_{l3}) - F_{1X}^{(1)}(X_{l3}) \right].$$

We can illustrate that $qg \ll 1$ and $qdg \ll 1$ for reasonable adoption and upgrading costs. This implies Eqs. (11) and (12) will be satisfied at a high accuracy if we approximate ϖ_3 with $\varpi_1 + \frac{1-\phi_3}{1-\phi_2}\varpi_2$, where ϖ_1 and ϖ_2 are the solutions to the basic Eqs. (15) and (16). Thus, the solutions to the two subsystems are consistent with high accuracy for reasonable adoption and upgrading costs. Table 1 presents numerical examples to illustrate the extent of consistency between the solutions to the two subsystems, where the parameters are set so that both the subsystems have solutions. In the illustration, only $C_{u0}^{(1)}$, $C_{u0}^{(2)}$, and C_{u1} are varied because the condition for solvability of the basic Eq. (16) is the most difficult to be satisfied of the three for solvability of the basic Eqs. (15)–(17) within the reasonable range of costs, and the relative surplus of C_{u1} to $C_{u0}^{(2)} - C_{u0}^{(1)}$ is the main determinant of the relative value of $(1 - \phi_2)(K_3 - K_4)$ to K_{12}, i.e., whether there exists a solution to Eq. (16) and the accuracy of approximating ϖ_2 by neglecting the nonlinear part of Eq. (16). From Table 1, we find that for a moderate value of C_{u1} (example 1), the solutions to the two subsystems are highly consistent. The extent of consistency decreases as we decrease or increase C_{u1}. For example 4 and 6, K_{12} and $(1 - \phi_2)(K_3 - K_4)$ are so close that we cannot say the solutions are consistent and approximate ϖ_2 or ϖ_3 by letting $\frac{\varpi_3-\varpi_1}{1-\phi_3} = \frac{\varpi_2}{1-\phi_2}$. However, the high consistency is recovered when we adjust $C_{u0}^{(1)}$ and $C_{u0}^{(2)}$ accordingly.[4]

4. The Probability Model of Adoption Timing and Numerical Illustrations

With the above preparations, we now investigate the adoption timing of innovations and compare the results under different assumptions about data recording.

Denote the time to adopt the innovation by T. Denote stopping at first hitting time of the underlying process of technology progress by $T_{h1} = \inf\{s : X_s = X_{h1}\}$ for $X_0 < X_{h1}$, and stopping at first exit time by

---

[4]Actually, for $C_{u0}^{(1)} = 0.95$, $C_{u0}^{(2)} = 1.85$, and the default parameter values, the more reasonable value range for C_{u1} is that between 0.935 and 1.225. However, the condition for solvability of the basic Eq. (16) cannot be satisfied over this range.

Table 1. The consistency of the solutions to the two subsystems.

Examples	1	2	3	4	5	6	7
$C_{u0}^{(1)}$	0.95	0.95	0.95	0.95	0.95	0.95	0.935
$C_{u0}^{(2)}$	1.85	1.85	1.855	1.85	1.825	1.825	1.805
C_{u0}	1.30	1.425	1.425	1.265	1.265	1.235	1.212
K_{11}	0.175	0.175	0.175	0.175	0.175	0.175	0.175
$K_2 - K_3$	0.238	0.238	0.240	0.238	0.228	0.228	0.228
K_{12}	0.107	0.107	0.107	0.107	0.107	0.107	0.116
$(1 - \phi_2) \times (K_3 - K_4)$	0.114	0.131	0.130	0.108	0.113	0.108	0.123
K_{13}	0.307	0.307	0.307	0.307	0.307	0.307	0.307
$(K_2 - K_3) + (1 - \phi_3) \times (K_3 - K_4)$	0.351	0.369	0.370	0.345	0.342	0.336	0.330
mqw	1.000000	1.000000	1.000000	1.003048	1.000000	1.002252	1.000000
mqf	1.04×10^{-12}	1.22×10^{-5}	7.26×10^{-6}	3.70×10^{-3}	1.07×10^{-12}	4.09×10^{-3}	6.25×10^{-13}
$mqdf$	1.19×10^{-10}	1.40×10^{-3}	8.36×10^{-4}	1.90	1.23×10^{-10}	1.74	7.17×10^{-11}
mqg	3.00×10^{-9}	6.00×10^{-7}	1.26×10^{-6}	1.68×10^{3}	1.58×10^{-10}	5.22×10^{1}	1.92×10^{-12}
$mqdg$	3.44×10^{-7}	6.90×10^{-5}	1.44×10^{-4}	1.93×10^{5}	1.81×10^{-8}	5.98×10^{3}	2.19×10^{-10}

$T_{l1,h1} = \inf\{s : X_s \notin (X_{l1}, X_{h1})\}$ for $X_0 \in (X_{l1}, X_{h1})$ and $T_{l3,h2} = \inf$ $\{s : X_s \notin (X_{l3}, X_{h2})\}$ for $X_{h1} \in (X_{l3}, X_{h2})$. Under the assumption that 1FI as well as CI emerges over the recording period and the recorded sales are the total sales of CI and 1FI, the relevant probabilities are

$$P_{(0,t_1)}(X_0) = \Pr\{T \le t_1 | X_0, X_{T_{l3,h2}} = X_{l3} \text{ for } X_{h1} \in (X_{l3}, X_{h2})\},$$
(18.1)

$$P_{(t_1,t_2)}(X_0) = P_{(0,t_2)}(X_0) - P_{(0,t_1)}(X_0),$$
(18.2)

$$P_{(t_2,\infty)}(X_0) = 1 - P_{(0,t_2)}(X_0).$$
(18.3)

Seven numerical examples are presented to illustrate the extent of consistency of the solution to one subsystem with the solution to the other. The default parameter values are $\alpha = 0.01$, $\sigma = 0.03$, $r = 0.07$, $r - \delta = 0.06$, $X_0 = 1$, $p_0 = 1.0$, $\mu_1 = 1.0$, $\mu_2 = 1.0$, $\nu_1 = 0.2$, $\nu_2 = 0.5$, $C_e = 0.825$, $C_{d0}^{(1)} = 0.80$, $C_{d0}^{(2)} = 1.00$, $C_{l1} = 1.75$, $C_{d1} = 1.70$, and $C_{l2} = 2.625$. $E(T_h)$ is increased from 0 to 26. X_{h1} is set in accordance with the various levels of $E(T_h)$, and $X_{h2} = X_{h1}^2/X_0$. For these parameters, $\beta_1 = 133.50$ and $\beta_2 = 1.17$. mqw is the value of qw with maximum absolute difference from 1. mqf, $mqdf$, mgf, and $mqdg$ are the maximum absolute values of qf, qdf, gf, and qdg respectively. We find that for a moderate value of C_{u1} (example 1), the solutions to the two subsystems are highly consistent. The extent of consistency decreases as we decrease or increase C_{u1}. However, the high consistency is recovered when we adjust $C_{u0}^{(1)}$ and $C_{u0}^{(2)}$ accordingly.

In above probability model, the trigger X_{l2} will not be used. Equation (18.1) is represented as

$$P_{(0,t_1)}(X_0) = P_{(0,t_1)}^{(1)}(X_0) + P_{(0,t_1)}^{(2)}(X_0),$$
(19)

where $P_{(0,t_1)}^{(1)}(X_0)$ and $P_{(0,t_2)}^{(2)}(X_0)$ denote the likelihood to adopt CI before t_1 prior to the arrival of 1FI, and the likelihood to adopt 1FI or CI before t_1 if CI is not invested prior to the arrival of 1FI respectively.

For $K_{11} < (K_2 - K_3)$ and $K_{13} < (K_2 - K_3) + (1 - \phi_3)(K_3 - K_4)$, we have

$$P_{(0,t_1)}^{(1)}(X_0) = \begin{cases} 1 & \text{for } X_{l1} \ge X_0 \\ \Pr\{T_{l1,h1} \le t_1, X_{T_{l1,h1}} = X_{l1} | X_0\} & \text{for } X_{l1} < X_0 \end{cases},$$
(20.1)

$$P_{(0,t_1)}^{(2)}(X_0)$$

$$= \begin{cases} \Pr\{T_{l1,h1} \le t_1, X_{T_{l1,h1}} = X_{h1}|X_0\} & \text{for } X_{l3} \ge X_{h1} \\ \dfrac{\Pr\{T_{l1,h1} + T_{l3,h2} \le t_1, X_{T_{l1,h1}} = X_{h1}, X_{T_{l3,h2}} = X_{l3}|X_0\}}{\Pr\{X_{T_{l3,h2}} = X_{l3}|X_0\}} \\ & \text{for } X_{l3} < X_{h1} \end{cases}.$$

$$(20.2)$$

For $K_{11} < (K_2 - K_3)$ and $K_{13} > (K_2 - K_3) + (1 - \phi_3)(K_3 - K_4)$, $P_{(0,t_1)}^{(2)}(X_0) = 0$ and $P_{(0,t_1)}^{(1)}(X_0)$ is represented as (20.1).

For $K_{11} > (K_2 - K_3)$ and $K_{13} < (K_2 - K_3) + (1 - \phi_3)(K_3 - K_4)$, $P_{(0,t_1)}^{(1)}(X_0) = 0$ and $P_{(0,t_1)}^{(2)}(X_0)$ is represented as

$$P_{(0,t_1)}^{(2)}(X_0)$$

$$= \begin{cases} \Pr\{T_{h1} \le t_1|X_0\} & \text{for } X_{l3} \ge X_{h1} \\ \dfrac{\Pr\{T_{h1} + T_{l3,h2} \le t_1, X_{T_{l3,h2}} = X_{l3}|X_0\}}{\Pr\{X_{T_{l3,h2}} = X_{l3}|X_0\}} & \text{for } X_{l3} < X_{h1} \end{cases}.$$

$$(20.3)$$

For $K_{11} > (K_2 - K_3)$ and $K_{13} > (K_2 - K_3) + (1 - \phi_3)(K_3 - K_4)$, $P_{(0,t_1)}^{(1)}(X_0) = 0$ and $P_{(0,t_1)}^{(2)}(X_0) = 0$.

Denote $\mu = \frac{1}{\sigma}(\alpha - \frac{\sigma^2}{2})$, $a_1 = \frac{1}{\sigma}\log(X_{l1})$, $a_2 = \frac{1}{\sigma}\log(X_{l3})$, $b_1 = \frac{1}{\sigma}\log(X_{h1})$, $b_2 = \frac{1}{\sigma}\log(X_{h2})$, $x_1 = \frac{1}{\sigma}\log(X_0)$, $x_2 = \frac{1}{\sigma}\log(X_{h1})$, and $u_1 = x_1 - a_1$, $u_1' = b_1 - x_1$, $w_1 = w_1' = b_1 - a_1$, $u_2 = b_2 - x_2$, $w_2 = b_2 - a_2$.

According to Borodin and Salminen (1996), we have

$$\Pr\{T_{l1,h1} \le t_1, X_{T_{l1,h1}} = X_{l1}|X_0\}$$

$$= \exp(u_1' - w_1') \cdot L_\gamma^{-1}\left(\frac{1}{\gamma} \cdot \frac{sh(u_1'\sqrt{2\gamma + \mu^2})}{sh(w_1'\sqrt{2\gamma + \mu^2})}\right) \quad \text{for } X_{l1} < X_0,$$

$$\Pr\{X_{T_{l3,h2}} = X_{l3}|X_0\} = \exp[\mu(u_2 - w_2)] \cdot \frac{sh(\mu u_1)}{sh(\mu w_1)} \quad \text{and}$$

$$\Pr\{T_{l1,h1} + T_{l3,h2} \le t_1, X_{T_{l1,h1}} = X_{h1}, X_{T_{l3,h2}} = X_{l3}|X_0\}$$

$$= \exp[\mu(w_1 - u_1 + u_2 - w_2)]$$

$$\cdot L_\gamma^{-1}\left(\frac{1}{\gamma} \cdot \frac{sh(u_1\sqrt{2\gamma + \mu^2})}{sh(w_1\sqrt{2\gamma + \mu^2})} \cdot \frac{sh(u_2\sqrt{2\gamma + \mu^2})}{sh(w_2\sqrt{2\gamma + \mu^2})}\right) \text{ for } X_{l3} < X_{h1},$$

$$\Pr\{T_{l1,h1} \le t_1, X_{T_{l1,h1}} = X_{h1}|X_0\}$$

$$= \exp[\mu(w_1 - u_1)] \cdot L_\gamma^{-1}\left(\frac{1}{\gamma} \cdot \frac{sh(u_1\sqrt{2\gamma + \mu^2})}{sh(w_1\sqrt{2\gamma + \mu^2})}\right),$$

$$\Pr\{T_{h1} + T_{l3,h2} \le t_1, X_{T_{l3,h2}} = X_{l3}|X_0\}$$

$$= \exp[\mu(w_1 - u_1 + u_2 - w_2)]$$

$$\cdot L_\gamma^{-1}\left(\frac{1}{\gamma} \cdot \frac{\exp(u_1\sqrt{2\gamma + \mu^2})}{\exp(w_1\sqrt{2\gamma + \mu^2})} \cdot \frac{sh(u_2\sqrt{2\gamma + \mu^2})}{sh(w_2\sqrt{2\gamma + \mu^2})}\right) \text{ for } X_{l3} < X_{h1},$$

$$\Pr\{T_{h1} \le t_1|X_0\} = \exp[\mu(w_1 - u_1)] \cdot L_\gamma^{-1}\left(\frac{1}{\gamma} \cdot \frac{\exp(u_1\sqrt{2\gamma + \mu^2})}{\exp(w_1\sqrt{2\gamma + \mu^2})}\right),$$

where $sh(x) \equiv \frac{1}{2}(e^x - e^{-x})$, and $L_\gamma^{-1}(\ )$ represents inversion of the Laplace transformation with respect to γ, which can be numerically computed (Bellman and Kalaba, 1966).

Figures 2–4 display three numerical illustrations about the impacts of the speed of technology progress on adoption timing, under different assumptions about data recording. We find that while the impact of the speed of technology progress on the likelihood of adopting before t_1 and after t_2 is monotonic when only 1FI is expected and it is not available during the period of sales recording, there is a significant turning point in the impacts when 1FI does emerge over the recording period. However, the impacts are much less nonmonotonic when a further generation of improvements is expected. In Fig. 4, the nonmonotonic impacts even disappear.

In Fig. 2, the probabilities that a firm adopts the current innovation before a time point over a time period and after a time point are shown as functions of $E(T_h)$, the expected arrival time of the future innovation. Figure 2(a) is under the assumption that only 1FI is expected in the future, the sales data are adoption records of CI and 1FI was not available over the period of recording. Figure 2(b) is under the assumption that only

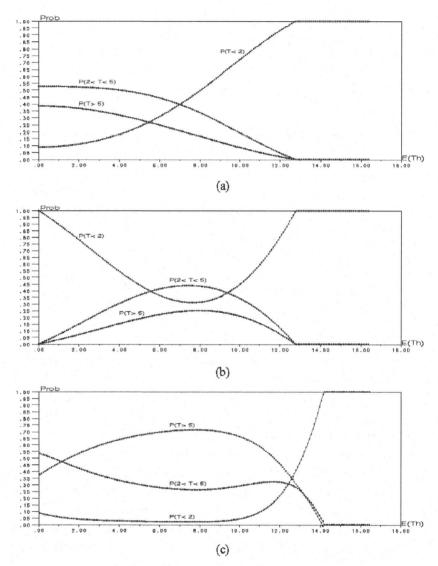

Fig. 2. The effect of the speed of future innovation arrival on the likelihood of current innovation adoption.

1FI is expected, 1FI does emerge during the period of sales recording. Figure 2(c) is under the assumption that both 1FI and 2FI are expected, 1FI emerges but 2FI is not available over the period of sales recording. The state of technological progress of an innovation is assumed to follow a

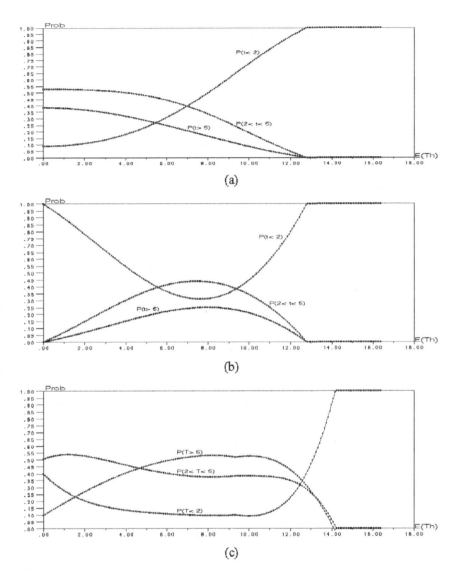

Fig. 3. The effect of the speed of future innovation arrival on the likelihood of current innovation adoption.

Geometric Brownian motion. It is shown that there is a significant turning point in the impact of the speed of technology progress on the likelihood of adopting before t_1 and after t_2 when only 1FI is expected and it emerges during the period of sales recording. However, the impacts are much more

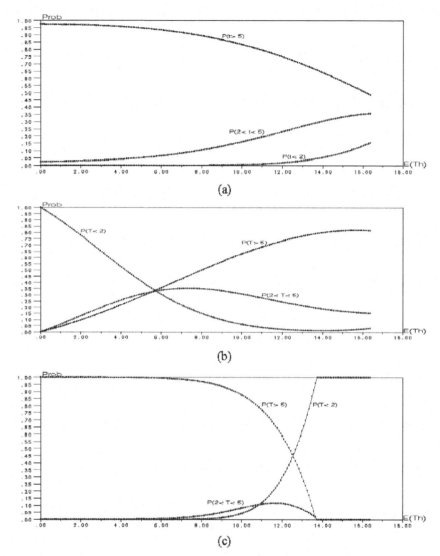

Fig. 4. The effect of the speed of future innovation arrival on the likelihood of current innovation adoption.

monotonic when a further generation of improvements is expected. The default parameter values are $\alpha = 0.01, \sigma = 0.03, r = 0.07, r - \delta = 0.06$, $X_0 = 1, p_0 = 1.0, \mu_1 = 1.0, \mu_2 = 1.0, \nu_1 = 0.2, \nu_2 = 0.5, C_e = 0.825$, $C_{d0}^{(1)} = 0.80, C_{u0}^{(1)} = 0.95, C_{u0}^{(2)} = 1.85, C_{l1} = 1.75, C_{d1} = 1.70$,

$C_{u1} = 1.30$, and $C_{l2} = 2.625$. $C_{d0}^{(2)} = 1.00$ means there is no value of CI after the arrival of 2FI. X_{h1} is set in accordance with the various levels of $E(T_h)$, and $X_{h2} = X_{h1}^2 / X_0$.

In Fig. 3, it is shown that there is a significant turning point in the impact of the speed of technology progress on the likelihood of adopting before t_1 and after t_2 when only 1FI is expected and it emerges during the period of sales recording. However, the impacts are less nonmonotonic when a further generation of improvements is expected. The default parameter values are $\alpha = 0.01, \sigma = 0.03, r = 0.07, r - \delta = 0.06, X_0 = 1, p_0 = 1.0, \mu_1 = 1.0,$ $\mu_2 = 1.0, \nu_1 = 0.2, \nu_2 = 0.5, C_e = 0.825, C_{d0}^{(1)} = 0.80, C_{u0}^{(1)} = 0.95,$ $C_{u0}^{(2)} = 1.85, C_{l1} = 1.75, C_{d1} = 1.70, C_{u1} = 1.225,$ and $C_{l2} = 2.625$. $C_{d0}^{(2)} = 1.00$ means the value of CI is minus after 2FI emerges. X_{h1} is set in accordance with the various levels of $E(T_h)$, and $X_{h2} = X_{h1}^2 / X_0$.

In Fig. 4, it is shown that there is a significant turning point in the impact of the speed of technology progress on the likelihood of adopting before t_1 and after t_2 when only 1FI is expected and it emerges during the period of sales recording. However, the nonmonotonic impacts disappear when a further generation of improvements is expected. The default parameter values are $\alpha = 0.01, \sigma = 0.03, r = 0.07, r - \delta = 0.06, X_0 = 1, p_0 = 1.0,$ $\mu_1 = 1.0, \mu_2 = 1.0, \nu_1 = 0.2, \nu_2 = 0.5, C_e = 0.825, C_{d0}^{(1)} = 0.80,$ $C_{u0}^{(1)} = 1.00, C_{u0}^{(2)} = 2.05, C_{l1} = 1.75, C_{d1} = 1.70, C_{u1} = 1.225,$ and $C_{l2} = 2.625$. $C_{d0}^{(2)} = 1.00$ implies the value of CI is negligible after the arrival of 2FI. X_{h1} is set in accordance with the various levels of $E(T_h)$, and $X_{h2} = X_{h1}^2 / X_0$.

5. Conclusion

Since the technology progress is an unceasing and uncertain process, firms are generally confronted with a sequence of innovations. The investment decision of a technology innovation can be viewed as a link in a chain of real options. Thus, the adoption decisions of innovations are strongly influenced by the technology environments, which determine the values of the sequence of real options.

Based on previous studies, this article extends the concept of real option chains by investigating the impact of the speed of innovation arrival on adoption timing when firms expect two generations of future innovations. Our numerical illustrations show that while there is a significant turning point in the impact of the speed of technology progress when only one generation of future innovation is expected and it emerges over the recording period, the impact becomes much less nonmonotonic or even monotonic when a further generation of improvements is expected. This confirms the intuitive and our previous empirical results.

This article can be extended in two ways. Firstly, empirical characterization and analytical explanation of the interactions patterns of developing strategies of suppliers and adoption strategies of demanders under differing innovation environments are very important to complete understanding of technology innovation and diffusion of innovations, and to making policies regarding the development of high-tech industries.[5] Secondly, empirical and theoretical characterization of strategic adoption timing of technology innovations in competing environments may also prove to be interesting.

References

Alleman, J. and Noam, E. (eds.), 1999. *The New Investment Theory of Real Options and Its Implication for Telecommunications Economics*. Kluwer Academic Publishers, Boston.

Amram, M. and Kulatilaka, N., 1999. *Real Options: Managing Strategic Investment in an Uncertain World*. Harvard Business School Press, Boston, MA.

Balcer, Y. and Lippman, S.A., 1984. Technological expectations and adoption of improved technology. *Journal of Economic Theory*, 34, 292–318.

Bellman, R.E. and Kalaba, R.E., 1966. *Numerical Inversion of the Laplace Transform*. American Elsevier Publishing Company, New York.

Bollen, N.P., 1999. Real options and product life cycles. *Management Science*, 45, 670–684.

Borodin, A.N. and Salminen, P., 1996. *Handbook of Brownian Motion-Facts and Formulae*. Birkhauser Verlag, Basel.

Brennan, M.J. and Schwartz, E.S., 1985. Evaluating natural resource investments. *Journal of Business*, 58, 135–157.

---

[5]Bollen (1999) develops a framework to value the options to contract and expand capacity when the market demand of a product is governed by an exogenous stochastic product life cycle of Bass type. However, our previous results show that the life cycle patterns of new products are strongly influenced by technological expectations and thus suppliers' R&D investment strategies. Therefore, a richer model should allow the life cycle of innovations to become endogenous.

Copeland, T., Antikarov, V., 2001. *Real Options: A Practitioner's Guide*. Texere, New York.

Dixit, A.K. and Pindyck, R.S., 1994. *Investment Under Uncertainty*. Princeton University Press, Princeton.

Farzin, Y.H., Huisman, K.J.M., and Kort, P.M., 1998. Optimal timing of technology adoption. *Journal of Economic Dynamics and Control*, 22, 779–799.

Grenadier, S.R. and Weiss, A.M., 1997. Investment in technological innovations: an option pricing approach. *Journal of Financial Economics*, 44, 397–416.

He, J. and Zeng, Y., 2001. Investing in technology innovation: empirical evidence and model fitting. Working paper, The Chinese University of Hong Kong.

Huisman, K.J. and Kort, P., 1999. Strategic technology investment under uncertainty. CentER Discussion Paper 9918, Tilburg University, CentER, Tilburg, The Netherlands.

Huisman, K.J. and Kort, P., 2000. Strategic technology adoption taking into account future technological improvements: a real option approach. CentER Discussion Paper 2000-52, Tilburg University, CentER, Tilburg, The Netherlands.

Ingersoll, J.E., Jr. and Ross, S.A., 1992. Waiting to invest: investment and uncertainty. *Journal of Business*, 65, 1–29.

Kaplan, R.S., 1986. Must CIM be justified by faith alone? *Harvard Business Review*, 64, 87–93.

Myers, S.C., 1977. Determinants of corporate borrowing. *Journal of Financial Economics*, 5, 147–175.

Nair, S.K., 1995. Modeling strategic investment decisions under sequential technological change. *Management Science*, 41, 282–297.

Pindyck, R.S., 1991. Irreversibility, uncertainty, and investment. *Journal of Economic Literature*, 29, 1110–1152.

Rajagopalan, S., Singh, M.R., and Morton, T.E., 1998. Capacity expansion and replacement in growing markets with uncertain technological breakthrough. *Management Science*, 44, 12–30.

Rosenthal, S.R., 1984. Progress toward the 'factory of the future'. *Journal of Operations Management*, 4, 203–229.

Trigeogis, L. (eds.), 1995. *Real Options in Capital Investment: Models, Strategies, and Applications*. Praeger, Weatport, CT.

Trigeogis, L., 1996. *Real Options — Managerial Flexibility and Strategy in Resource Allocation*. MIT Press, Cambridge, MA.

Weiss, A.M., 1994. The effects of expectations on technology adoption: some empirical evidence. *Journal of Industrial Economics*, 42, 341–360.

Developing Low Carbon Economy
Is a Systematic Project

Jianxin You

Chinese Academy of Science & Technology Management,
Tongji University, No. 1239 Siping Road,
Shanghai, China
yjx2256@vip.sina.com

As a strategic option to prevent global warming, energy conservation and emission reduction have become the key to the healthy development of the world. Every country is making vigorous efforts to boost the development of the low carbon economy (LCE). However, the development of LCE, being a systematic project, cannot be carried out by considering as it stands, and it must see that the progress of the LCE is promoted comprehensively, where the people's ideological awareness is considered as an important element. In addition, the developing countries should notice the resource value of "Carbon Dioxide Emission Rights", and the industrialized ones should respect the resources power of the former. As pointed out, the management subject has a vital role to play in developing the LCE.

Keywords: Low carbon economy (LCE); Systematic project; Ideological awareness; Resource value; Emission rights.

1. Energy Conservation and Emission Reduction Is the Key to Economic Development

1.1. 10 years of Kyoto Protocol

A team of experts, including members of the UN's Intergovernmental Panel on Climate Change (IPCC) from America, Europe, Australia and China, considered reports dating back to 1970 and found that at least 90% of environmental damage and disruption around the world is attributable to the rising temperatures driven by human activity (Ian Sample, 2008). As declared, global warming is changing the world. Climatic change has become a significant global issue of worldwide concern.

As a matter of fact, international society had begun formal cooperation on addressing global climate change since 1992. Especially on 11 December 1997, 149 countries ratified the Kyoto Protocol at the third Conference of the Parties to the United Nations Framework Convention on Climate Change (UNFCCC) (COP 3) held in Kyoto, Japan. Under the Protocol, 36 industrialized countries and the European community agreed to adopt legally binding commitments to reduce their emissions by an average of five percent against 1990 levels over the five-year period 2008–2012 (UN, 1997). Developing countries did not have to commit to reductions. In December 2007, COP13 was held and it has been 10 years since the adoption of the Tokyo Protocol. During that period, in 2005, the treaty entered into force in the form of international law and it was the first time in history to limit the greenhouse gas (GHG) emission, which marks a milestone with regard to the international cooperation in dealing with climatic change with the efforts from the international society. The governments had subsequently been putting in place legislation and policies. Then a carbon market was coming into being. Meanwhile, how to tackle the climatic change after the protocol expires in 2012 has gradually aroused wide concern. COP13 (Bali roadmap) and G8 held in July 2008 both focused on the new framework for global climate regime to ensure reductions of greenhouse emissions in the long term in post-Kyoto era.

1.2. Developed countries bear the obligation to take the lead in the implementation of cooling down the earth

The targets for reducing emissions under Kyoto vary according to the level of development. The reason for requesting industrialized countries to accept higher reduction standard differing from developing ones is that the increase of GHG emission is closely related to human production and social life. More than 100 years of industrialization has made some countries becoming rich first, but destroyed the environment we lived in and consumed the enormous quantity of natural resources, especially energy resources at the same time. Accordingly, it behaves the developed countries continuously leading the industrial revolution to take the lead to commit to cooling down the Earth (Karen and Mun, 2007).

1.3. Reducing GHG emissions is the common responsibility of all mankind

The Kyoto Protocol provides China with a good excuse to postpone fulfilling its commitment, as it is a developing country. Nonetheless, China will assume the responsibilities of a world power.

A responsible country should regard reducing emissions as a duty, not as a slogan, and not continue to pollute and destroy the environment by right of the Protocol. China should make a clear head that "Made in China" is not to leave pollution but to benefit the country and the descendants.

China has always implemented its obligations under the Convention and Protocol since ratification. The Chinese government has made environmental protection as a fundamental state policy and adopted a series of proactive policies and measures regarding environmental protection and climate change (NDRC, 2007). Moreover, the government took the initiative to set the goal of reducing total emissions of major pollutants by 10% during its 11th Five-Year Plan period (2006–2010).

1.4. Energy saving is as important as emission reduction

High-energy consumption is a by-product of rapid economy growth, which results in a serious shortage and a sharp rise in price of resources, and is an important source of increase in emissions. Thus, high-energy consumption has become a major bottleneck for developing countries to seek further development, because it has been leading to some negative effects on development, as the development cost increased and hindering the improvement of the people's living standards.

1.5. Energy saving and emission reduction is to better improve economic development

Does energy saving and emission reduction mean "not to seek for development"? No, it is not a standstill at all. It is not advisable to follow the traditional development mode with high-energy consumption and emission reduction. Hence transformation of economic development mode and pursuance of health are the common problems faced in developing countries.

Striving for both quality and speed of growth is the guiding ideology of China's economic development in new period. By encouraging energy saving and emission reduction, developing the LCE is a crucial selection of innovating development mode.

2. Developing the LCE is a Systematic Project

2.1. Enhancing the ideological awareness, being steadfast

Human resources are the basis of developing the LCE, which most important in the awareness that is the scientific attitude and comprehension of economic development along with energy saving and emission reduction. So the primary task for developing the LCE is to enhance the public awareness.

The Chinese government is urged to arm the head with scientific outlook on development and rectify the guiding ideology in economic development and persevere in improving the people's living standards wholeheartedly. For urbanization and contemporary rural area construction, modern industry and development of modern service, which including the various aspects of reform and opening-up, should improve the quality of people's life and realize the healthy development as the final goal (People's Republic of China, 2007), and take resource conservation and environmental protection as two basic state policies. The government should maintain giving prominence to building a resource-conserving and environment-friendly society in the course of its industrialization and modernization, striving to enhance the capability for sustainable development of China (IOSC, 2007).

2.2. Joint administration of all levels

It is baton and action principle to obtain policy environment support for energy saving and emission reduction. Innovating development mode needs government support, which is important guarantee for super-conventional development (high/low speeding).

Energy saving and emission reduction are not just internal affairs of any country, but a common task that the whole world is faced with.

The developed countries and regions should not only take the lead in the implementation of its obligations but also bear the duty to aid the developing ones in common promotion of energy saving and emission reduction.

2.3. Adjusting the industrial structure and innovating development mode

Energy saving and emission reduction do not mean to cease developing but change and innovate the development mode.

The industrial structure adjustment is a critical part of further economic development for many regions, but not everyone can realize this. For example, in some regions that are unsuitable for heavy and chemical industry, some leaders of local government and corporate are still keen on boosting such kind of project. Therefore, it is a complicated and arduous job to adjust the industrial structure and the mode of development.

2.4. Advancing science and technology of enterprises

Advancement of science and technology is a vital force in transforming the pattern of economic development and realizing energy saving and emission reduction. Enterprises should be encouraged to take the initiative in carrying out innovation to promote advancement of science and technology.

China should not only strive to win supports from developed countries and regions in advanced achievements and resources of science and technology but also strengthen the construction of human resources and actively promote independent innovation.

Besides, in order to improve the competitiveness of enterprises, the management of science and technology should be strengthened and its great importance should be attached to the resource value of independent intellectual property rights.

3. Paying Attention to the Resource Value of "Carbon Dioxide Emission Rights"

3.1. Attaching great importance to the resource of "Carbon Dioxide Emission Rights"

The mechanisms of emission reduction provided in the Kyoto Protocol can be summarized as "technique-based" and "market-based" mechanisms.

"Technique-based" mechanisms mean cutting GHG emissions through improving the efficiency of fossil fuel utilization or realizing the substitution of energy through developing renewable energy with techniques called "new energy".

For "market-based" mechanisms, the countries with technological advantages can procure carbon dioxide (CO_2) emission rights through exchanging by providing technological supports for developing countries, and thus helping decreasing the emission of toxic and harmful substances based on the principle of the clean development mechanism (CDM).

3.2. CDM project in China

The CDM projects in China had obtained issued CERs (Certified Emission Reductions issued by the Executive Board) of 36,371,368 tCO2e (total CO_2 emission) till February 2008, accounting for 31.33% of the total CERs issued and exceeding India (30.02%) firstly.

Till 16 January 2008, the sum of CDM projects approved by National Development and Reform Commission (NDRC) is 1,068 altogether, the total amount of estimated CERs being 261 million tCO2e/y.

3.3. Negative effects of CDM

The original intention of CDM is that developed countries would obtain CERs through investing in CDM projects in developing countries through technology transfer and/or direct investment. But according to the actual situation of CDM project in China, most are capital transfer from developed countries, which means purely transaction of CO_2 emissions right, while technology transfer is rare. CDM projects would bear in danger of becoming the cheap facilities for developed countries to reduce their emissions on current trends.

3.4. Establishing long-term effects of CDM

The developed countries have applied large amounts of the reduction opportunities with low cost and the low price of CERs, which would probably make it hard to compensate developing countries for the cost of commitment with the revenue of CDM projects. Developing countries should insist on the principle of the priority of technology progress when selecting the projects and development mode of CDM, actively boost the sustained development of reduction and guarantee the national welfare.

CDM can help developing countries spurring economic growth and obtaining advanced technology, but at the same time, dominated by benefits drive of market economy, it is hard for these countries to acquire what they deserved for usually being deprived of the discourse power.

Advocating independent innovation is not only helpful for developing countries to advance technology progress but also critical in acquiring the discourse power in CDM so as to withstand market risks, and thus improve the people's living standards through energy saving and emission reduction.

4. Management Subject Will Play an Important Role in the Development of LCE

Great emphasis should be laid on the implementation of promoting energy saving and emission reduction, as well as advocating "both quality and speed of growth", which should not only be confined to slogan. For whether industry sphere or service industry, what the development goals of management subject incarnates is always the efficiency, quickness and economics, which comes down in one continuous line with the nature of emission reduction. So the management subject will be sure to play a vital role in the development of LCE.

References

Ian Sample, M., 2008. World's wildlife and environment already hit by climate change (15 May 2008). Guardian, London.

Information Office of the State Council of the People's Republic of China (IOSC), 2007. China's Energy Conditions and Policies (10 Jan. 2007). Beijing.

Karen, F.-V. and Mun, S.H., 2007. How do market reforms affect China's responsiveness to environmental policy? *Journal of Development Economics*, 82, 200–233.

National Development and Reform Commission (NDRC), 2007. China's National Climate Change Program (June, 2007). Beijing.

People's Republic of China, 2007. Constitution of the Communist Party of China (CPC). People's Press, Beijing.

United Nations, 1997. Kyoto Protocol to the United Nations Framework Convention on Climate Change, 10 Dec. 1997 in Change, U.N.F.C.o.C., editor. U.N.Doc.FCC/CP/1997/L.7/Add.1.